W9-BPN-282

A NARROW DOORWAY

Women's Stories of Escape From Abuse

by Fern Martin
editing by Anne Mokros

Published by

1 Main Street, Burnstown, Ontario, Canada K0J 1G0
Telephone 1-800-465-6072 Fax (613) 432-7184

ISBN 0-896182-43-7
Printed and bound in Canada

Layout and Design by Leanne Enright
Cover Design by Tammy Anderson

The opinions expressed in this book are those of the author and are in no way the responsibility of Lanark County Interval House.
Royalties from the sale of this book will be donated to Lanark County Interval House.

Copyright ©1996

The General Store Publishing House
Burnstown, Ontario, Canada

No part of this book may be reproduced, stored in a retrieval system or transmitted in any form or by any means electronic, mechanical, photocopying, recording or otherwise, except for purposes of review, without the prior permission of the publisher.

General Store Publishing House gratefully acknowledges the assistance of the Ontario Arts Council and Canada Council.

Canadian Cataloguing in Publication Data

Martin, Fern
    A narrow doorway: women's stories of escape from abuse

ISBN 1-896182-43-7

    1. Wife abuse. 2. Wife abuse--Case studies.
3. Abused

HV6626.M38 1995   362.82'92   C95-920864-X

First Printing March 1996

DEDICATION

This book is dedicated to the ten wonderful women who shared their stories and to all the women who have stories to share.

I would also like to dedicate this book to the memory of three Lanark County women who didn't survive their partners' abuse.

Vera Presley, 78, Innisville

Vera was shot by her husband in their village home on July 26, 1988, in a murder/suicide. She had stayed at the shelter for two weeks in 1985. When disposing of her belongings, Vera's niece discovered notes from her stay at Interval House hidden with her Bible and $200.

Thelma Fokuhl, 65, Beckwith Township

Thelma died on December 13, 1992, following a beating by her common-law partner. Earlier that day, Thelma had made arrangements to go to Lanark County Interval House. Because no cause of death could be found, Oliver Baptiste was convicted of aggravated assault and sentenced to eight years in prison. A long-time police detective said the beating was the worst he had ever seen and suggested she may have died of fright.

Donna Barr, 43, Perth

Donna was shot by her ex-husband in her home on January 13, 1996 in a double murder/suicide. Also murdered was a friend of Donna's, Steven Young. Donna had separated from her abusive husband two years before. He was convicted of assault and uttering threats and sentenced to three years probation.

ABBREVIATIONS/ACRONYMS

AA   Alcoholics Anonymous

Algonquin   Algonquin College, a community college centred in Ottawa with campuses in Lanark County.

CAS   Children's Aid Society

CHEO   Children's Hospital of Eastern Ontario, located in Ottawa.

mother's allowance   Government financial assistance for unemployed women who have dependant children.

Rideau Regional   The Rideau Regional Hospital of Eastern Ontario; a large facility in Smiths Falls built to house individuals who are developmentally delayed.

The Royal Ottawa ROH   a psychiatric hospital in Ottawa.

TABLE OF CONTENTS

Abbreviations...4

Acknowledgements...7

Foreword by Dr. Peter Jaffe 8

Introduction..11

What is Abuse?...18
The Seven Types of Abuse: Emotional Abuse, Environmental Abuse, Social Abuse, Financial Abuse, Physical Abuse, Sexual Abuse, Ritual Abuse.

Life In A Shelter 24
A History of Women's Shelters, Lanark County Interval House, Security, The Rules, Jobs and School, Life in a Shelter for a Woman, The Children, Staffing, The Crisis Counsellor's Shift.

Jane's Story..32
Jane grew up in a supportive family atmosphere. Trained as a nurse, she supported her family. Her husband's alcoholism and extreme violence finally drove her away.

Why? 44
Why Do Women Stay? Why Do Women Leave? Why Do Men Abuse?

Susan's Story..50
When Susan's mother had a nervous breakdown, her children were separated and sent to foster homes. Susan became pregnant and married a man she hardly knew. Within a week the physical assaults began.

Minimizing Abuse 66

Donna's Story 68
Childhood sexual abuse cut short Donna's education. She supported her family with her cleaning skills and endured her husband's alcoholism and violence.

Counselling...78

Lauren's Story 81
Lauren was well educated and her husband seemed resentful of that fact. His abuse appeared to start as a result of a head injury. He continued to harass her long after the separation.

The 'isms 105
    F'ism, L'ism

May's Story 108
    May's husband raped her shortly after their wedding and continued to
    abuse her. Following a rape by her husband's business partner, she
    suffered a nervous breakdown and was given shock treatments. Her
    religion helped her survive.

Pills 123

Cindy's Story 125
    Orphaned at birth, Cindy endured an abusive childhood and married a
    man who became physically and sexually abusive. In order to escape, she
    had to leave her two young sons behind.

Support Groups 138

Rachel's Story 141
    From the age of six, Rachel was sexually abused by an older brother. She
    used her attractiveness to support her two daughters and her addictions,
    meeting many abusers along the way.

Humour 162

Elizabeth's Story 163
    At age seven, Elizabeth became the housekeeper for her father and two
    brothers. Gutsy and determined, she survived her husband's physical
    abuse and repeated gang rapes by his friends.

Burn-Out 184

Lois' Story 188
    In spite of a very unstable childhood, an early pregnancy and two more
    children, Lois managed to provide a home for her family. Her life fell
    apart when she met Fred.

The Strange Women 201

Jackie's Story 204
    Jackie had a good job and seemed to be in control of her life until she met
    Jonas. A charming but extremely abusive man, he used religion to justify
    his abuse and to support his belief that it was his duty to procreate using
    many women.

Is There Any Hope? 219

Seven Types of Abuse 222

Suggested Reading 227

Women's Shelters in Canada 229

ACKNOWLEDGEMENTS

The author has many people to thank including:

The ten women who gave of their time and who persevered through the pain.

My niece Deirdre (Martin) McKennirey for alloting every Tuesday evening during the winter of 1989 to meet with me and start the editing process.

Friends who encouraged me for several years by asking, "How's your book going?" Mercifully, they eventually quit asking because it became too embarrassing for us all to hear the same reply: "Well it's not finished yet."

Anne Mokros who volunteered to help me get back on track. She came to my house every Thursday morning during 1994. I supplied lunch and she supplied her knowledge of editing. We worked line by line, and she kept asking the all-important question, "What are you trying to say here?" I am also most grateful to Anne for encouraging me to return to my pursuit of publishers.

General Store Publishing House, which bravely took the risk. Tim Gordon who only two weeks after receiving the manuscript said, "I feel obligated to publish this book." What a relief. He must have felt the vibrations of my pounding heart. It was a pleasure to work on the final edits with Susan Code and John Stevens.

The superb board, staff and volunteers of Lanark County Interval House, many of whom took time to read, comment, encourage, correct and endlessly support me in this task, in particular Helen Blair, Dianne Czerwinski, Ida-Jane Graham Routliffe, Ella Hamilton, Donna Johnson, Jane Laut, Janet Mosier, Joan Perkins, Thelma Peterson, Joni Seligman, Carole Smith and Jane Szepesi.

Special, special thanks go to Catherine Cunningham-Huston, Joan Gawn, Hinda Goldberg, Olive Millett and Linda Lombardo for their very careful perusals and excellent suggestions.

Gloria Dyck, Suzanne Mayrand, Kate Ryan and Susan Mackey for their sleuthing and legal advice.

My niece Christa Giles and Donna Hall of Amethyst for their input.

Helen Levine who endorsed this book. Her support was truly appreciated.

Dr. Peter Jaffe for taking the time to write the excellent foreward. His knowledge of the issue and commitment to the cause add much stature to this book.

Last, but not least, is a sincere thank you to my treasured family—my husband, Peter, for his computer help, and our children Linda, Selina and Rusty, and even son-in-law David. Wonderful people whose love and encouragement I devour.

FOREWORD

Fern Martin has provided an invaluable resource in *A Narrow Doorway*. She has taken us beyond the litany of statistics on violence against women and into the reality of women's lives. These lives are a tribute to courage, perseverance and surviving years of terrorism.

When people hear statistics (like the recent Statistics Canada report that suggests that twenty-nine percent of all Canadian women face violence in an intimate relationship—ten percent face violence so severe that they worry for their own safety and lives), they recoil in horror and then move into denial. The numbers are too high. They didn't define violence properly. They must be feminists who hate men. What about violence against men? This denial can reassure the average person that they needn't worry about themselves, their daughters, sisters, colleagues at work, friends or neighbours. Fern Martin offers a different perspective with the voices of ten women who represent thousands of women across Canada whose homes have become war zones. These women's stories offer tremendous insights and wisdom to readers about how individuals are forced to cope with incredible levels of pain and trauma.

The women's stories are a reminder of how much energy our communities must commit to eradicate violence. In my travels across the country as part of the Canadian Panel on Violence Against Women, the messages we received from 139 communities and 4,000 people were consistent. Silence is the number one friend for maintaining the status quo and tolerating or ignoring violence. As long as we pretend that the problem doesn't exist or only happens in other places—big cities, that part of town, that family—there can be no safety for women in their own homes.

Perhaps Lanark County was the perfect place for Fern Martin to create this book. There can be few more beautiful places in Canada that inspire a real sense of the quaint, quiet, and peaceful. Driving through Perth, one senses a total tranquillity and the antithesis of violence. Fern reminds us of the reality of what happens behind closed doors in peaceful communities and how far we need to go to involve the whole community in preventing violence. Perhaps one day there will be signs on the roads that enter Lanark County that say Welcome to Lanark County, where peace and safety begin at home.

Peter G. Jaffe, Ph.D., C. Psych.
Executive Director
London Family Court Clinic
Associate Professor, Psychology/Psychiatry
University of Western Ontario

INTRODUCTION

It was the summer of 1979. In the past year, I had helped establish a shelter for abused women in Lanark County and was now a board member and a volunteer.

Late one night my phone rang. It was Sandra at Interval House. Something had come up. Could I attend a meeting first thing in the morning?

The morning sun warmed my back but could not remove the chill of apprehension I felt as I rang the doorbell at Interval House. The shelter had only been open for a few months and now something was wrong. Sandra unlocked the front door, ushered me quickly into the dim hallway and indicated that the meeting was upstairs.

I met a new woman on the landing. Although her face was swollen and bruised, she shyly returned my smile. The baby in her arms was restless, and several children peeked at me from behind her skirt.

I joined a dozen women in the sunny second-storey porch. The group was sipping coffee and talking in hushed tones. I learned that the police had brought Jenna and her four children to the house. The police had wanted us to know the danger we were in. Another volunteer made room for me on the tattered couch. She leaned over and whispered, "Did you see her?"

"Yes," I replied, "He really did a number on her."

Sandra entered the room and sat cross-legged on the carpet. No one interrupted as she relayed the police officers' message.

Sandra told us that Jenna's husband was bad news. He had no fear of anyone, including the police. He would do anything to get his wife back. If he found out where she was staying, we would all be in danger. This man had beaten others, but they were too terrified to testify against him. He had beaten Jenna for years, but this last time he used a tire iron. When the eldest child tried to protect her mother, he grabbed the child and twisted and sprained her arm. After he left for work, Jenna called the health nurse for help because she was afraid for her children's safety. The nurse called the police who took the family to the hospital and then brought them to Interval House. Jenna was covered in bruises and had recurring headaches.

Sandra took a deep breath and started pulling tufts out of the rug. She then began telling us what she had learned from Jenna. Jenna's husband had caused two of their infants to die. One baby was born prematurely when he pushed Jenna down the stairs and then kicked her abdomen with his work boots. She started to bleed that night. The fetus was too young to survive. The other infant was born mentally and physically disabled. Jenna's husband had beaten her abdomen constantly during that pregnancy. The day she brought the baby home from the hospital, he put it in the crib and kept her away from the room until it died.

As Sandra described Jenna's husband, I glanced out the window to check the driveway below looking for the man whose portrait was now engraved on my mind. The word bastard echoed around the room. I turned to the woman beside me and we held each other.

The group of staff and volunteers decided it was essential to double up on shifts so that if he did break down the door, there would be an extra person to call the police. We scheduled the shifts for the week and left for home.

I sat in my car for a while, shaking. Such extreme violence was a revelation to me. I had helped establish the shelter because I believed that women should have an alternative to living with physically and emotionally abusive mates, but I was not prepared for this. Perhaps I held a genteel notion of wife abuse: a push, a slap, threats. I could not comprehend the brutality Jenna lived with nor did I want to know. I had a peculiar desire to faint.

As I drove home that day I started to worry. What if he did break in? What about the safety of the other women and children in the house? And then there were the neighbours. What if he went to the wrong door? The board had recently spent a long evening assuring an angry community that it was quite safe to have an Interval House in their residential area. As a board member, I shared legal responsibility for the operation of the house. As a volunteer, I was in physical danger.

In the sixteen years since the shelter opened, I have learned there is another side to the old boundary sign that proclaimed Lanark County as quaint, quiet and peaceful. I'm not shocked anymore to hear that male friends and acquaintances punch and choke their wives or girlfriends. I can listen to an abused woman tell her story and recognize that, generally, she's minimizing the cruelty she's endured. I've become aware of the epidemic of rape and sexual assault of women and children, most of whom do not report it. Instead, they carry the shame and anger that can cripple their emotional well-being. Above all, Lanark County Interval

House has opened my eyes to the incredible perseverance, courage and strength of women.

There's one other crucial lesson I've learned: it is silence that allows abusive men to continue their violence and abuse without being challenged. It is a silence that we have all been a part of, consciously or unconsciously.

Lanark County is situated approximately forty kilometers west of Canada's capital city, Ottawa. It is a beautiful area. The famous Rideau Canal bisects the town of Smiths Falls in the south. The lovely Mississippi River meanders around the northern part of the County, through the town of Carleton Place, over the magnificent falls in Almonte and under North America's only five-arch stone bridge in the pretty village of Pakenham. Perth, the County seat, has a wonderful collection of stately homes and a graceful park in the centre of town complete with a band shell where the Perth Citizen's Band has performed for more than 125 years.

Lanark County was settled in the early 1800s, in the main by Scottish and Irish immigrants. Today's population of approximately 54,000 includes descendants of those original pioneers as well as European immigrants who came as a result of war, back-to-the- landers who arrived in the '60s, and more recently, city folk attracted by the beauty of the area or small-town life.

A mix of occupations has developed in the County due to the variety of geographical features of the area. Deep, fertile soils support dairy and beef farms. Coniferous and deciduous trees on the rocky Precambrian Shield harbour some forestry industries. An abundance of sugar maple trees produce the sap that enables Lanark County to promote itself as The Maple Syrup Capital of Ontario. Hospitals, schools and small businesses employ people locally. A large number of Lanark County residents commutes daily to Ottawa to work for the federal government or the many high-tech companies in the region.

I am part of the half of the County population who live on farms or are isolated from close neighbours. This environment shapes our characters, and we either thrive or are inhibited by it. What is privacy to some is isolation to others, especially if they don't have their own transportation. What is self-sufficiency to some is poverty to those who have no choice.

As one of the descendants of Scottish and Irish pioneers, I treasure this County: the land and its people. I also, at times, despair about the abuse that exists here.

It would be comforting to read that abuse only happens to the 'others'—people who are not a part of our particular social group, people who are not like us. But the truth is, abusers come from all walks of life: the educated and the illiterate, the affluent and the poor, the city dwellers and the inhabitants of rural areas. So the risk of being abused is as great for women and children in Lanark County as in any other region of the country. Lanark County cannot be categorized as 'the other.' In fact, for many, it is an ideal place to work, live and raise a family.

I was born in 1945, the third daughter of Lanark County dairy farmers. That same morning one of our Holstein cows delivered a heifer calf. My parents had two names picked for females. The calf got Gloria.

My sisters and I attended the one-room rural school near the end of our lane and graduated from the local high school in Almonte. I became a hairdresser. I married my high-school sweetheart in 1965 and had two daughters and a son in quick succession.

Always an activist, I was very involved in my community. I worked to establish a day-care centre in Almonte and joined the local auxiliary of the Children's Hospital of Eastern Ontario (CHEO) to raise funds to build the new hospital. It was during that time, in the early '70s, that the women's movement really took hold of me. The CHEO meetings gave young mothers an opportunity to share, and we found we had much in common. Although I did not yet call myself a feminist, I embraced feminist ideals. It all just made so much sense. And for the first time in my life, I had women friends. Discussions at parties crescendoed as we women argued with the men for our right to be employed, to be educated and to be treated as equals in society and at home.

In 1974, members of the CHEO auxiliary and a low-income women's group, The Neighbourhood Club, worked together to establish a women's centre and thrift shop in Almonte called The Hub. The thrift shop was a great success, and we were able to use the profits to finance local needs such as sending children to summer camps and buying books for the library. The discussions on women's rights continued. When the United Nations declared 1975 as International Women's Year, we took advantage of available government grants and organized a conference in Almonte called Women's Day. One hundred and seventy women attended. Two years later we organized another conference in Pakenham and even more women came. It was heady and exciting. We were going to change the world.

Soon we were hearing about women's shelters. There was one in Toronto, another had just opened in Ottawa. Were husbands beating their wives in Lanark County? Unthinkable. But in 1978 we got a grant to find out. A woman who had been abused by her husband was hired to do a study. If anyone could get results, it would be this woman. She was unstoppable. Following her report, a public meeting was held where women and men from the County formed committees to work on establishing a shelter. One women's group, The Exchange, pledged to pay the first six months' rent on a house that had been selected in Carleton Place. A few months later it was open.

That was when my eyes were opened. That was when I became aware that even friends and acquaintances were being abused by their husbands. As long as it was 'other' women, abuse was just an issue. But when it was friends who were being abused, it really hit home.

I have learned much in the past sixteen years, and it is the women who came to the shelter who have been my teachers.

Some women in particular were pivotal to my education. I think that is true for all women who work in shelters. It could be the first woman who tells you of bestiality or ritual abuse, or it could be the woman whose background is very much like your own, and you realize that her story could easily be yours. You can tell when a woman is especially significant in your life because you have a strong reaction. In spite of years of hearing about abuse, one woman's story will have an important impact on your life.

Public education has always been a part of my interest and duties at the shelter. I initiated the program when I was a volunteer and continued doing it while working as a crisis counsellor. I now concentrate on that area. My duties as Public Education Coordinator for Lanark County Interval House include speaking to groups as well as writing a column for five weekly newspapers on the issue of violence against women and children. Occasionally, women staying at the house share their stories for the column. These personal accounts always have the most impact on readers. It is an effective way to help the public understand why a shelter is needed. It also lets other women living in abusive situations know that they are not alone.

I have written this book so that you can learn about some of the realities of abuse as I have learned them. Often, when talking of wife assault, many people give me the distinct impression that they believe the woman must be equally at fault. They remind me that I'm probably biased, and the old clichés come out: "It takes two to tango, you know"; "There are two sides to every story." When I'm told this, I always feel a deep hurt for all the women I have met who bent over backwards to make their marriages work, often staying in the relationship longer than was safe, and who, once they left, faced that lack of sympathy. In fact, twenty-nine per cent of Canadian women have been physically or sexually assaulted by a marital partner at some point during the relationship, and each year, more than 100 women in this country are murdered by their spouses or boyfriends.

I believe these stories are valuable not only because of their information about abuse but also because they represent a history of Canadian women from the 1930s to the present. We learn about the women's childhoods, the events that brought them to Interval House and how they have fared since leaving the shelter. Through their stories, we get a glimpse into their mothers' generation and see the results of limited choices, unwanted pregnancies and inadequate social supports. We also witness the short-term and long-term effects of the abuse on their children.

I am enormously grateful to these ten women for sharing their stories. It was a difficult task. Each woman had left the shelter two to ten years before doing the interview, and yet to talk of the abuse was to relive the horrors and to again feel the humiliation and pain.

I started working on these stories in 1987. I had just taken a leave from the shelter because the work had become too stressful and I was burnt out. Some women I approached directly. Others responded to a letter I had written to editors of local weekly newspapers inviting former residents to contact me if they were interested in participating in the project. I did not deliberately seek out women with horrendous stories. In fact, I am somewhat ashamed to say, my intention was to provide stories of abuse that would be easy to stomach. What I found, however, was that the women simply had not revealed their whole stories during their stays in the shelter.

As are most women who come to the shelter, these women were wonderfully frank and truthful, admitting to their own frailties and taking responsibility for their choices. There is little editing. The stories are told in the women's own words and without further analysis because the women's words speak for themselves.

The interviews were taped. After typing the transcripts, I returned to see each woman two or three times in order to clarify details and to ensure her story was correct. With each return visit, all of the women had more memories to share.

I have added short essays to give you a clearer picture of life in a women's shelter and to illustrate some of the issues faced by abused women and shelter workers.

Although I always knew the stories were powerful and important, it was several years before I found an interested publisher. When General Store Publishing House expressed encouragement, I thought it best to revisit each of the women for an update on their lives. At first I was embarrassed that it had taken so long to get to this stage, but I see now that the six to eight-year period between the first interview and the update gives the stories more depth. Several of the women have had dramatic changes in their lives, and there have been changes in the lives of their children. The updates were done in the summer of 1995.

All the names of all the women, children and men in the book have been changed. The women selected the names to represent the people in their stories and we worked together to modify some situations in order to protect identities. Each woman has read the final draft and has given permission for her story to be published.

The women shared their stories in the hope that this knowledge will give other abused women the courage and strength to find their own narrow doorway through which escape is possible, hence the title of the book. I recorded their stories with the idea that it would raise the awareness of those who could provide the necessary support and assistance.

What happened to Jenna? She stayed at the shelter for five days, called her husband and went back home. Her husband had a good job and provided well for the family, and she reasoned that she could not support the four children on her own. She also knew that if she didn't return, he would eventually find her and kill her. Jenna felt it was safer for her to live with him than away from him. This was confirmed when she spoke to her husband on the phone. He told her if she didn't come home immediately, he would find her and cut off her legs.

Jenna returned to Interval House several months later. This time we quickly transferred her to a sister shelter because her husband was now aware of our location. When she went back to her husband the second time, he moved the family to western Canada. At that time, there were few protective services for women in the west. I wonder if she is still alive.

WHAT IS ABUSE?

This will not be an easy book to read, especially if you have little or no knowledge of abuse.

My co-workers and I learned about abuse in small doses. The women who came to our shelter usually didn't tell all, and in the early days, we shelter workers didn't ask many questions. There were several reasons for our reluctance to delve into a woman's life. We simply didn't know what questions to ask, and we were afraid to unlock information and emotions that we felt ill-equipped to deal with. We also believed, and still do, that a woman has the right to her privacy and that it is up to her to choose when she will deal with her own difficult issues.

In later years, as we gained experience and comfort, and as the women felt more comfortable with us, we started to inquire and soon were hearing of unimaginable degradations such as incest and bestiality. We became aware that some of the women, having been sexually abused as children, had developed multiple personalities. We witnessed women experiencing flashbacks: cowering, shielding, trying to protect themselves from their attackers.

In order to broaden our knowledge and increase our counselling skills, we attended workshops. At one workshop we were introduced to the most horrific abuse of all—ritual abuse. I am still trying to come to terms with that disturbing reality.

Learning about abuse can be distressing. It is upsetting to know that such cruelty exists. As I wrote at the start of this section, I learned about abuse in small doses over a long period of time. This book does not give you that luxury of learning gradually. So read it at your own pace—one story a day, or a week, or a month. Anne Mokros, the woman who helped to edit this book, had an interesting observation. She said that the first time she read the stories, she felt depressed. The second time, she felt angry. The third time, she began to see the strengths of the individual women and enjoyed reading about their survival and accomplishments.

It may help you to know that most of the women are doing quite well now.

The Seven Types of Abuse

As Public Education Coordinator of Lanark County Interval House, I have talked to many groups about abuse and violence against women. When trying to explain just what abuse is, one of my most effective tools is a paper entitled *The Seven Types of Abuse*. This paper originated at an Ottawa men's group named 'New Directions'. Many of the men attended the group as part of a court order after having been convicted of assaulting their partners. Some attended the group on their own initiative (usually after their partners left them). One of their tasks was to list the abusive behaviours they used in order to control their wives or girlfriends. The behaviours were then arranged under six categories or types of abuse: physical, emotional, sexual, financial, social and environmental. With help from victims, co-workers and members of the Lanark County Coalition Against Family Violence (representatives of agencies who work with abusers and victims), the original list has doubled in length. We added several subcategories such as Abuse During Pregnancy and Abuse in a Vehicle as well as a seventh type—Ritual Abuse.

One act alone may not be abusive. What is important is the intention behind that act. Most abusers use many different tactics to manipulate their partners' behaviour and repeat those techniques over a long period of time.

We give this same paper to every woman who comes to Interval House for shelter and ask her to identify the abusive behaviours that pertained to her relationship. Some women mark almost every line. It is often an eye-opener for them to realize that there is more to abuse than physical assault.

I will introduce and summarize the various abuses here. A full listing can be found in the appendix at the back of the book.

The words he or him are used to describe the abuser and she or her to describe the victim. There is no intention to hide the fact that women also abuse their male or female partners but, in marital or intimate relationships, the abusers are most often male and their victims are most often female.

Emotional/Verbal/Psychological Abuse

This type of abuse is the most common. The abuser is able to undermine the woman's self-confidence by continuous and often subtle put-downs such as calling her names and comparing her to others. He may snap his fingers and expect her to serve him or blame her for everything that goes wrong.

Emotional abuse often accelerates during the woman's pregnancy and after the birth. He may insult her body, deny that the child is his, blame her because the infant is the 'wrong' sex, and sulk or make her feel bad for the time she spends with the baby.

Emotional abuse can be just as serious as physical abuse. In fact, many women say it feels worse because the pain lasts longer. Broken bones heal, but the pain from hurtful words continues. Some report that their partners continue to be emotionally abusive long after they have stopped being physically abusive.

Environmental Abuse

Environmental abuse is not about kicking trees, it is using the victim's environment or surroundings to make her feel afraid or upset. He often targets items that have a special significance to her—he will rip her best dress, break the antique dishes she inherited from her mother, harm her pets or mow over her rose garden. Some abusers come home angry and smash the furniture or punch the walls.

Environmental abuse can also take place in the family vehicle. The person who drives the car also controls the environment of the passenger. He may drive too fast to frighten her or push her out of the car while it is in motion. He may tamper with the engine or chain the steering wheel to prevent his partner from using the car (this could also be social abuse).

Social Abuse

Social Abuse includes abusing a partner in public and preventing a partner from socializing with others. The abuser controls what she does, who she talks to and where she goes. He censors her mail and phones frequently to make sure she is where she is supposed to be (at home or at work). Sometimes he deliberately makes a scene in public so that she is reluctant to go out with him again.

He may use the children to socially abuse his partner by teaching them to call her names—bitch, ugly, bad mother. Using the children often reaches a peak during separation or divorce proceedings with such activities as buying the children off with gifts and encouraging them to undermine their mother's plans.

Sometimes religion can be used to socially abuse, especially if her faith is an important aspect of her life. He declares what is acceptable and punishes her for her "sins."

Social abuse leaves the victim feeling embarrassed and humiliated. It can keep her isolated from family and friends, afraid to go out in public, and is an effective way to control her life.

Financial Abuse

In Canada today, many women in the workforce still earn much less than their male counterparts. Women who work at home raising their children don't receive a wage. The result is that women are often financially dependant on their husbands. When this is the case, the abuser can exert power and control over his wife by withholding money from her or by refusing her a say in how the money will be spent. Some women are threatened until they hand over their pay cheques or baby bonus. Sometimes the abuser gives his pay cheque to his wife to manage but then blames her if there is not enough money left over for his activities. It is a sad fact that some women never have any money of their own until they get the old-age pension or until their partners die.

Physical Abuse

This type of abuse is the easiest to recognize and gets the most press. It ranges from standing too close (intimidation) to murder. It can start with a push but increases in frequency and severity if the relationship continues.

Physical abuse can start during pregnancy or may increase while a woman is pregnant. The punches or kicks are directed at her abdomen, perhaps in an effort to cause a miscarriage, or she may be tripped or pushed down the stairs for the same reason. The abusive man who does not want to become a father can be very dangerous indeed.

Sexual Abuse

For many years it was believed that one of a wife's responsibilities in marriage was to provide her husband with sex whenever he wanted it. Indeed, it was only in 1983 that Canadian law made it illegal for a man to rape his wife. But old traditions die hard. The sexual relationship in many marriages is not based on equality or choice, and positive change in the immediate future looks bleak. Date rape is a major problem, and young women still report tremendous pressure to "put out" if their dates spend money on them or take them out for dinner.

Sexual abuse is very degrading, hurtful and a difficult topic for most women to discuss. It ranges from sexual jokes and name-calling (whore, slut) to forced sexual intercourse. The abundance of pornography doesn't help. Women report being told by their abusers that they are not normal if they refuse to mimic acts depicted in pornography. Some are forced to pose for pornographic photos. Pornography misinforms men about women's sexuality and serves to undermine women's self-confidence. Pornography also misinforms men about their own sexuality, about what to expect of themselves in terms of potency, dominance, etc.

Ritual Abuse

Ritual abuse is happening in Eastern Ontario as it is in many parts of the world. We know this from survivors who have called our crisis line as well as from counsellors with expertise on ritual abuse. The statements from survivors reveal a horror most of us find difficult to believe or comprehend.

We have many rituals in our lives, ceremonies that we repeat at certain times of the day or year. Teatime in the afternoon or a particular Christmas celebration are rituals. The Christian communion is a ritual that reenacts the Last Supper, using wine to symbolize the blood of Jesus and bread to symbolize his body. A cult may perform the same ritual but uses real blood and the actual flesh of a person or animal.

Ritual abuse is most often performed by a group of people who are usually, but not necessarily, members of a satanic cult, a so-called Christian sect or other religious group. They use rituals as a means to control, to intimidate or to justify abuse.

As in most religions, men dominate the group or cult, although women are involved in the rituals.

Some groups or cults have little knowledge of ritual or are unorganized in their activities. Others are highly sophisticated and include respected members of our communities. Some have been linked to involvement in criminal activities such as pornography, drug trafficking, illegal adoptions and illegal abortions. Their victims may be members of their own families—children and women—or transients who are labeled expendable.

The sophisticated cult or group is expert at brainwashing. It uses deliberate and calculated methods such as isolation, deprivation, torture, and repeated chants and phrases to make people submissive. Mind-altering drugs are often used. The purpose of the brainwashing is to ensure that the victim will stay with the cult, and that the cult will continue.

Cults start with young children. The children are given a pleasurable activity, but along with that activity, they are made to witness a traumatic event—the mutilation of another child or the killing of an animal. The process is repeated in different forms so that the child is no longer able to experience pleasure without also feeling pain. Later on, the child is forced to take part in the mutilation or killing so that he or she feels responsible and guilty and is unlikely to tell anyone about the experience. Sometimes trickery is used to give children the illusion that a murder is taking place. Sometimes actual killings do occur. Either way, the result is traumatic for the child.

Survivors talk about being isolated in closets or boxes. Snakes, leeches or spiders may be put in the box with the child or used in an abusive ritual.

The rituals may be performed by people dressed as doctors or police officers so that the child is less likely to ask for help from people in those professions or anyone in authority.

In order to deal with the extreme trauma, children may develop multiple personalities. It is a coping mechanism. During the trauma, a different personality takes on the role of the child who is being hurt so that the real child can escape into a safe fantasy. Some children have developed many personalities. Getting in touch with the various personalities is an important part of healing.

The only reference to ritual abuse in this book can be found in Elizabeth's story. One of her tormentors, Frank, was suspected of dabbling in ritual abuse.

LIFE IN A SHELTER

A Condensed History of Women's Shelters

In North America, Britain and Europe, the women's movement of the 1960s and early '70s gained momentum as women gathered together to discuss issues that affected our lives. Child care, barriers to higher education, barriers to employment, and inadequate health care were among the hot topics of the day. Women established drop-in centres where they could meet and discuss issues and share information. In England in 1971, one such drop-in centre became the impetus for the first women's shelter. Some of the women who had come to the centre had eyes blackened by their husbands' fists. They refused to leave. Home was no longer safe for them or their children. Erin Pizzy chronicles the development of the first women's shelter in her book *Scream Quietly or the Neighbors Will Hear* (Penguin Books, 1974).

In 1973 Canadian women established the first women's shelters in North America in Toronto and Vancouver. By 1979, when Lanark County Interval House opened its doors, there were approximately sixty women's shelters in Canada. Today, in 1995, there are approximately 280 shelters for abused women (see appendix).

Most shelters evolved in a similar fashion. When women found out that other women were being beaten in their community, they got together to organize fund-raising projects, applied for government grants and battled local zoning by-laws in order to open shelters. Usually the shelters filled rapidly, and this was always a surprise to each community. There had been little apparent evidence or knowledge of wife assault. Abused women had kept silent about the violence they experienced until they were given a safe alternative.

The fact that the shelters included children was particularly significant. Mothers would not leave their children behind. For many, the reason they left their partners was to protect their children.

The shelters were truly a grass-roots, women's initiative. Governments and academics were slow to acknowledge the reality of spousal abuse. Even as late as 1982, members of parliament laughed when MP Margaret Mitchell announced that one in ten Canadian men beat their wives. That laughter spurred public outrage and eventual government response.

Most women's shelters are called Transition House or Interval House, or are named to recognize a woman who was significant to the history of the shelter, the community or the country. For example, the Emily Murphy Transition House is named in honour of one of the women who led an action to have Canadian women declared persons.

When we realized that a shelter was needed in our community, we sprang into action, and Lanark County Interval House was opened within six months. The need was so great, in fact, that several abused women were already settled in the shelter before the official opening could be held.

Lanark County Interval House

Lanark County Interval House is located in an old two-storey brick house in a residential area of Carleton Place. The main floor contains a modern kitchen, a dining room with a large pine table, a comfortably furnished living room, a bathroom and a much used laundry room. A recent addition holds a bright, fully equipped playroom. The two-car garage has been converted into a staff office and counselling room. Upstairs, there are four bedrooms and two more bathrooms. The backyard is fenced around a marvellous play structure.

Ideally, each family has a bedroom to themselves—their only real privacy. The bedrooms contain single beds, sturdy bunks and cribs. Rooms must be shared when there are more than four families or adults in residence. The single woman or smallest family is usually the one to be moved around to accommodate the newcomers. There are a total of fifteen beds at Lanark County Interval House, three of them are cribs, but occasionally more than twenty people at one time have made it their home.

The women divide up the household chores and the cooking duties at a weekly residents' meeting. A shopping list is made so that a volunteer can purchase the necessary items. If a woman has special dietary needs, efforts are made to obtain the cooking ingredients that she requires. The smells from the kitchen are often heavenly. It is very tempting to work overtime in hopes of getting an invitation to share in the evening meal.

Security

Security is an important feature in a shelter so all doors are solid and always locked. The windows have security glass, and the house is air-conditioned so that windows and doors can stay locked even during heatwaves. There is a direct emergency signal to the local police station. If abusive partners step on the property, the police are called. However, it was not always so.

For several years Lanark County Interval House allowed abusive husbands to come to the door to pick up their children or, if the women wished, to talk with their partners. Some shelters even allowed repentant husbands to visit with their wives inside the house. In 1988, a husband shot and killed his wife while meeting with her in an Ontario shelter. It was a horrific reminder of the danger facing the women and shelter workers. After that episode, all shelters increased their security.

A good relationship with the police is crucial to a shelter's security. The Carleton Place Police Service is always notified of potential problems, at which time they step up their surveillance. They are quick to respond to calls for help, sometimes arriving within seconds of a call.

The community also provides a measure of security. There is no sign to advertise the shelter's location, but of course, most Carleton Place residents know where it is. When a stranger, a man, asks for directions to the shelter, the locals will suggest that he go to the police station for assistance. Then they will phone Interval House to notify the staff of the inquiry. Even if the man is delivering a $500 donation from his service club, it is a precaution that the staff appreciates, and which safeguards the women and children.

The Rules

All shelters have rules, the most important being a) no violence and b) no illegal drugs or alcohol allowed on the premises. There is a curfew and usually a limit on the length of time a family can stay. There are other rules, written and unwritten, necessary for families to live cooperatively and to maintain health standards.

The no-violence rule can be a problem for moms who use spanking as part of their discipline. As soon as the children realize that mom can no longer spank them, they test her to the limit. The children's workers help both mother and child to adjust to other methods of discipline, but it is often tough going.

Jobs and School

Women are free to come and go. Those who are employed continue to work once they have established their safety or started legal proceedings. Employers are often very supportive and understanding and allow women to take a leave of absence until it is safe for them to return to work.

If they can, the women often plan to leave abusive partners when it will least disrupt their children's lives. Those with school-age children try to hang on until the summer holidays or other school breaks.

Although one thinks of the shelter as being for women, the majority of residents are children, mostly preschoolers. Those who attend school do so as soon as it is safe or when interim custody agreements have been arranged. They may attend school in Carleton Place or, if transportation can be arranged, they go to their home school. If it is not safe for the child to leave Interval House, teachers send class work to the shelter. School bus drivers, taxi drivers, teachers and school staff all share in the job of protecting Interval House children. At times a police escort has been required to get the children safely to school.

Life In A Shelter For a Woman

Women may stay in the shelter only one night or, in cases of extreme abuse, for several months. Some come back a second or third time. There is a cycle. The first time a woman leaves her partner, she usually calls him within the first week. He is often remorseful, cries, begs her to come back, and promises to get help and change his behaviour. She too wants the relationship to work and she returns. Unfortunately, unless he follows through and goes for counselling, he is unable to change his behaviour and starts abusing again. The woman will return to the shelter, this time staying for a longer period as she prepares to live independently. Most women don't stay longer than six weeks.

As you can well imagine, a women's shelter is a lively place. It is definitely not a holiday for the woman. She has to care for her children, take turns at household chores, cook meals and try to live cooperatively with the other families. At the same time, she has to cope with the abuse she has suffered and make important decisions about her future.

At this very traumatic time in her life, she must also wade into the complications of the legal system: custody agreements, peace bonds (a promise from her partner that he will stay away and keep the peace for a year), separation agreements. If her husband is charged with assault, she will be required to talk to the police and the Crown Attorney and then testify against her partner in court.

If the woman has no money, she must deal with the welfare system and forms that require detailed information about her finances. And in a very short period of time, she needs to find housing: a safe, affordable place for herself and her children.

There are lots of tears in a women's shelter. It may be the first time the woman has talked about the abuse she has endured. Sometimes memories of childhood abuse or dating violence flood to the surface because now she is in a safe place and has time to reflect.

While at the shelter, most women go through a period of depression: mourning the death of the relationship, the wasted years, the loss of hope. But the women also begin to find their former selves. It has been months or even years since they have been free to laugh, to be silly and to have fun. Often strong friendships develop between the women in the shelter.

There are also accomplishments. A woman who has lived for many years with an abusive, controlling man may not have been allowed to make many decisions beyond what was to be cooked for supper. And sometimes even that decision was rejected and the meal actually thrown in her face. It can be a major achievement and self-confidence boost, then, to phone a lawyer, call a real-estate agent or prepare a meal that receives praise and appreciation. One woman told me that the first time she had money of her own was when she was given the small weekly allowance at Interval House (currently about $20). It gave her a great deal of satisfaction to buy some personal items and still have some money left at the end of the week.

The Children

The children in the shelter present special joys and challenges. The joys are numerous as they explore new friendships and new toys, and delight in the freedom to play or spill juice without fear of punishment. Babies are especially precious, some only a few days old. The toddlers soon learn the route to the office where, with innocent smiles, they try to get their sticky fingers on a keyboard or climb up onto a welcomimg lap. Older children revel in the Nintendo games, the outdoor play structure or a bike ride with the children's workers. The teens (young men and women) are often thoughtful and want to talk with counsellors about their own feelings and worries.

But . . . after escaping from an abusive husband, Mom naturally expects her children to be grateful to her because now she and they can live happily ever after. Sometimes that is true. However, children more often become angry with their mother because it is safer to express their anger against her than against their father. They blame her for staying too long, for removing them from their neighbourhood and friends, or for not protecting them from the abuse.

Children, especially boys, often mimic their fathers' behaviour. The lessons they have learned are dramatic. I witnessed a baby, less than a year old, choke his mother in a most unbaby-like fashion. I observed another child whose behaviour chilled my optimism. This four-year-old boy strutted and swore and lashed out at others in December 1989, the same week Marc Lepine murdered fourteen women in Montreal.

Staffing

Lanark County Interval House is staffed twenty-four hours a day by women who work as crisis counsellors. There are also children's workers, administrative workers, an overall coordinator, and coordinators of the volunteer program, the follow-up and advocacy program and the public education program. High-school students assist with child care, while university and college students often work in the follow-up program. Carefully screened and trained volunteers assist in all areas of the work.

The Crisis Counsellor's Shift

There are few calm moments for a crisis counsellor. After all, it is crisis work. When a family has just arrived, they need undivided attention. The process goes like this: Welcome them to the shelter. If she wants it, give the woman a hug. Get her a cup of coffee. Give the children a box of toys and some juice until they feel comfortable enough to go with the children's worker and explore the playroom. Help the woman talk about her situation. Find out if the abuser is looking for her. Is he dangerous to others? Does he have weapons? If so, inform the police. If she's been injured, find someone to take her to the hospital. Show her around the house. Introduce her to the other women and children. Help her get settled in a bedroom. Give her towels. Lock up any medication for safe keeping. Sit with her and listen some more. Tell her about the house rules. Have her sign the confidentiality agreement.

The next day, listen again. Answer questions. Assign her household chores. Help her find a lawyer. Help her assemble the questions she needs to ask about obtaining interim custody of the children. Call the welfare worker to come and assess the woman's financial situation. Fill out forms to designate who to call in case of an emergency or to note any special needs. Ask her about the history of the abuse. How were the children affected? How are the children settling in? How is she feeling—about herself, about her partner? Does she have any plans? Does she have other supports—family, friends? Do all this in a relaxed manner. Give her lots of time to talk.

The counsellor also finds time to talk with the other women in the shelter. All are at different stages. Some are looking for apartments ("I can't afford that much rent!") or negotiating with their partners for a reconciliation or attending court or trying to deal with difficult children. Laughing, crying, needing to share.

The shelter operates a busy twenty-four-hour crisis phone line. The phone rings. It's a call from a woman. She's crying. "He pushed me around last night, called me a slut, told me I was a rotten mother, won't let me take a night class, said it isn't his job to babysit, thinks I'm running around with every man in town."

Or it's a call from a woman who has started having nightmares and flashbacks—memories of childhood sexual abuse: "I can't believe this is happening. I feel like I'm going crazy."

Or it's a call from a woman who has just left our shelter: "My husband keeps following me. He tried to run me off the road. I called the police, but they don't think it's serious."

Or it's a call from a man who demands to speak to his wife: "I know she's there. You should know she's crazy. She should be committed. You shouldn't believe anything she says."

Or it's a call from a welfare worker needing information from one of the residents.

Or a call from a lawyer: "Could Mary come to the phone?"

Or a call from a woman who thinks her neighbour is being abused: "What should I do?"

Or a call from another women's shelter: "Do you have room for a woman and her three children?"

Or a student: "I'm doing a project on wife abuse. Can you help me?"

Or a supporter: "Our church had a tea and we've got leftover sandwiches and cookies. Can you use them?"

Or a former resident reporting an achievement: "I was just accepted to go to college!"

Or, occasionally, it's the dreaded call from a woman contemplating suicide: "I can't take anymore." Help her to talk. Try to build up her self-esteem. If she's going down, get her address, call the police on the other line, keep her talking until they arrive.

As in every household, but more so in a shelter, the appliances and plumbing test you: the toilet is plugged, the stove won't turn on, the washing machine quits.

The doorbell rings and rings. It's a woman returning from getting a prescription filled, or a volunteer arriving to drive a woman to a lawyer's appointment in the next town. Or it's the woman with the donation of sandwiches and cookies from that tea, or a child who's been playing in the sandbox and needs to go to the bathroom. Or it's a woman who is trying to look brave: "Is there someone I can talk to?" Arrangements are made with a volunteer or the admin. staff to answer the crisis line so the counsellor can give this woman uninterrupted time. Get her some tea, a box of Kleenex and help her to feel comfortable. "Where would you like to begin?"

If there's a lull, read. There are minutes from Interval House committees or the board of directors meeting, newsletters from other shelters, information about federal initiatives or provincial grants, research papers.

Files need to be written—of the residents' progress, the crisis calls, the chores that need to be done during the next shift.

There's a half-hour shift exchange: a time to brief the next worker on the day's events, the emotional and physical states of the residents, who got missed and needs extra time, crisis calls she should be aware of.

That's the day shift. The evening shift is almost as busy, and unfortunately, there is no office staff to pitch in when needed. The door bell rings less frequently, and there are no phone calls from other agencies. It becomes calmer when the children are settled in bed. The evening is a time for the women to sit with a cup of tea, go over the day's events, get to know each other, play cards and talk.

The overnight shift is the quietest of all. There are few calls between the hours of two and six. Sometimes a woman can't sleep and needs to talk, or a child wakes up sick and requires medication. Sometimes the doorbell rings, and there is a family, dressed only in their pyjamas: "He had a gun. We had no time to change."

After this brief overview of abuse and life in a women's shelter, it is time to meet the women that this book is all about.

JANE'S STORY

As I approached Jane's neat frame house, I could hear the dog—loud barks that changed to a menacing growl when I knocked. The door opened and Jane, gripping the dog's collar, smiled and invited me in. The dog eyed me carefully before deciding I was harmless then wandered off to chew his bone.

Lanark County Interval House had only been open a few months when Jane and her teenage children sought shelter in the fall of 1979. Jane valued the security the house gave her and the support she received from staff and residents. She spoke glowingly of the day one of the volunteers took the family for a Sunday hike: It was wonderful—just what we needed. It had been so long since we'd been able to relax and laugh together.

I've come to know Jane better through our work together on various committees. I have never heard, nor could I imagine, Jane raising her voice. Not because she's timid, but because she is a truly gentle woman.

Jane is a very private person and so I was surprised when she offered to share her story for this book. It was very difficult for her to relive those painful memories but she persevered.

Here's her story.

I was born in 1934 on a Lanark County farm. My mother had ten children in twelve years. I was the third one. Our large farm home had six bedrooms, a big kitchen and an outhouse in the back. As well as farming, father cut logs and trucked cattle.

Christmas was a happy time. There always seemed to be something for everyone under the tree. We'd get carrots from the basement for the reindeer, and before we fell asleep, we could hear sleigh-bells ringing outside. Of course it was father shaking the bells. In the summer we helped with the garden and picked berries.

When my youngest brother was born, mother became quite sick and was in the hospital for what seemed to be a long time. That was when I got my first taste of being a housekeeper.

My two oldest brothers didn't go to high school, but I always wanted to be a nurse so I boarded with a family in town and got my grade thirteen. Then it was off to Kingston for nurse's training.

The first year I was in training, I knew my mother wasn't well, but the doctor just said her blood was low. She died of cancer when I was in my last year. My little brother was only ten years old. I intended to stay home and help the family, but my father and sister insisted I finish. It was hard, you know. My sister went to school and looked after the five young ones. Dad had no insurance so there was a big hospital bill to pay as well as provide for the family.

After graduation in 1956, I came home and looked after the family so my sister could go to business college. I worked at the local hospital on weekends.

During high school I had several boyfriends for short periods of time. I didn't go out much. I went to Saturday-night dances with my two brothers. While I was in training, I just went out the odd night to a show or something. I guess I was thinking of the younger ones at home and how my sister was getting along. I really didn't feel like living it up. I went home on my days off as often as I could, to help my sister.

I met Dave on a blind date. My first impression was that he was a good dancer. He worked in Ottawa at the time, so we saw each other on Saturdays or Sundays. One Saturday, we were to go to a reception. When he came in through the door, I thought he looked kind of strange. He sat on a chair and dropped a cigarette on the floor, and that struck me as being kind of different. But I wasn't used to anybody who drank so I didn't know what it was.

Dave's friend drove us to the dance. Dave didn't say too awful much on the way to the hall. It was just a short drive anyway. When I went to get out of the car, he was sound asleep beside me. So I asked his friend what was wrong, and he said that Dave just had too much to drink. That just made me very mad. I asked the friend to drive me home, and I told Dave never to come back again if he was going to let that happen. He came the next day and apologized. He said it would never happen again. And it didn't. There was never a time when we were dating that I was aware that he was drinking.

That fall my sister finished college so I went back to Kingston and became a full-time nurse. I came home every night. It was about an hour and a half drive. During the winter months, I didn't come home if the weather was bad or if I had to do shift work.

Dave and I dated for nearly two years, and it was getting serious. Although in the back of my mind I had reservations, I couldn't seem to make any sort of reason why. We argued a lot. He wanted me to work closer to home. He was Catholic and I was Protestant and that was another one of our arguments. We got engaged the summer I was twenty-five years old. In those days, if we were to marry, one of us had to convert. I gave in and took the religious classes.

About two months before the wedding, Dave smashed his car. He told me he was crowded off the road, but I found out six months later that he had been charged with impaired driving. At the wedding rehearsal it seemed as though he had been drinking, and that bothered me. We were married the next morning and he seemed fine.

There weren't any sort of problems until about a month after we were married. Dave started drinking and he wouldn't be home in time for supper. I'd had enough of this and was ready to leave him until I found out I was already pregnant.

Dave was sort of mad that I got pregnant right away. We weren't using any precautions. He seemed to sort of straighten up then. He didn't have anything to drink in the house at all. Heather was born ten days early by Caesarean section. It was kind of an upsetting time for me. I thought everyone would be counting on their fingers. *(At that time it was considered a shameful thing for a woman to have a baby within nine months of her wedding.)* Dave seemed to be proud of being a father and was good to help with the baby. I went back to work two months later.

Dave's father offered to let us build a house on his farm. We worked on it all the next summer. Dave's mother, Mrs. White, babysat Heather once we moved. We went to dances and parties and everything seemed to be fine. We had a happy home life. I grew to love my husband.

The next pregnancy was planned and we were both quite happy about it. Carol was also born by a C-section in December, and in two months I was able to go back to work.

That February I found out I was pregnant again! All of a sudden Dave got cross and ugly and started belittling me. He said I was stupid to get pregnant, that it wasn't his child; he didn't want another child, we couldn't afford it. Which, you know, I was aware of too, but I didn't get pregnant on my own! The rhythm method was our only means of birth control. It wasn't an ideal situation because after having a section for each of the girls, I wasn't looking forward to having another baby in eleven months' time. I had a lot of tears and a lot of unhappiness during that pregnancy. I was run down. That winter Dave lost his licence for impaired driving.

Our son Robert was also born by C section. He was small but he was healthy and I was back to work in two months. We could have gotten by with me staying at home except that Dave was drinking more and more.

Dave often acted like a spoiled child. If he saw something he wanted it didn't matter if he didn't have the money, he bought it anyway. My salary would have to cover all the other expenses.

The next summer Dave went to Montreal to work. The second weekend he came home rip-roaring mad. He was crazy. He slammed his fist on the stove and shouted and roared. He pushed me out through the back door and yelled at me for not packing his clothes properly so he could go out in the evening. He wouldn't let me take the kids. I ran to his mother's and asked her to help me get the kids. It was very frightening. She went to our house and returned with the children. She said he was crazy.

We all stayed in the barn for part of the night. I asked Mrs. White what I should do. I said we couldn't live like that: it wasn't good for the children. She explained that that was how it used to be for some families in her younger days. I had the feeling that her father was physically abusive. She never did say that he was ugly or mean but he was a drinker. Her parents were separated and he lived with another woman without a divorce, which was quite a thing in those days.

Dave came and apologized the next morning. He said they'd been drinking on the drive home.

Over the next ten years Dave lost his licence many times to drinking, and then I'd have to drive him to work and come back home to get ready for my job. On Fridays I'd have to stay in town and wait for him to come out of the hotel. In the early days, the hotel closed at six and didn't reopen till seven, so it wasn't too bad. But later it never closed. I'd sit outside in the truck, waiting. If I didn't and went home, he'd be furious. If it looked like he was going to be late, I'd have to call my mother-in-law and ask her if she could keep the children longer. The Friday night routine gradually stretched out to Thursdays as well.

I was so tired. Sometimes, at a house party, I'd sit in a corner and if I dozed off that would be a disgrace. Dave would get ugly—maybe throw a beer bottle at me from across the room to wake me up. He'd chew at me all the way home. He didn't hit me or anything at that point.

I couldn't cry in front of him; he'd just belittle me more. Sometimes I cried on my way to work. It was a twenty-five-minute drive. The head nurse would ask, "Are you alright? You look like you've been crying."

I'd say, "I must be getting a cold."

One Friday night in 1966, Dave came home in good time. He had his licence at that time and didn't appear to be drunk. The kids had already eaten and were bathed and put to bed. Out of the blue, Dave accused me of sleeping with another man. He was shouting and pounding me—it seemed like forever. He went to bed and slept, but I stayed up half the night. I had multiple bruises and a black eye. When he left the next morning, Heather, who was about six, ran to Mrs. White's to get her to come and see me. Heather still remembers this. I think Mrs. White was upset—she didn't know what to say. I remember sitting out on the back step. I didn't want anyone to see me like that. I didn't want my family to know. I just kind of sat there in dread of what Dave would do when he came home. I didn't know what to do. He came home and had supper as if nothing had happened. He never said a word about it. I phoned into work and said I had the measles and wouldn't be in for a week.

Times after that Dave avoided hitting my face; he generally punched my arms. Meanwhile, he was coming home from the hotel with bruises and cuts from fighting.

I was able to get a daytime nursing job. It was a relief to be finished with shift work.

In 1970 Dave had a car accident and he was hospitalized for two weeks with a broken jaw; it was wired shut. After that, he was much freer with his slaps and kicks. I asked the doctor if Dave had had a head injury because he seemed to be much more irritable. I also wondered if it was because he couldn't fight at the hotel for fear of breaking his jaw again that he took it out on me. My legs and arms were so badly bruised that I had to wear pant-suit uniforms and sweaters during the summer. The odd time, he hit my face.

More and more, I guess your self-respect and morale goes down. I wondered what I was doing wrong. I tried my best to bake something special or to make sure he always had a steak. Dave liked steak and I remember one time I had prepared his favourite meal. He'd been drinking all day and when he came to the table he upset it and yelled, "Cook me something better than this slop." It wouldn't matter if it was the best steak in the butcher shop.

There were times when he fell asleep, I'd be so full of hate that I'd wish I had the courage to hit him with a bat for all the horrible things he said to me and about me. I wondered why Dave's parents didn't do something, but I guess they were afraid of him as well.

Dave ridiculed my family, especially my father. He said, "Your father's always here with his crooked nose. He's nosy."

My dad was very polite but he told me later, "There were many times when I drove away I could hear Dave shouting at you and I'd wonder if I should go back, but I was afraid it might make things worse."

My brothers told me, "I wish you had said something." They saw him get ugly at dances but didn't realize that he was worse when we got home.

There were times after he was sort of being verbally abusive, we'd get into bed, and he was loving and kind. But I was turned off—I couldn't. He was never sexually abusive.

One Thursday night in 1975, Dave was really drunk and wanted me to cook him a steak. When I placed it on the table, he got out a long hunting knife and sort of cut the steak with it as he was sitting beside me. He said the steak was too tough and reached over and threatened me with the knife. I stayed awake all that night.

When he went to work on Friday I called my sister and asked if we could come for the weekend. The kids and I put our clothes in the car and after work I picked them up at school. I told my sister what was going on. My father came over and I spared him most of the gory details. Mrs. White phoned and said that Dave was looking for me. On Sunday a neighbour phoned and said, "Don't come home, he's got a revolver."

I went to see my employer and he persuaded me to charge Dave with assault. I was crying and he said, "What's become of you; where's your backbone?" It helped me see that I was worth something. I had been degraded for so long.

The police picked Dave up at work on Monday and I faced him in court on Tuesday. I felt sorry for him: he was unshaven and dressed in his dirty work clothes. The judge asked if Dave could speak to me. Dave was full of apologies and promises. He said he'd keep the peace, he'd stop drinking, he would go to church. He had to sign a peace bond for a year.

The kids and I went back home and we had a year with no beatings. But the verbal abuse, if not worse, was just as bad. He said I was lazy and good-for-nothing, I couldn't cook. He said the kids weren't necessarily his. When the year was up he went right back to the old ways.

In the summer the kids often slept outside in a tent. They enjoyed sleeping out there. If they heard Dave roaring and shouting, they'd go to their grandparents'. If he was quiet, they'd sneak into the house and go to their own bedrooms. Sometimes he'd be so wild, if I could get away from him, I would go to the White's as well. If he came over, we'd slip out the back door and hide in the barn. During the winter, the children slept upstairs three to a bed, in the only bedroom where they could escape out the window and onto the porch roof.

Some nights Dave could go on all night long. Sometimes he just yelled at me. It wouldn't be a prolonged beating but he'd punch hard enough to leave a bad bruise. Many nights I didn't get to bed. I had to keep myself alert during the day.

Dave got bouts of pancreaitis. It's a drinking illness. He was hospitalized for a week and then didn't drink for a month. It was a nice time. We'd actually go for Sunday drives and do things together the way normal people do. It was a peaceful period, seemed to make life worth living.

Two years later his gall bladder was removed and he had two operations on his pancreas. He was having problems with the combination of painkillers and nerve pills and alcohol. Whenever he could, he talked the doctor into giving him more prescription drugs or he would run to emergency for a shot. If the doctor said, "No," Dave became more abusive. He didn't work after that and got a disability pension. This meant he could drink all night and sleep all day. I rarely got a full night's sleep.

The kids were getting older (in their teens), and Dave told them they were too fat and too lazy. If Heather wanted to go to a high-school dance he'd say, "Get your tin pants on; we don't want any babies around here." Heather was almost finished high school when she started dating. She'd always be home by midnight and if she and her boyfriend stood outside on the step for even two minutes, Dave would shake his fist and say terrible things to her when she came inside.

That summer Robert was fifteen and he stayed home every evening to protect me. Even when he was little, Robert took on the father role. He was only six when the porch step broke. He ran to get a hammer and said, "Don't worry, I'll fix it for you Mom."

Dave began molesting Heather and Carol during his drinking spells. The girls didn't tell me this until after we'd left home. The girls told me that before I'd get home, he'd want them to get him something to eat and then he'd reach out and rub their backs and try to rub their breasts. It was always when he was really drunk. I felt really angry. I asked, "Why didn't you tell me sooner?"

They said, "We knew it would worry you and we knew it wouldn't go any further because we could get away from him." They didn't tell Robert either because he would have killed him.

There were weekends when Dave didn't appear to be drinking but his behaviour was peculiar. At that time I didn't think about it because I knew he wasn't drinking. He used to say, "If the doctor isn't going to give me something for the pain I know where I can get something that works a lot better."

One day he tore my nightie to shreds and then he choked me until I was nearly unconscious. It was a frightening feeling. I could feel myself blacking out and I thought, This is it. It was like he was possessed. I found out later that he'd been getting drugs from a neighbour.

In September of 1979, Heather was away at her first year of college. Dave came home on a Tuesday night and he was just wild beyond imagination: kicking at anything and everything. I shoved him backwards. It was the first time I was brave enough to push back. The kids and I ran to the White's and he was right behind us. He pounded on the locked door: "Let me in, let me in." We heard him say he was going to get a gun and that scared me. I called the police. They got there in half an hour. It seemed like a long time. I think Dave heard me phoning because he went back home and turned the lights out. The police arrested him the next morning.

The kids and I went to my employer's home for the night and the town police patrolled the area. I laid an assault charge the next day. The police told me about an Interval House that had recently opened in the next town. I didn't want to put my family (my sister) in any danger, and even though I knew little about Interval House, we really had nowhere else to go.

We were given the largest bedroom. The kids were relieved to see it had a fire escape out the back window. There were two other families at the house, yet we could all sit down peacefully and eat together. At that time the meals included deer meat and goat's milk because the house didn't have much money and relied on donations of food. It didn't matter. For the first time in months we could go to bed and feel safe and actually sleep. I felt so much better even though my mind was twirling.

I cried a lot while I was at Interval House. I was ashamed at what the kids had gone through. But the moral support I received from the staff and the other residents helped me realize that I didn't need to feel so ashamed. It wasn't such a big disgrace.

I got my car and clothes the next day while Dave was in jail. Still, when he was released I was afraid to drive to work. After two days, I drove the kids to high school and went on to my job. Dave showed up at the school and Robert was called to the office to see him. Dave demanded that Robert tell him where we were staying. That night Robert was in tears. The next day I called the principal and Dave wasn't allowed to harass the kids again.

We stayed at Interval House for ten days and then moved to an apartment my employer found for us. He and his wife were a wonderful support and kept in touch. Heather came home from college on weekends.

For the first few months I cried after the children were in bed. I was ashamed at what they had gone through.

In November Dave started calling me at work. He said he'd learned his lesson; he wanted to see the kids; he couldn't live without us, and he wouldn't drink anymore. He said he loved me and begged me to return before Christmas. We moved back in early December. I suppose I still had some hope that he would change but something inside me told me it would never work. Everything was quiet and he really tried. He even had supper started when I got home from work.

On Christmas Eve, Dave bought liquor and beer. He said he'd need it if friends visited during the holidays. He drank a little on Christmas Day and during the week. He was going down day by day. One day he was in the process of skinning a beaver in the basement when he turned to me with the skinning knife in his hand and said, "If you ever call the police on me again you'll never live to tell the tale." That night I told the kids to pack and secretly put their stuff in my car. The next day they went off to school and I went to work. I phoned him that night and said we wouldn't be back. Fortunately, we were able to move back into our apartment.

Dave kept phoning and phoning me at work. I had an unlisted number at home. When his begging didn't work he became quite angry.

In February, Dave admitted himself to the Kingston Psychiatric Hospital. His father asked me to go with Dave for marriage counselling, but I refused.

In March, Mrs. White was visiting Carol and I. Dave came to our apartment, supposedly to pick his mother up but he pushed his way inside and demanded that Carol go home with him. He started pounding me and tried to throw me out the window. Carol attempted to protect me but I told her to leave. She ran to a neighbour's and called the police. When they arrived, Dave had left through the back door. They found him two days later. I had to take time away from work. I had three broken ribs. Dave was charged with assault and sentenced to three months in jail.

I had the full support of the police. If Dave was banging at the door, I'd phone and the police would be there in minutes.

Dave phoned me repeatedly at work. He threatened, "You just watch when you go out that door at night—I can see you. You know how good a shot I am." I had difficulty sleeping.

In May Dave beat up his father and was jailed for fourteen days. His father was astonished at his son's violence.

In July he beat up his mother. He burned her arms with his cigarette and threatened to drown her. He was sentenced to six months in jail.

The day after Christmas, Dave punched his father in the stomach because he wouldn't take him to buy booze. Shortly afterwards his father was hospitalized and several months later died of a bowel obstruction.

In January 1981, Dave broke his seventy-six-year-old mother's arm. He was sentenced to eighteen months in jail. The kids and I looked after Mrs. White. It was great; it was peaceful.

Dave was sent to the Clark Institute in Toronto for psychiatric assessment. The psychiatrist called me for information about Dave's childhood and the only thing I could come up with was that he was an only child and sort of spoiled. I know that when Dave was a teenager and Mr. White was away, Dave would take his father's car even before he had a licence. If Mr. White questioned the change in mileage, his mother would cover up by saying she'd lent the car to a neighbour. But otherwise I didn't think he was treated badly. It seems to me that he had to have somebody else to blame when he smashed up his truck or whatever he did.

When he got out of jail he was warned not to contact his mother, but he did. She had moved into town and he just tormented her. He beat her up badly on Christmas Eve and was sentenced to two years. She lived in fear during her last three years of life.

Dave is still around and is still driving. In fact, he just bought a new truck. I don't know where he gets the money or why a dealer would sell to him. I don't know how, with all his drinking, he hasn't killed himself. A neighbour once told me, "The devil gives much stronger protection than God."

The last time Dave really bothered me was four years ago. I was walking home and he drove slowly past me. My heart was pounding. I called the police when I got home and he hasn't bothered me since. I'm still afraid he'll come up behind me or try to run me down. I carry a corkscrew in my hand when I walk home at night and I'm very watchful.

I still shake inside telling you about all this and I'm angry with myself for not leaving earlier. I was degraded for so long. I was afraid to stay and I was afraid to leave. I feel angry that my children missed a good childhood: violence and running and being afraid. Mrs. White used to say, "Well he never did anything to hurt the kids. Why are they afraid of him?"

My children get together and talk about it. "Do you remember the time he did such and such," they say. It hurts their spouses to hear these stories so they do their reminiscing when there are just the three of them. My son is still angry with his father and is afraid Dave will do something to hurt me. I think he still feels he should have done more to protect his sisters and I. As far as I can tell, my children are non-violent and have married non-violent people. One of my daughters is a nurse.

My life is full. My workdays are long but I enjoy my job and the close relationship with my employer and his wife. I have women friends; I attend church, and I see my children and grandchildren often. My father is still alive and I enjoy visiting him, as well as my brothers and sisters.

I have a little dog that doesn't like men and barks loudly if anyone comes to the door. I feel comfortable going to sleep knowing that my dog will wake me.

But I don't think I'll ever have that weight off my back until Dave is dead and in the ground.

I visited Jane for the update. This time her little dog was tied in the backyard, but it alerted her to my presence. She said, He's still a real good watchdog. He's eleven—the same age as my oldest grandson.

Jane's husband died in 1991. He had been living at a retirement home as well as "boarding" with a woman. Jane said, One lady told me that the woman probably drank along with him and that would please him. She bought things for him, including a truck. That would keep him 'peaceified.' The woman came home from work late at night and found him dead in bed. I'm sure he died of an overdose of pills and drinking. The police phoned Robert and he called me right away at 4 a.m. He said, "He's dead." I said, "Who's dead?"

The next day I actually called the funeral home and asked, "Is it him in the casket?" The woman at the funeral home said I could come in the back door and see him to be sure, but I said no, I believed her if she said it was him.

Nobody went to the funeral. A forty-second cousin went to the wake. She said she just wanted to be sure he was dead.

He died on our wedding anniversary. Carol said, "Don't you think he did that on purpose?" I just thought, I can breathe again. It was a relief for all the children too. It was the only way.

After he died, I heard from some of the staff at the retirement home. They had an awful problem with him coming back and demanding pain pills and tranquillizers.

Jane continues to work as a nurse.

Jane's father has been sick. And, just as in the past, Jane and her sister take turns taking care. He just wasn't eating. He said, "I think I just got lazy." But, you know, living alone . . . He's living at my sister's. I take him back to his own house every weekend to give her a break. So I spend every Saturday and Sunday with him.

Jane takes delight in her eight grandchildren who are all nearby. Her daughters have good marriages, but Robert and his wife have separated. She found somebody else. I think that's the main reason they separated, but I don't know. He has the children every second weekend and one or two evenings every week.

Two years ago, Jane took up square dancing. My son-in-law's mother invited me. She said she'd dance the man's part if I could dance the woman's part. It was quite a fun evening. This lasted for a year and then she got married. So a year ago, I started dancing the man's part with another woman. It's two hours of good exercise and fun every week. Some nights when I get home from work, I'm tired and I think I won't go. But then I have a bath and I feel better and I'm always glad I went. When you get home from square dancing you feel invigorated.

I asked Jane for her advice to other women. Don't put up with more than one thing of abuse. Get out and get help for yourself and for your partner if he'll go. Or put him out—whichever works best. Usually getting out is safest. Don't try to hide it. Don't be ashamed that it's happened. Ninety-nine per cent of the time it's not your fault.

Jane told me that she had just met an abused woman that day in the grocery store. She could see the bruises on her arms, neck and legs. Jane asked her if she'd been hurt and the woman told her that her boyfriend had hit her. I just said, "Have you got a safe place to be?" and she said she'd been at her sister's. I asked, "Have you reported him?" and she said, "Yes." I suggested she call Interval House and she said the police had already told her about it.

WHY

Why Do Women Stay?

When I talk to groups about abuse, the question they most often ask is, "Why do women stay in an abusive relationship?" One could spend many hours outlining the socialization of women and men, the roadblocks and lack of supports for women to actually leave, and the special ties found in intimate relationships. But I often like to turn it around and ask the questioners if they have ever been in a similar predicament. For example, have they ever stayed in an unsatisfactory job too long?

Consider this scenario: You discover that because of the stress of your job you have developed ulcers and yet you stay at it. Why? The reasons could include economic necessity, the status linked with being employed or the social perks in working with others.

Or perhaps you have your own business and it's not doing well financially. How long is it before you declare bankruptcy, and why do you delay? Could it be in part because of the shame of your supposed mismanagement, or the hope that conditions will change and the business will take a turn for the better?

Or perhaps your job is physically quite dangerous. For example, farming and mining are both considered high risk and yet people continue to choose those occupations. Why? Could it be because of family pressures (to maintain the farm in the family name), or because it is the only job available in the area or because you optimistically believe that it will be different for you and that you can minimize or sidestep the danger?

The reasons for staying in an unsatisfactory job are among the many that can apply to staying in an abusive relationship. There are others.

Many women stay for the sake of the children. They accept society's ideal of a two-parent family regardless of how detrimental that arrangement may be to the health of all.

There are financial concerns: If you don't have a job, how will you support yourself and your children? One woman told me she delayed leaving an abusive partner in the early '70s because of her avocado-coloured stove and refrigerator. She knew if she left she would have to give up her middle-class house and her middle-class life and go on welfare. This would mean poverty and loss of opportunity for her children as well. It was a most difficult decision.

There is a great fear among abused women that, if they leave, they will lose their children. The woman is more likely to feel responsible for the children, and the abuser knows that threatening to call CAS is an effective way to keep her in line. Often, in abusive relationships, the children are harmed, directly or indirectly, by one or both parents. Neglect, emotional abuse and physical assault are common.

A woman may stay in an abusive relationship because she knows she made a mistake—she chose the wrong mate. Feelings of loyalty or a fatalistic attitude make her feel she must live with the consequences. Resigned, she says, "It's my lot in life." Or she may have chosen this partner over the objections of her parents and now feels bound to prove them wrong.

Ongoing emotional abuse can damage a woman's self-confidence and leave her uncertain about any decision she might make.

If the woman is physically assaulted, especially about the head, the physical injury can cause confusion. Several years ago I was in a car accident and suffered a minor head injury. For a week after, I felt as though my brain was scrambled. I could not think clearly and certainly could not have made an important decision.

An abuser may require his partner to participate in activities she finds repulsive. Out of fear, or to ease herself out of the situation, she cooperates. If her partner's behaviour becomes particularly bizarre, her shame in being involved may ensure her silence. She'll be reluctant to leave and open herself to exposure.

Alcohol is often a factor in abusive relationships. The victim accepts the abuse because, "He was drinking and didn't know what he was doing." When alcohol is involved, there appears to be a gender difference that is illustrated by a common statistic used by addictions agencies: when the man is the alcoholic in the family, nine out of ten women stay in the relationship; when the woman is the alcoholic, nine out of ten men leave.

Some women turn to alcohol or drugs in order to cope with the pain of emotional or physical abuse and are thus unable to make a decision.

Some abusers threaten to commit suicide or to kill their partners if they leave. Or he may threaten to kill the children, her parents, friends or anyone else who might support her. Women know these threats are often real.

If the abused woman has a physical disability, her dependency is multiplied. In order to contemplate leaving the abuser (and her caregiver), she must find a shelter that can accommodate her particular needs. She also needs to know that there is other accessible accommodation in her community and other caregivers.

An immigrant woman faces special obstacles. She may not yet be able to read or speak English or French and therefore does not know what services are available to her. She may feel that she cannot trust the police. Probably her greatest fear is of deportation, especially if her husband is her sponsor.

An aboriginal woman may delay leaving because finding a safe place means leaving her community and all her supports. In the north, it can mean a move of several hundred miles and limited communication with her family. If she moves to the south, she must cope with an unfamiliar culture.

There are particular religions and cultures that give women little status and place great emphasis on a woman's duty to keep the family intact. When a woman leaves her husband, she not only incurs his wrath, but the disapproval of the whole community. She may be shunned or even attacked by others.

Furthermore, of course, there is always the hope that the abuse will stop, and that her partner will change for the better. On top of all that, she may still love him. She recognizes his vulnerabilities and knows that he needs her support. How can she leave him now?

Change is difficult. There is a saying: Better the devil you know, than the one you don't. An abused woman who leaves a relationship will have many devils to face.

But, surely, no one still believes that a woman stays in an abusive relationship because she likes being beaten. Some women may be so wounded in their self-esteem that they feel that they deserve the abuse, but no one likes it.

Rather than dwelling on why women stay, I think the more important question is, why do they leave?

Why Do Women Leave?

A woman may endure an abusive relationship for one, twenty or even fifty years and then leave. What is the final straw?

You'll see in these ten stories that most of the women felt that the abuse had escalated to such an extent that if they stayed much longer, they would be killed. Some saw it as escaping an emotional death. Some sought advice and left as a result of that advice and their own sense of survival. Some left because there was now a place of safety (Interval House) for them and their children.

Several years ago I attended a workshop in Montreal where a McGill researcher reported on her study of this very question. When she asked women why they had left their abusive relationships, the most common answer was that they finally realized that the relationship would never improve. The researcher felt that this loss of hope was a key factor in the decision to leave.

While many women stay for the sake of the children, it is also a key reason why they leave. If her partner starts to abuse the children and is no longer a good father, or if she sees that his abuse of her is starting to affect the children, that is when she gets out.

She may leave because a significant person has suggested it. This person could be a doctor, a police officer, a parent, a friend, a counsellor or her child. When a woman calls the shelter to talk about the abuse, you can hear the despair or fear in her voice. Sometimes you need only say, "You are being abused. You are in danger. It is important that you leave. I will help you." Although she has taken the first step by making the phone call, the counsellor's affirmation of the abuse gives the woman permission to make the move.

Our society still places great pressure on women to keep the family intact. However, there is almost equal support for women to leave abusive relationships. There are role models—prominent women who have left and who have shared their stories of abuse. There is also the co-worker or the woman next door who has demonstrated that she can survive on her own and who is willing to share her knowledge.

Sometimes a woman leaves intending to return soon, after she and her partner renegotiate and renew the relationship on a more positive footing. But if her partner becomes more abusive, he may make it impossible for her to return.

Women leave when they develop a measure of self-confidence. Some find this increased self-assurance when they get a job, return to school or take on a task in the community. They realize that they are capable and are worthy of respect. The abuser often sees this new independence as a threat to his control and increases his abuse, thus prompting her to leave sooner.

If the pattern of abuse involves alcohol and the abuser only beats her when he's drunk, the first time he beats her when he is sober is often an eye-opener for the woman. She leaves because there is now no excuse for his behaviour.

There are many other reasons that impel a woman to make such a drastic change in her life. I remember a phone call from a woman who had just been told that she had six months left to live. She decided that her last six months were going to be abuse-free. She phoned to talk about the arrangements she needed to make in order to leave her abusive husband.

There are many reasons why women stay in or leave abusive relationships but I think the most important question to be asked is, why do men abuse?

Why Do Some Men Abuse?

The word some must be emphasized because only a minority of men abuse women and children. But their actions have a ripple effect, causing much havoc and fear among the wider population. Too often, they are supported in their violence by the silence or inaction of their brothers.

In my fifty years of life I have learned that men are shaped by their environment, as are women. So the young boy who observes his father and other men receiving deferential treatment grows up to expect the same. When he hears the female gender being degraded, it is natural to copy the language. With the abundance of pornography and the sexual portrayal of women in mainstream media, it is easy for him to adopt the same limited view of their role. By omission, he rarely has the opportunity to learn of the contributions of women to his world and so he is unlikely to have a natural respect for their abilities. And if his father verbally abuses and/or physically assaults his mother, he learns that that is how you handle women.

I know all this. And yet, I do not truly understand. I do not understand why some men degrade and abuse the women they profess to love. I do not understand why some men fear women and especially fear women's achievement of equality. I do not understand some men's anger and self-centredness. I do not understand their fascination with war and guns and their need to dominate and control. I do not understand violent sports, in particular, boxing. Most of all, I do not understand rape.

In discussing this issue, a male friend suggested that our culture promotes male violence. He pointed out that men are even more likely than women to be attacked or abused by other men. It was his contention that we should be exploring how some men are able to resist this socialization and live their lives as gentle men. What went right in their lives? What can we learn from them? This is a fine idea, but I want to leave it to the men. I want them to take it on with the same energy and commitment that women have devoted to the protection of our sisters. I want them to use their outrage to make a positive difference. But it is rare to hear men even ask the questions or show any lasting concern.

It is easy to feel depressed by this issue, but I have found hope in an article written for *Science 82* about U.S. anthropologist Peggy Sandry. In her study of rape-free and rape-prone societies, she found that there were many societies where women are not abused, as well as societies where violence against women was very pronounced. There is a common thread in the violence-free societies: the deity was female or a non-gendered spirit, and there was no threat of famine or war.

Whatever the reason the society is rape-free, it is interesting to note that there are places where women, and perhaps men, are *not* abused. It reinforces my belief that culture dictates behaviour and that men are not born violent. It also follows that, with a change of culture, women could live without fear.

Imagine that.

SUSAN'S STORY

Susan has a wonderful, happy face—the kind that breaks into a smile with little provocation. But that smile disappears when she talks about her teen years. The memory is painful.

After my first interview with Susan, I went over my notes and discovered that she, like so many women, had minimized the physical and verbal abuse she suffered at the hands of her husband. During the second interview, she shared more information but simply did not dwell or elaborate on the years of physical hurt and emotional humiliation.

Then I interviewed Olive, the Interval House counsellor who was on shift the night Susan arrived, and learned about the depth of degradation that Susan had survived. Olive said:

"I remember listening to Susan and thinking she looks like the kind of woman who would never be beaten. She looks like the neighbour across the street who would always have supper ready on time. She had such a gentle face and yet there she was, telling me about the most horrendous abuse—it just poured forth. The most shocking incident took place after a party. Suuan hadn't wanted to attend; her husband had been drinking all day but he insisted she accompany him. Before long, he got in a fight and the host made him leave—actually put him out the door. While Susan was driving him home, he punched her and called her names. He blamed her for making him leave and said, 'Wait till we get home.' When they got in the house, he really went after her. She fell down and he kicked her head several times until she started to bleed. She dragged herself onto the bed and bled so much the mattress had to be thrown out. He had the nerve to say, 'Now look what you've done.'

"I don't remember sleeping on that shift. I think she talked all night and then she didn't talk about it much again while at the house. She didn't want me to tell anyone about that particular beating. I think it was just too humiliating.

"Susan berated herself for not leaving her husband a note—for not being fair, upfront, honest, direct. She was quite certain she should phone him in the morning and tell him that she had 'his' son. But she was afraid of what his reaction would be and the names he would call her. I role-played the phone call with her and used the most degrading names I could think of, including fucking cunt, but she said he would use worse. I then suggested she could always hang up on him. This was so foreign to her, so impolite. So I said, 'What is the worst thing that can happen to you if you hang up? Will you get struck by a lightning bolt?' It sounded so ridiculous that she had to laugh.

"When she did call her husband, she hung up when he became verbally abusive. She was elated, and there was no lightning bolt."

Susan stayed at Interval House for about two months and was so certain that she had chosen the right course, she was one of the few women who didn't return home to give their husbands a second chance.

Here's Susan's story.

I was born in 1951. I was the third child in a family of eight. Father was thirty and mother was seventeen when they got married.

My father was in the armed forces so we moved many times. He was a heavy drinker you know, but he wasn't abusive. He was loud and strict and far from being perfect, but he wasn't cruel. We got lickin's if we deserved them. We all loved and respected him, but we feared him as well.

I remember hearing my father talking to my mother after he'd come home from the hotel. He'd talk about war memories. His drinking buddies were also veterans. He cried when he talked about scraping through the remains of his friends who'd been hit by bombs—looking for their dog tags. Mother would hold his hand and quietly listen to him. We kids often watched this scene through the stove-pipe hole in the bedroom floor.

Father never drank at home. He always drank at the hotel or at other people's homes.

My mother was very quiet and lenient with us—maybe to balance my father's strictness. I used to think my mother was fat you know, but now I realize she was always pregnant. She had several miscarriages as well. Father was Catholic and wouldn't hear of birth control. I remember her holding a bloody sheet between her legs and father telling us he had to take her to the hospital. Mother cried a lot. She had several nervous breakdowns and had to be hospitalized.

When I was fourteen, my mother had just been hospitalized with another nervous breakdown. All of a sudden one day you get called to the office at school and, "Would you mind coming with us please?" We were driven home and our clothes were put in a bag and myself and my six-year-old sister were driven twenty-six miles away to the country and dropped off at a farmhouse. We were divided up in twos. My two oldest sisters didn't have to go because they were over sixteen.

I felt terrible. You know we were Catholics and I always felt we were close. And then again, about four months later, I came home from school and my little sister had been moved. I wasn't told about that either. She had been very withdrawn. We never got together. I learned where my middle brother and sister lived and I wrote to them.

I found my youngest sister three years ago. I located her myself. The adoption didn't work out I tell you. She didn't get along with her adoptive mother at all. She has a child and she's on mother's allowance in Toronto. I'm still searching for my two youngest brothers.

I still don't know the details. I think Father asked the Children's Aid for help when Mother was hospitalized, or it could have been a relative; anyway he obviously signed the papers. The Children's Aid probably investigated and decided he wasn't a fit parent. I was never able to ask him what happened. I didn't want him to feel I was blaming him. I didn't want to hurt him. I blamed him and yet I didn't want to open old wounds. He never talked about it. Father died five years ago.

I never asked Mom about it either. She's had enough hurt. I don't think she ever slept with my father after that. She never got pregnant again. When she was released from the psychiatric hospital, she came home to no children except for her two oldest daughters. It sounds unbelievable. She's fine now. I mean, she's still on medication you know. It's hard to talk to her. She drifts off.

The people in the foster home were very nice but I just felt I was a housekeeper. They tried in their own way I suppose, but it was all so new. I felt foreign. I was from town and this was a sheep farm! I was there for a year and then they sold the farm and I moved with them to town. I finished high school there and got my grade twelve.

When I was eighteen, I moved to a town in Lanark County and found a place to board and got a job on an assembly line. I didn't know anybody. Oh yeah, I got to know people at work, but I mean not really anybody outside of work. So I was lonely. Obviously that loneliness didn't work out.

I didn't go out with George for long; I gave in quite quickly. I think I had too much to drink. To be honest with you, I needed that to relax because I wasn't comfortable. You know, you get your nerve from a bottle. I'm not a very outgoing person; I was even less then. The drinking was pretty much new too.

When I found out I was pregnant, I didn't want it. I thought, I hardly know this guy. I told George. You know I was surprised because he said, "We'll have to get married." What do you do? Catholic girls didn't get pregnant and have babies on their own, no more than they had abortions or anything like that, eh?

The wedding was very small—his family and two of my sisters. I wanted to get out of that church. I didn't want to be there, but I felt like I had to you know. I was nineteen and he was twenty.

We moved to a trailer outside of town.

One week later came the first pow. He was drinking. That was the night after his parents gave us one of those country receptions. It was their wedding gift. After we came home it was, "You didn't talk to people enough," you know, "Say thank you to so and so." I mean these were all total strangers to me and I was even more withdrawn. I just put my coat on and proceeded to walk out the door. I didn't get very far. "You're my wife now; you're my property" type thing. "You're here for the duration." He grabbed me and hit me right on my cheekbone. I felt like nothing—like numb—like what have I got myself into? I couldn't leave. We were in a trailer and there was only one door out. I didn't know at the time that he had a drinking problem from an early age.

Life went on. The work ran out and I was laid off. I didn't have any transportation so I just stayed inside the trailer all day. I was very shy. I didn't know anyone in the trailer park.

At the start it was mostly verbal abuse, whenever he was drinking, usually on the weekends. Once the pregnancy started showing he'd say, "That kid's not mine. It can't be mine." That went on right up until John was born. The baby came two weeks early. Then George said, "That kid's definitely not mine. He doesn't even look like me. He looks like you." Oh God.

George usually used his fist in my face. Oh yeah, there were bruises. Well, I didn't go anywhere anyway. I didn't have a [driver's] licence at the time.

When John was a year old, George said I had to get a job because he wanted to buy a farm. So I found a job and a babysitter and that's that. George bought the farm and drove me to work on the way to his job. We were even more out in the country now and I still didn't have a driver's licence.

George started drinking during the week with his buddies and staying up all night. He didn't always go to work. He quit making payments like he was supposed to, so he put the farm up for sale and sold it at a profit. We moved closer to town. Instead of putting the profit into something else, he bought rounds for his buddies for weeks and weeks and weeks. He squandered it all.

I guess this was about the time I started feeling alright. I finally got my driver's licence because half the time George wasn't there. If I needed to take the baby to the doctor or to get groceries, he was never there.

Our arguments were mostly one-sided. George was the type who was always right and nothing I said mattered. I would never fight back. Oh, I thought of leaving him all the time but I didn't have the courage to do it. He always used to say to me, "If you leave, you'll never take my son alive." And now it's his son you know.

I'd go to work, bring home a pay cheque, look after my son and do the housework and just be there.

Even though George drank a lot he was able to keep his job. His boss was an alcoholic too. They were drinking buddies.

The abuse got worse. I never told anyone what was going on. I explained my shiners usually by saying, "I walked into a door." He generally hit my body but when he was real bad he punched me anywhere. I felt he wasn't angry at me but at someone else. He'd come home from the hotel really angry and I'd get it. If I was lucky, he'd be so drunk he'd just pass out. He beat me about twice a week.

He lost his licence and then he had to hitch-hike to work.

My eighteen-year-old brother called to see if I could help him get a job. He lived with us for about six weeks. He was shocked with George's treatment of me and couldn't understand how I could put up with the abuse. After that, I confided in my brother. I helped him get a job and he eventually got his own apartment. I visited him often.

I found out George was seeing other women. I started getting calls from Bell Canada: the bill was overdue. I found the bills under the seat of the truck. There were a lot of calls to Ottawa. The bills were phenomenal: over 100 bucks. I found letters from women as well. You know, George was an attractive-looking man—on the loose. I was too afraid to say anything.

One night when he wasn't there, a woman phoned and asked for him. I asked her, "Who is this?"

And, "It's none of your fuckin' business. What right do you have to ask me—you're only his wife!"

The phone bills never came in the mail anymore. He always picked them up.

Then I got pregnant. I could hardly believe it. We so rarely had sex. George wouldn't believe it either and it started all over again you know, "This one can't be mine." He even punched me when I was pregnant. I sometimes wished it would bring on a miscarriage. I didn't want to bring another child into this mess. I felt like that with the first pregnancy too.

Tanya was born in 1978, and surprise, surprise—she looked exactly like George! There was no denying. He thought she was the greatest thing in the world. But she was petrified of him—even as an infant. If he was drunk and tried to hold her, she would scream. That young. You'd wonder how they know, but they know. She was fine other times when he was sober.

I had my tubes tied because I was toxic during Tanya's pregnancy. I went back to work two months after she was born and now I had two children to take to a babysitter. George didn't help out at all as far as child care. He was still Good-Time Charlie—going out to the bars and everything. Most of his buddies were single or divorced.

In 1980 I had a hysterectomy. I'd always been healthy. I just had a bad pap test so they sent me for more tests. I had irregular cells. They were precancerous they said. They gave me a choice—either a partial or a complete. I decided I might as well have it done all at once. I bounced right back; six weeks off work. I was fine, no problems. George was still abusing me.

One day my brother visited and said to me, "If you don't leave or do something, you're going to go out of here in a box." The only place I could go to was to George's relatives and it wouldn't be getting away from him. My brother was younger and I didn't really want to involve him eh? I had been reading about Interval House in the paper all the time and one night George was out and it just clicked on me: If you don't get out now, right this minute while it's on your mind, you'll never leave. I phoned Interval House and Olive answered and I said, "Do you have to have money to go there?"

She said, "Just come."

I called my brother. He said, "You're finally going to do it eh? I'll be right there." I grabbed armfuls of clothes and threw them in garbage bags.

It was scary cause I didn't know what I was going to, really. I had a lot of mixed feelings. I thought they might not let me stay because I didn't have enough bruises. I put the kids to bed at Interval House and they weren't upset you know. It was kind of like an adventure to them. The house was clean and warm and I knew George didn't know where we were, so we were safe for a while. It was quiet, peaceful, and there I was pouring out my soul to a total stranger. My childhood was bad enough but I went from bad to worse. I felt I was a wimp; I was in a daze, a stupor. I had no backbone.

The Interval House staff helped me feel accepted and welcome. The house was empty when we went there. We started a roll; it was full by the end of the week.

It was a week before George located us. The first place he went was my brother's eh, but my brother said he didn't know where we were. It was George's lawyer who suggested that maybe she went to 'that' place. George had never heard of Interval House. The lawyer phoned and asked for me and whoever answered the phone said she didn't know—you know the whole bit. *(When someone phones the shelter and asks for a woman, they are given a set statement , "It is the policy of Lanark County Interval House to not give any information as to who is or is not here")* And then the counsellor told me it was up to me to call him back if I wanted to. By this time I already had applied for interim custody so I figured it was safe.

His lawyer must have phoned my lawyer and said that George had a right to see the kids. I was afraid to let the kids go; but at the same time I knew that he'd never taken any time to care for them before and I knew that he wouldn't be looking after them. He'd be taking them to his mother's.

By now I'm feeling a bit better, more relaxed. And then he wants to see me—to talk to me! I went with the kids to meet him in a restaurant. He's wearing a three-piece suit. And he's making all these promises if I come back: he's going to change and all that stuff. He wasn't going to beat me anymore. But I'm not biting. He didn't promise to stop drinking.

He took the kids all weekend. He got them every weekend. John was nine and Tanya was two. Brought them back with new toys and this and that. He was a great guy eh? More or less trying to buy them. He didn't have the money for it.

John gave me a hard time. He wanted to go with his dad. He didn't want to go to a different school. It was kind of hard, especially at the end of the week. It would take you all week to get them settled down and then it would be time for George to come and visit again. It was Dad, Dad, Dad. "Dad said this," and "Dad said that." "Dad wants us to come back home." "Dad loves you." With all those new toys you know, you forget about the nights you wakened up in your sleep and you heard your parents—screaming and crying.

My sister-in-law visited and told me that her husband took George to file for personal bankruptcy. I told my lawyer about this because I had co-signed a $2,000 note with George. He advised me to file bankruptcy also so that I wouldn't be held responsible for George's debts. There was a fee for filing and my only income at the time was my income tax refund—over $300. I gave them my T-4 slips and my refund went to the trustees.

I had good days and bad days you know but I started to feel better about myself. If I could get a counsellor by myself and talk it out . . . but sometimes it was pretty busy you know. I stayed at Interval House for two months. I went to my sister's place but that was a big mistake. We were given a room in the basement like, for the three of us and, you know, she went to work every day, and her husband went to work every day and that left me more or less housekeeper again and no job and no income. So I went to Manpower and looked for employment but there was just nothing available. So we only stayed there a month.

You're not going to believe this but when I was living at my sister's, George still came for the weekend to visit the kids. I mentioned my problems to him and he found me this apartment. And he moved us back! By this time we had about six garbage bags full of clothes.

I phoned back to my old job and they said my job was there anytime I wanted it. They'd just put a girl in temporary for me. They took me back at the same rate of pay.

George hassled me after I came back here. He'd phone at all hours and stuff. Drunk, you know. Ask you to go back type thing. That didn't stop until I went to a lawyer and finally filed for divorce. Since we've been divorced I've had no problems with him. We get along fine when he comes to pick up the kids. If I have any problems with the kids or the kids need anything that I can't afford, all I have to do is pick up the phone and there's no problem as far as financial. He's good with support and he never forgets. Mind you, it's not a lot. I get $140 a month, which I got from the beginning, and I've never asked for an increase but like I say, at Christmas time he goes overboard and for birthdays. He paid for my son's driving school this summer. Anything they need, all I have to do is ask.

George has cirrhosis of the liver. Thirty-eight years old and his doctor told him if he doesn't stop drinking he won't see forty-five. He has less than twenty per cent of his liver now. He stopped drinking for almost a year and then . . . When the pain gets too bad he goes off it for a while. He's always sober when he comes to pick up the kids.

Actually, he sees the kids more now than he ever did. Tanya and George are very close and damn me if I say a word against her father. It sounds real screwy on paper but I was thinking to myself how rotten it was at the beginning and how things have more or less come full circle as far as the relationship with the kids and how we get along. We just should never have been married in the first place. It should never have happened.

John gets disgusted with George's drinking. He says he should know better. I don't know, touch wood—I've got a sixteen-year-old. He's not perfect, but God he's good for a teenager. You know I'm really lucky. He's so polite, he does well in school, he keeps a job, he buys his own clothes and everything he needs. He has nice friends. He's a lot like me—quiet but good-natured.

Tanya does well in school and she has lots of friends. She's always putting on shows. She makes me sit on the toilet while she performs in the bathtub. The shower curtain is her theatre curtain.

Money is a problem with me. I make enough to keep a roof over our heads but there's not much left over at the end of the week for extras. I mean, lets face it, I have a steady job but the pay is not that good. I'm a lead hand and I only make $8 an hour. But you know, I don't have to depend on anybody else. We don't have a lot. I mean, I may never get a car of my own, I just can't afford it until I get my kids raised, but it doesn't matter to me. I've got friends who pick me up at the door to go to work and I'm only ten minutes away from the grocery store so a car would be a big luxury item. I don't know, maybe I'm pattin' my own back but I know a lot of girls that are on mother's allowance and welfare, which is fine, but I'm able to work you know, and maybe I don't earn a lot of money but I mean I've got my pride. A lot of people say, "How do you do it on what you make?"

When we moved in here I didn't have hardly anything—a bunch of old second-hand furniture. The $140 pays for my babysitter and you know, I've been figuring it out. I've been paying for a babysitter for fifteen years and I still have a few years to go yet before I can leave my daughter alone. She's got to have somebody to care for her before school and someplace to go at lunchtime and some place to go after school. You know you just don't leave a little girl alone when all is said and done. I don't like to see kids comin' home to an empty house and nothing to eat in the fridge and nothing to amuse them even—no one to talk to even. Kids need that when they come home: "How was your day and what did you do?"

I'm proud of myself. I can say "No" to anybody and I like it. I can go to bed when I want and I get up when I want on the weekends. I don't have to have my sleep disturbed by someone coming in, stumbling over furniture and stuff. I make the rules around here. Not that I'm a dominating person with my kids, because I'm not. If anything, I'm still very lenient with them. But if I want to play bingo or something . . . Not that I go out a lot, because I don't. I stay in more than anybody I know because I work ten hours a day and I'm so tired. I work a four-day week. It's a long day but it's worth it. You get three days off.

So if I want to stay in my nightgown or housecoat till eleven o'clock before I go uptown and do what I have to do, I do it. Or I sit in the bathtub and soak for an hour. I have my own leisure time now. My kids aren't small anymore so they can do for themselves. There's not that constant doing for them.

All my girlfriends work too so they're not the type that are at your doorstep for coffee all the time 'cause they have their homelife too and they have their work to do in the evenings too.

One thing that I really enjoyed was the purchase of my new bed—no one else had slept in it! After all the years of sharing a bed with sisters and foster sisters and husband and children, I finally had a bed that was mine alone.

My brother still lives nearby and although we'd do anything for each other, we're not close. We have a biological link but we've had eighteen years apart so we have nothing really in common. When I found my younger sister I was really happy, but again there's a difference.

I didn't date anyone for twenty-two months. That sounds like a long time but I didn't want anything to do with men for a long time. I've been seeing a fellow for the last, well, over two years. He's separated and he lives in another town so I only see him on weekends. It was a blind date through one of the girls at work. He is her brother. I'd never been on a blind date in my life. All of a sudden, thirty-five years old and going out on a blind date and I'm just like a sixteen-year-old kid, scared to death.

But it's worked out very well. I mean he's a Sagittarius—he's a very strong type of person. He's a big man. He's reliable. I just feel safe with him. He spends the weekends here. There's no talk of marriage or anything permanent. He's going through a rough time. His wife took off on him so he's hurting too. My kids get along well with him. My ex-husband thinks he's terrific! He's even told him so and he's told the kids. They seem to have a respect for one another.

I have a lot of resentment for the wasted years. It really turned me off marriage and that's not right because I know there are a lot of good marriages. *I asked her to tell me how many she actually knew of.* Well I don't know of any (much laughter). Most of them are outward appearances to other people.

Some of my friends are in the position I was in years ago. I try to give them advice but, I mean, that's their life. The day will come when they've just had it and can't take anymore. And somebody can't tell you; you've got to do that for yourself. Is this all there is to life? There's got to be more—even if it is just that uninterrupted sleep at night. Basically all that I wanted was a family and a home. I didn't want anything fancy—just that security I guess.

Susan showed me her file—given to her when she left Interval House. (Personal files are no longer given to residents but are destroyed once each woman leaves the shelter. This is done because of a concern that in a legal dispute there is a possibility that information in her file could be used against her). The following excerpts taken from Susan's file document some of the highs and lows she went through. Writings by various Interval House staff clearly illustrate the change in attitude of her son and the very difficult pressures felt by women trying to separate from their partners.

Day 1

Susan has been married for 10 years. She's thought a lot about leaving and now has decided to do it. The column in the paper certainly helped her to decide—especially the one about the effects on children of living in an abusive situation. Her brother, his wife and another sister-in-law are very supportive. Her mother-in-law tells her to stick it out.

Her husband is an alcoholic. He has been charged twice with impaired driving. Her life has consisted of working all day at a paying job and then coming home to work at childcare and housework all night. This woman is worn out!

He is abusive, not just when he drinks—but it's worse then. He first hit her just a week after they were married but she's tried to stick it out. . .

She is concerned that her mother-in-law will push her husband to demand custody of the children, so needs to contact a lawyer quickly about an interim custody order . . .

Day 2

Susan's brother called to say her husband was out looking for her last night . . . Said he'd phone the police and report her as a missing person. Susan thinks she ought to phone him to say she and the kids are okay—but she's scared to do this and needs support. She says, "I'm a coward." But in fact, I think she's a brave person who has every right to be frightened of this man.

Day 3

Susan did phone her husband . . . The kids are getting along well and cooperating very nicely. John seems very devoted to his mother. This is a worn-out woman.

Day 5

Susan took the completed legal aid form to the lawyer's office today so interim custody is underway. She also met with the school principal, so John will start tomorrow. He is somewhat nervous—understandably so.

Day 7

John's a dream—we did the shopping together and he was so helpful—such a considerate person. Susan should be proud of him and of herself for doing such a good job of parenting, especially with all the hardships she's coped with. John seems to really like his new school and has told me he has two new friends.

Day 9

Susan's husband went yesterday to file bankruptcy. Susan will have to do this too or be stuck with his debts. Her husband's lawyer called and harassed her—told her George was entitled to access, and asked why her lawyer had not contacted him. She was pretty shaken. She now seems quite aware of the games lawyers play and will talk to her lawyer on Monday. The court date for custody has been set. She's very nervous about seeing her husband there and would like company if possible. She went out with her brother this afternoon. He gave her an envelope of money collected from colleagues at work. Guess they like her as much as we do. Nice eh?

Day 13

Susan went to deal with the bankruptcy. Her lawyer advised her that she does not have to go to court re custody. Her husband wants to settle out of court!! It was a great relief to Susan.

Day 16

Her husband came (in a three-piece suit!) to pick up the children, who will stay at his parents for the night unless Tanya gets upset and wants to return. Susan was quite nervous both before he arrived and after he left. She made a lot of jokes but seemed at a loss without John and Tanya around . . . (Later) . . . Susan is getting used to being without the kids—she kinda likes it. She slept like a log and seems to be really pleased with herself.

Day 17

John and Tanya returned laden with gifts and candy and promises of more gifts and candy. Both children were very hyper and cranky all evening. I think that Susan had trouble coping with John's chattiness about weekend events, new toys, money from Dad, etc., and that she probably needs lots of support so she won't feel intimidated by her husband's bribing of the children. Susan had a very bad headache this evening but managed to retain her special good-naturedness.

Day 23

Susan's sister has said she could live with her. Susan doesn't know what to do and is feeling incompetent about her inability to make decisions. People have made decisions for her all her life. Where to live and where to work seem to be the main questions . . . She is especially at loose ends right now because Tanya and John have gone off with their father until tomorrow.

Day 24

John gave her a hard time tonight on returning from Dad's. Didn't want to go to bed—said he'd go to live with his father where he could stay up till eleven.

Day 37

Susan is fed up with having to deal with her husband when he comes to get the kids. She feels his begging and "suckiness" constitute harassment in violation of their agreement. It's not simply five or ten minutes—it's the anticipation of it and the after-effects on both Susan and the kids. Even though she has been consistently straightforward with him and does not allow him to manipulate her into complicated arguments, it is definitely taking its toll on her. We agreed that staff should meet him at the door, and if he asks for Susan, simply tell him she does not want to talk to him although we will relay his message to her. It would help if her lawyer would relay this message to him formally, and I suggested she get him to do this. She is also interested in finding out about divorce. Will Legal Aid pay for divorce? Can she get him to pay for it if she files? He cashed her family allowance cheque. I told her she should let her lawyer know this also and have it included in any list of things he owes her. He could be charged with forgery or fraud. She has arranged to pick up furniture and clothes tonight while he is away with the kids. Her brother has a truck, and storage is being arranged. I think Susan is nervous about possible repercussions as this is a very concrete reminder to him that she means business and will not be talked into returning. Her plans are to go to her sister's at spring break, but continued aggravation by her husband may encourage her to go sooner.

Day 38

Susan returned from her trip to her old residence perfectly disgusted at the state of affairs. The place was a pigsty. Her brother couldn't get a truck so she didn't get very much of her stuff.

Day 41

Susan's children went with their father for supper. I let them out when he arrived so Susan could avoid confrontation. This worked very well. John returned with the report that all furnishings have been moved and the china is at Susan's mother-in-law's.

Day 54

Susan was really down in the dumps. She has a lot of concerns about John. We talked about how she could help John with his attitude.

Day 56

Susan not as cheerful as usual. John pulled the Dad's-not-like-that routine when Susan tried to be very firm about getting homework done.

Day 59

Susan is in good form. She says she is beginning to look forward to weekends without kids.

Day 60

Susan went out with her brother to see the movie '9 to 5'. She seems cheerful. I hear she's been throwing popcorn at the staff . . .

(another staff entry) Yep. She said it shows she's now assertive enough to deal with the world. First staff, then the world.

Day 63

We had popcorn last night. Susan restrained herself.

Day 66

Susan is concerned that once she has left here, her husband will feel he has demonstrated his good behaviour and quit being so responsible about bringing the kids back on time.

Day 67

Susan talked with her husband about her move in two days. She didn't want to spring it on him at the last minute. She reports that he took it quite well.

Day 68

Susan talked quite a bit about plans when she moves; in particular, about trying to get some counselling for herself and John. She feels he is giving her a pretty heavy time of it.

Day 69

Good luck, Susan.

When I visited Susan for the update, she was living in the same place, dating the same boyfriend, working at the same job and smiling the same smile.

Her son got married last year and both he and his wife have good jobs. They are saving money for a down payment on a house. Susan likes her daughter-in-law's outspokenness.

Her daughter will soon graduate from high school. Susan describes her as: A handful, but no worse than any other teenager. She's like her father—she has the same temperament. She looks like him, she talks like him, she acts like him. She doesn't like me to say this.

Susan's ex-husband is still drinking and hasn't paid child support for three years. He was late weeks and weeks. I phoned him and asked him about it and he was so verbally abusive I said, "Fine, I'll never ask you for another cent again." So if my daughter wants something I say, "You ask your father," and he generally comes through.

This lack of financial support creates a real hardship for Susan because she makes less than $10 per hour. It will be compounded when her daughter becomes eighteen and is no longer eligible for the baby bonus.

Susan and her boyfriend plan to take a trip together this summer. I don't want marriage and I don't think he does either.

Susan's best news concerned her family of origin. She found her two brothers. Four years ago, legislation changed so that siblings and grandparents could now register with CAS and begin the search. Susan registered and, a year later, was elated to receive a phone call from one of her missing brothers. All eight children had a reunion and continue to meet in order to get to know each other.

Susan's mother is still alive and is physically healthy.

Susan's advice to other women is, Don't take any shit off a man. That sounds really sexist doesn't it? I hear so much of it every day from other women and I say, "Why?" I find so many women are hung up on material things. Maybe because I never had a lot of material things, it didn't really matter to me that much. I mean, I like nice things as well as the next one but . . . They're staying because of the vehicles and babysitters for the kids so they can get out once in a while.

Susan, maintaining her positive outlook, adds:

There are some decent men out there. My bosses are super nice guys. And my brothers. And my boyfriend.

Susan initially included another man in the above list. She had said, Even my ex-husband. Deep down he's a very good person.

In our last conversation she asked me to remove him. He just pulled another one.

MINIMIZING ABUSE

Wife abuse remained hidden in our society for hundreds of years, partly because everybody minimized it.

The abuser minimized the effects of his actions. He told his wife that it was her fault or that her complaint was exaggerated, or he ignored the situation.

The victim minimized his intentions, her feelings and her pain—he didn't really mean it, she should have tried harder, at least the bruises won't show this time.

The doctor, faced with a woman who had unusual bruising, accepted the explanation that she walked into a door and thus minimized the risk of serious injury.

The psychiatrist, listening to a tearful and depressed woman on the couch, minimized her situation by subscribing to one of many psychiatric theories, perhaps labelled her masochistic for staying and prescribed tranquillizers for her depression.

The police, when called about a domestic, separated the husband and wife, talked to both parties, minimized the danger by not charging the husband or by expecting the woman to lay the charge, and left when they felt the situation was under control. Or they dramatically minimized it by not showing up.

The neighbours, not fully aware of the danger and not wanting to get involved, minimized the situation by ignoring it or blamed the woman for staying (she must like it) or for causing the abuse.

The victim's family minimized the abuse by requiring her to keep silent so as to not bring shame on the family. Or they placed responsibility on her shoulders by telling her, "You made your bed, you lie in it" or encouraged her to forgive her husband and work harder to keep him content.

If the case ever got to court, the judge minimized the danger faced by the victim and gave the abuser a far lighter sentence than would be given a person who assaulted an unrelated victim. The abuser was given a simple reprimand or a suspended sentence or was required to sign a peace bond. And so on and so on.

Until recently, there was little or no recognition of wife abuse in the medical schools, in the law schools, or even in schools of social work.

Many of these conditions are still true today.

We minimize because, as individuals and as a society, we don't know what to do about wife abuse. The situation is very complicated and is unlikely to be resolved with one particular remedy. So, if we can't handle it and can't see an immediate solution, it is easier to dismiss it or minimize what we do know.

To a certain extent, even the stories in this book minimize the reality. You will notice, sometimes, that one sentence is used to summarize ten years of rape or physical assault. As Jane explained, her information just skimmed the surface.

When we minimize abuse, we allow it to continue. Facing the reality is a first step toward finding solutions.

DONNA'S STORY

Donna couldn't read the questions on the Interval House intake form and her writing skills were limited to signing her name. She explained that due to her uncle's abuse, she had been removed from school at eight years old. If Donna's reading and writing abilities were limited, there was nothing wrong with her common sense. She was the one who, after Interval House staff puzzled about why the refrigerator quit, looked behind it and announced, It's not plugged in!

A strong woman, Donna liked to work and she was an extremely efficient and thorough house cleaner. The rooms sparkled when she was a resident—quite a feat considering the number of small children spilling orange juice and pressing their peanut-butter fingers against the windows.

Donna had a kind and honest face. Her shy smile revealed a few lonely teeth—the others were smashed out of her gums during various beatings. Although she had little self-esteem, she loved to laugh and could poke fun at herself and others without being hurtful. She told us a wonderful story about the day she painted her bathroom. Shortly after she had finished this task, her husband started yelling. He stomped towards her, dropped his pants and displayed a white circle on his bottom. Donna had many funny stories to tell.

When she was very young, Donna had been sexually abused and she was determined that her children would never be subjected to the same mistreatment. The recent discovery that her daughter had been enduring sexual abuse by an elderly family friend, broke the straw of Donna's defences. She arrived at Interval House extremely distressed. I can still recall her cry—almost a wail that seemed to flow from the depths of her soul. While at the shelter, she had to be hospitalized for a week due to her depression.

Donna's daughter, Laurie, was sent to live at a Children's Aid foster home until Donna could get back on her feet. Several weeks after Donna came to the shelter, the girl was scheduled to visit her mother for a day. We all shared Donna's excitement in anticipation of the reunion. But as soon as Laurie arrived, she launched into a verbal attack at her mother—calling her stupid and sounding like an echo of how Donna described her husband's verbal abuse. Even though we understood the dynamics of a family living with an abuser, it was a relief when Laurie finally left.

Donna gradually felt more comfortable at the house. It was gratifying to watch her self-assurance develop as she found that people genuinely liked her and valued her company and talents.

After two months, Donna was ready to leave, but her confidence waned as she agonized over the difficult decisions ahead. That was when we learned she had an old friend—the bottle. Our only comfort in watching her depart was knowing that she had an excellent Adult Protection Worker who would give her emotional support in the months to come.

Two years later, I visited Donna in her tiny but predictably spotless apartment. She was wearing new glasses and said that soon she'd be getting teeth as well. She had been working at writing her life story as part of a literacy program.

Donna and I sat beside the china cabinet, the only piece of her furniture her husband hadn't sold while she was at our shelter. A collection of salt and pepper shakers, carefully arranged on the cabinet shelves, included some precious sets that had belonged to her mother and her aunt.

Here's Donna's story.

I was born in 1948. When I was about six, my parents broke up. They were alcoholics. We were all divided up. So my sister lived with my aunt; my older brother went to my grandmother; my brother went to Dad's, and I went to my other grandmother's.

My father moved in with his three brothers to a sort of barn that was down a lane behind her place. A bootlegger lived up the street and my uncles would take me along to get their booze. They gave me some to drink too. They even took me to a hotel once. They waited till my grandmother went to work or somethin' and then they asked me over to the barn and they molested me. Or they'd come to visit and they'd get grandmother to go downstairs to cook them somethin' to eat and then they'd climb into bed with me. I guess one uncle was a teenager, the others were older. Sometimes they had intercourse with me. It went on for quite a few years. At that time I didn't know who to go to. Like, I wanted to talk to my father but he was livin' with this other woman and they had kids together. He gave me a couple of dollars and told me to go and get lost or go to the fair or do somethin' by myself.

My mother died when I was seven. They took me to the funeral. I don't remember much about her except that she had red hair. I was told that she died in a car accident, but when I was older, I found out she was stabbed. The man that did it only went to jail for a year.

The year after my mother died, my oldest brother drowned.

My aunt came up one day and she caught my uncle in bed with me. She told my grandmother what's goin' on so my grandmother didn't know what to do. She knew a man that worked at the Rideau Regional and she was talkin' to him about it and that's why I was put away at the Rideau Regional 'cause she didn't know what to do. I must have been about eight then. I was in grade three. They put me on wards to help with the other patients. I didn't go to school again.

So I was there for about a year and they shoved me out to work. They put me out to help and clean at a nursin' home. I stayed there I guess for a couple of years. I was livin' there. I guess the staff looked after me. Well, I worked there till I was about thirteen and then I worked at another nursin' home till I was sixteen.

I was thinkin' I wanted to get married—I wanted to get away from everythin'. So I took off from there and they put me back in the Rideau Regional for a couple of months. And that's like when they took me into a conference room. There must have been about thirteen doctors there askin' all sorts of questions, but I thought at the time their questions didn't make sense. I think they were tryin' to find out if I wanted to kill myself. So then I guess I stayed there for a couple of months and then I went out to work at two hotels in Brockville. I cleaned rooms. I had to look after the owner's five kids too. And then I went down to my grandmother's and I looked after fifteen kids for my holidays.

So I thought I might as well try to hack it out for a while till I got married. I thought when I got married it was the answer to my questions.

There was one young lad that I used to like a lot. He was from Rideau Regional. He could write and speak thirteen different languages. And he escaped from the hospital and came down to Brockville and that night he drowned. So I couldn't get over it. And I guess I still have feelings for him.

When I was eighteen, I met Gary in a restaurant. I was leavin' to go out for a walk and he asked if he could come with me. So we just started goin' out together for about a year. We got married in 1967. It was a marriage I jumped into too fast. Gary wanted me to give up work but I thought, Well, I've worked all my life and I want to keep on. So they gave Gary a job at the hotel but he was let go anyways. So then he got a job from the Rideau Regional.

He started runnin' around a couple of months after we were married. He drank a lot. I tried to hide the bottles but that didn't help. He beat me right from the start of our marriage.

I got pregnant. Gary started livin' with another woman. I was very upset. So when my baby was ready to be due the doctors told me to either stay with a friend or they were going to admit me to the hospital because like I was on thirteen different kinds of medication—because of my nerves, because of my diabetes, because of my health. I felt weak and tired all the time. One day I passed right out in front of a bus. So I went and I stayed with some friends till I had the baby. I called the baby Dennis. I stayed with them when I came out of the hospital and I worked for them.

Gary begged me to come back to him and so I thought I might as well give him another chance. So I went back and I got pregnant again and I had my daughter. I was going to call her Chance but I called her Laurie (laughter).

Gary and I were always fightin', like we couldn't get along. He was always drunk. He beat me whenever he was down in a depression, when things didn't go his way. It all depends on his mood. He always went to his family's, stayed away for a while and then he'd be back again. His father was an alcoholic. His mother died when he was quite young and he just couldn't get over it. I guess that's why he lived with an older woman. His brother even married an older woman.

When Dennis was five and Laurie was four we moved to another town. We lived there for eight years. Gary got a job in the next county and he only came home on weekends. My brother moved over with us and he helped out with the food or to dress the kids. I didn't have a steady job but I helped people out now and again: babysittin' and cleanin'.

Then Gary got a job in town. On weekends we used to go to the Legion or go out somewhere and and he'd leave first and drive home before me and lock me out. He threatened the kids that if they let me in the door they were going to know about it. So I used to have to sleep outside or try to find a place to stay. I kicked in the windows one night and got in.

Gary did queer things. Dennis had a habit of turning the TV off—he was quite young at the time. Gary got mad and swung this beer bottle and I got cut across the head. My head was bleedin'. He couldn't say he was sorry. He just went to his family's place, stayed away for a while and then came back. Or the young lad used to turn the vacuum cleaner on and off and Gary, like he got upset and he took the hammer to the vacuum. You didn't know what kind of mood he was goin' to get into. You didn't know which way to turn.

We couldn't talk; we never communicated.

Another time we were over at a friend's and Gary wanted Dennis to drink a glass of beer. Dennis was only nine years old. I tried to stop him. The friend got in the middle of Gary and me and she told Gary to just cool down for a minute. So when we got home that night I guess I was upstairs and Gary started swingin' at me, with his fists. So Laurie kept on saying, "Mom are you okay?"

One of the kids got on the phone and the cops came and they said to Gary, "The next time we come over Donna won't have to say a word." He says, "We'll charge you," and he says, "Donna," he says, "You're goin' down to the hospital." The cops were there about half an hour trying to cool both us down—cool me down. Well I guess because of my diabetes and that I was very hyper and upset.

It was like livin' on a funny farm.

He turned real bad shortly after his dad died. That's when it got the worst. He tied the kids up and started pounding them and everything else. I tried to get them out and he put me down and tied me up and started poundin' me. The neighbours heard the kids screamin' and myself and they called the police.

When Laurie was about nine, Gary went to the hotel one day instead of goin' to work. Some of his bosses showed up at the hotel for lunch and Gary bought them all drinks. He got fired (laughter).

Gary had to be put in hospital for a while for his nerves. We had no money and no food. I called the Welfare and a social worker came to visit and he helped us out. That was Peter.

I got a cleaning job at a company in Ottawa. I worked double shifts, I tried to keep the house up, I tried to keep the kids dressed and I paid all the bills. Gary didn't work at all. He stole my money to pay for his booze.

My favourite brother died in an awful car accident and he left me money. I bought nice furniture with it and put a down payment on the house. I really miss my brother.

Gary still had girlfriends. Some days I'd come home from work and some woman would be leavin'. I'd find their panties under my bed. This really hurt. I didn't much like sex with Gary: I would just think of all the other women he went to bed with. My friends at work said that I should have some fun and I started goin' out.

We lost the house because most of my money went to pay for the booze. We moved to another town.

Laurie was thirteen. She was having problems in school. A social worker talked to her and Laurie told her that she was sexually assaulted by a friend of Gary's. He was sixty-one years old! He'd take her for drives and make her suck him off or sometimes she had to have intercourse with him. He gave her money. One day he gave her $50! The social worker came and told Gary and me. I was really upset and Gary went crazy.

Gary wanted to go out west. I just got $300 from my income tax and I put it in the bank for Christmas. But he wanted it and so I lent him the money and he left. Laurie went to stay in a foster home. I had to go to court. It was very hard.

One day I got home and I opened my closet door, and Gary was standing in there. I was scared. He was so strange. I called the Children's Aid and I asked them if they would keep Laurie longer. I felt like I was goin' to have a nervous breakdown.

Peter took me to Interval House. I stayed there for two months. I didn't know which way to turn. They put me in the hospital. I was in there for a little over a week cause all I did was cry and bawl at the Interval House. I was upset. I hoped Laurie would have a better life. Gary sent me roses in the hospital but like I heard he was sellin' my furniture while I was away and that upset me too.

Why did you stay with Gary ?

I thought there was no one else like him. We came from the same background, we understood each other. Both of our families were alcoholics, both of us lost our mothers when we were very young. Drinkin' was a problem for me too. Remember my uncles took me drinkin'? We went places together but we always had to have a bottle between us. I remember our fifth anniversary—we were both drunk. We fell asleep in a Volkswagon near the township dump.

I went back home. I went to see Gary and we got into another fight. He was drinkin'. He sold my stuff while I was in the Interval House and while I was in the hospital. He gave my freezer away—just for a bottle! He sold my dryer for $25. And he took my unemployment cheques and he cashed them and he spent them. He was living with another woman at our place. I was very upset. Then I just felt I was closed in at the apartment, so I went and I stayed at a friend's house, and I babysat for them, I guess for a couple of months.

I went down to the hotel and Gary was in the hotel with an old girlfriend. He said he was going to spend the night with her. I said, "Well that was the end." I just had to get out.

I went to the motel and they said you can pick whatever room you want and you can get started whenever you want. So I lived at the motel for about a year and I cleaned for them. Gary phoned me the first couple of months that he wanted money. He didn't have enough money to pay his rent and to pay the phone bill. So I thought, well instead of being dirty, I'll loan him enough to pay for it. So he phoned me up on Christmas Eve and he says, "Donna," he says, "Can I borrow $20 off you?" So I thought, Well, I might as well take a walk and see what's going on. And that's when his girlfriend had moved in and I caught them in bed again. I was quite upset and I thought, I can't go back again.

I drank quite heavily. In January I was put in jail one night because I couldn't pay my taxi bill. I thought it was time I smartened up.

Peter wanted me to leave the motel. He said the people there were bad company for me. I was drinkin' with them. I went to Alcoholics Anonymous for a couple of weeks.

I met a fellow in April at the Singles Club dance. He drove me home. He came into my room and he talked to me about my drinkin'. He said I should forget Gary. Then he said something really strange. He said if I went out for a walk tomorrow my life would be changed. I laughed at him. I said, "You're crazy." (laughter)

So I got up the next mornin' and I asked the motel manager if there was any work and he said, "No."

So I went for a walk and I met Peter. He said, "There's a place for you in school in the Job Links [a government job-training program], and it starts next week." He said, "I'll help you get ready." And I looked at Peter and I thought, Well, I never really went to school and I didn't know how to read and write. It felt like I was in a great big dream—a dream I couldn't come out of.

So then I went back to the motel and I told the manager. So he said that would be the best thing because he was going to lose the motel and there'd be no work for any of us. So I went back into my room and I started packing some of my things. I made arrangements about goin' to school. So then I went and I stayed with a few friends till I got this place of my own.

I started school the next week. I went every day for six months and now I go one day a week and I work at Rideau Regional for four days. I'm learnin' how to read and write. I feel good but it's strange in a way. It's hard to believe, there's always somethin' you can learn every day. I've got my glasses now and soon I'm going to get my teeth.

We graduate in November. I'll feel badly because my favourite brother won't be there.

My daughter lives with me now. She moved in when I got this apartment. She goes very hyper sometimes. She don't like anybody drinkin'. I'm sorry she quit school. She's only got her grade 8.

My son, he's got a brain on his head. He's got a lot going for him. He's going to Algonquin and he's workin' at the Rideau Regional. He's got his licence. He's engaged. I like her. She's had a hard life. He drinks a bit. I don't see him that often.

Gary's goin' to get married—like he's engaged. His girlfriend's side of the family seems to have quite a bit of money.

I seem to be more settled now since I got my place. I got new friends at school. I don't drink as often as I used to. I go out and have a good time.

I want a bigger apartment and a steady job. I hope they keep me on where I'm workin' now. I don't want to get married right away. I still care for Gary. We went through quite a bit together. Sometimes I wonder how I lived through it all. It's a lot for one person.

A year after my first visit, Donna told me that Laurie had moved out. She was living with her boyfriend, a thirty-one-year-old alcoholic. The boyfriend had brutally beaten Gary because Gary had called him a wimp. The boyfriend asked Donna for her opinion of the beating and she said, I don't think much of it. *Donna returned home from work the next day to find her apartment had been vandalized and robbed. She suspected the boyfriend of the damage and her daughter of the theft.*

She said, Laurie's a lot like her father. You can never trust her and she don't always tell the truth. She plays mind games. She's even punched me. I can't take it anymore so I made her leave. My son tried to get in at 2:30 in the mornin' last week but he was drunk and I didn't let him in. They won't let me alone. Sometimes I think it will never end.

Donna continues in her literacy program and was made a permanent employee at a job she enjoys.

When I visited Donna for the update, she was living in a larger, two-bedroom apartment near the Rideau River and sharing it with her boyfriend of several years. He seemed like a kind man. Donna said, He's very nice. We do things together—go fishin' and campin'—like we go places. His kids are very nice to me, too, which means quite a bit.

My ex-husband sent his girlfriend up to get money from me, but [the boyfriend] said no. He said, "She doesn't have to keep dishin' money out."

Donna is living on a disability pension. She had health problems—diabetes and ulcers and she just had a hysterectomy—which prevent her from working. But she keeps busy. I go and help my neighbours and I help the landlord keep the hallways clean. There's always something to do.

Donna wasn't wearing her upper plate. My teeth don't fit that well.

Her son Dennis, now twenty-six, is the father of a fifteen-month-old child who he visits on Wednesdays. He had just been released from jail (convicted of car theft) and was living with them, 'till he gets his own place.

Her daughter Laurie, now twenty-five, has three children who have all been removed by CAS. Two of the children live with their father, the other child is in a foster home. She was livin' with a child molester. He was up on charges for it. The kids were taken away because they couldn't get along and he was drinkin' quite heavy. She told me she left him last Friday. She's just livin' down the road.

Donna was happy to tell me about meeting her younger sister. Her sister had traced her (they had last seen each other twenty-three years ago) and had also investigated their mother's life and death. She gave Donna copies of the police investigation, newspaper articles and a carefully typed summary of her findings. She learned that their parents began their marriage near Lanark County. Their father was transfered to a job far away and was rarely home. Their mother, who had four young children, was lonely and became involved with a group who "did considerable drinking." Up to that point she neither drank nor smoked. The marriage became strained and eventually she left home. She moved to Ottawa and had been arrested for prostitution. The day she was murdered, there was a drinking party in her apartment. She was stabbed and strangled. The autopsy report showed a high level of alcohol in her blood. She was thirty-six years of age. A twenty-three-year-old man was convicted of 'non-capital murder' (a new charge at the time) and was sentenced to prison "for the rest of his natural days." It is Donna's recollection that he was released after one year.

Some of it is quite hard to believe—the way that she lived. I was wondering about why she was dropping us kids off at my grandmother's. Now I understand it.

Donna told me that two of her uncles were dead (the ones who sexually assaulted her). One shot himself, the other died in a car accident. The third uncle is out west. It was obvious from the conversation that their abuse was still a difficult memory. Donna told me that her sister also has bad memories of the family.

I asked Donna if she had any advice for other abused women. The best thing you can do is get out of it. I kept thinkin' I should give him another chance and things got worse and worse. I got hurt and the hurtin' never goes away. Communication means a lot. Like my boyfriend now—we can talk. And now I see my kids goin' through it. My son—he's a lot like his dad. I think that's how he got into so much trouble.

I kept on blamin' myself for everything. Like I went around and I asked quite a few people and then I found out different. I learned it wasn't my fault. Gary's father was quite an abuser. His family wouldn't accept the boys but they accepted the girls. That's crazy.

COUNSELLING

I am often asked, "What qualifications do you need in order to work at a women's shelter?" I laugh and say, "Well, I was a hairdresser." Actually, my hair-cutting skills often come in handy at the shelter if a woman has no money or if it is too risky for her to venture outside to a hair salon.

I believe the essential qualifications for a shelter worker include a firm belief in women's equality, a non-judgmental attitude, an ability to listen, a willingness to learn, maturity, true caring and a sense of humour. Most shelter workers have worked at other jobs and all bring with them valuable life experience. For example, in Lanark County Interval House, there are former teachers, nurses, social workers, childcare workers and community workers. Many have the experience of marriage and motherhood. The staff members who have survived abusive relationships bring a particular empathy to the work.

Most shelters espouse peer counselling, that is, staff are not aloof from the clients but, for a short period of time, become a part of their lives as a friend or peer, giving the women the support they need. The common motto of shelter workers is, 'We support each woman in her choices.' There is a concerted effort to do just that and not place personal judgments on a woman's decisions.

When Lanark County Interval House was established, there were no courses on shelter work for counsellors so we had to learn by doing. We learned what kind of counselling worked and what didn't: what was helpful to the women and what hindered their healing. We learned that the most important thing we could offer was a listening ear and let the women know that they were believed. This sounds simple. But for a woman who has survived an abusive relationship, it is probably the first time in a long time that anyone has allowed her to talk about what is important to her. And it may be the first time in a long time that no one questions her truth. The highest mark of respect is to truly listen to another and to care about what they say.

Sometimes it is pointed out that because there are many counsellors, all working different shifts, abused women are compelled to repeat their stories. That does happen, but I see that as an advantage. Most women need to tell their stories many times. With each telling, the woman develops an objectivity about her situation that helps her come to terms with her reality. There are women who prefer to deal with only one counsellor, but when they feel more comfortable in the shelter and begin to trust, they usually start to share with the others.

We learned the importance of rebuilding the self-esteem of a survivor of abuse. Telling a woman that the meal she prepared was delicious or that you enjoyed the chat you just had with her can have an enormous positive impact on her self-confidence. Many of us see this as part of normal conversation, but it is rare for an abused woman to be given a compliment or even an acknowledgement of her work.

We learned that it is important to help each woman regain control over her own life by doing for herself. For example, if she decides to contact a lawyer, a counsellor shows her where she can find the phone numbers and demonstrates how the phone works. For someone who has not been allowed to do anything for herself, it can be a terrifying prospect to make such a call but a great ego-booster once the appointment is made.

We learned the importance of always dealing honestly with each woman. No matter how difficult the situation, only very rarely was anything done without her knowledge or involvement. For example, in Donna's story you read that there was a period when she was extremely depressed. Rather than calling the ambulance and having her carted off to the hospital, the counsellors talked with her and through the discussion she could see that she needed to be hospitalized. She was involved in making the necessary arrangements for her care and was assured that she could return to the shelter when her health improved.

Counselling takes many forms. Each counsellor has her own style, which she adapts to the woman's needs. If a woman was having difficulty in making a decision about returning to her partner, I liked to ask her to make a list of his good and bad characteristics. It sometimes helped her to look more objectively at the relationship. I remember doing this with Donna. At the time, she couldn't write, so I wrote as she dictated a long list of her husband's faults. When it came time to write down his positive aspects, she thought long and hard and finally said, "He's a good worker." And then she said, "But he hasn't worked at a job for five years." We chuckled for days about his only good characteristic.

When discussing their future, I liked to ask women to dream aloud about what they would ask for if they could wave a magic wand and have whatever they wished. Their fantasies were far from extravagant. Most simply wanted a secure apartment or a little house with a yard where their children could play and where they could all live in peace. Then we would spend time discussing what needed to be done in order to make their fantasy come true.

Some counsellors, like me, are huggers. But counsellors are careful to first ask the woman or child if they would like to be hugged. For some, human contact can be a great source of comfort. Others need to maintain their safe space.

Counselling can take place in many locations, such as in the office or more informally around the dining-room table with a group of women playing cards and discussing common concerns. Sometimes the conversation is about anything but abuse and that can be a refreshing change.

I often think the best counselling takes place between the women who are residents in the shelter. When they discover they have survived similar situations, it can have a powerful effect. I remember a conversation between a young woman, who worked for a time as a prostitute, and several residents. The young woman was enjoying their shocked responses as she educated the others about street life in the market area of Ottawa. It appeared to me that there was little common ground between her and the other women. "At least you got paid," was a comment from an older woman. The rest nodded. There was common ground after all.

An important aspect of the counselling is to help each woman build up her support system. Abusers are generally very effective at isolating their partners from families and friends. Women are encouraged to contact old friends, mend family relationships and get in touch with others who care.

The shelter keeps a good supply of books about abuse and most women take advantage of the opportunity to broaden their knowledge.

We encourage women to write about their lives. Some write powerful prose or poetry. Like speaking out loud about the abuse, writing it down contributes to the healing process.

Finally, as counsellors, we don't see ourselves as the only ones who can assist the women. Women are encouraged to seek the advice and support of others, whether therapists, spiritual counsellors, their hairdressers, doctors or lawyers. The women accept some advice and reject other suggestions. Each woman has her own perspective on life and her own problems to solve. What she needs is the opportunity to be heard and to feel respect for her choices.

I am continually impressed by the quality of counselling one finds in a women's shelter. It is first-rate. I am often told by ex-residents or women who used the crisis line that they found the counselling to be exceptional: helpful and kind, sometimes life-saving.

LAUREN'S STORY

Lauren, articulate and careful with her appearance, came to Lanark County Interval House in 1984 with her two children. She lived in a small rural village just outside Lanark County. She had only been at the shelter a few hours when two police officers knocked on the door asking for Lauren because they had been told by her husband that she was mentally unstable. They wanted to be sure that the children were safe.

This ploy has been used by several abusive husbands. Some declare their wives missing persons, or falsely state that their children have life-threatening illnesses that their wives are incapable of treating. The staff are then faced with the dilemma of how to preserve a woman's right to confidentiality without obstructing the police. At Lanark County Interval House, the officers' message is relayed to the woman. She must then decide how to respond. Usually she reassures the police about her decision and they in turn agree not to disclose her whereabouts.

Lauren made good use of the services of the house as she struggled with the decisions concerning her and her children's future. It intrigued me to learn that several years earlier, she had taken up running. This activity helped her develop the self-confidence she needed to leave her husband.

Lauren stayed at the shelter ten days, but returned home once her husband assured her that he understood why she had left. He said he would move out immediately. The counsellors cautioned her not to move back before he left, but she was worried about his emotional well-being and that of her seven-year-old daughter who was lonesome for her dad and her neighbourhood friends. The staff shared her concern for her daughter who seemed quite depressed. One day, while holding a kitchen knife, she talked of killing herself.

I was on shift about a year later when Lauren came back for a support visit. She wanted to separate from her husband, but her feelings were complicated by her attraction to another man. After listening to her dilemma, I commented that she seemed to be hoping that her new man would carry her off, thereby making her decision for her. I helped her sort out the various issues she was facing and together we separated the possible end of the marriage from the possible-new-relationship problem.

Lauren wrote powerful verse illustrating her feelings of imprisonment and loneliness in a loveless relationship. She brought some of her works that day. My favourite, SALVE-ATION, is a compelling example of her talent.

Here's Lauren's story.

I was born in a small town in the Ottawa Valley in 1950 and am the eldest of three. I had little connection with my brother and sister as they were both much younger. I don't seem to remember very much about my childhood other than the fact it was very unhappy. I was very much alone, very isolated.

There was a very tense atmosphere in our home, basically cold I guess. There was no real affection shown. My mother was always very uptight, always arguing with my father about this or that. She has always had trouble with her health. When I was little she was in and out of the hospital. She had rheumatic fever and I guess she had a recurrence of that every year. She's had more operations than anyone else I know. Frankly she's very wrapped up in herself and her problems. The rest of the family has very little sympathy for her.

My mom spent quite a bit of time with her mother. She lives in a neighbouring town. She's over ninety and has only just moved into a nursing home. Mom would go there and stay for a month or two and come back for maybe a few days and then go down there again. So she felt she was doing something worthwhile.

Dad worked at the mill all his life and was very active in sports. He had a coin collection and, any time that he could, he was always off in his room with his coins. He eventually put a lock on the door to keep my mother out. He just retired a few months ago and has a very, very busy life. He's still in sports: curls, plays golf. He has lots of friends and he likes to travel.

Mom and Dad are still together in the same house but there's really no interaction at all. Even now you feel uncomfortable if you're visiting them together. The children feel that too you know. They don't want to go there. You really have to work on them to get them to go with you to visit their own grandparents.

I was my Dad's favourite so Mom resented me. She seemed to feel that anything that was done for someone else took away from her.

Through high school I was very involved in many things but I was always in charge of events. I wasn't really involved with the people. I would still go home by myself. I was the brain. I was very shy really.

I met Ted when I was nineteen and he was twenty-two. I had a summer job and he started to work at the same place full-time. He asked me out. I wasn't immediately interested but when it was obvious how serious he was, it was just incredible for me. I hadn't had very much experience at all. He said I was different and he liked that. We talked and talked and we got sexually involved right away. That was basically a new experience for me as well. I went down to see his parents and it was a big thing for them. The whole family was there because he had never brought anyone home before.

That was another reason I was drawn to him, because of his family. His mother was a very warm person, very talkative. I really felt a part of that family, more than my own.

But what happened to really pull us together was due to unusual circumstances. We hadn't dated very long when Ted was involved in a car accident. His best friend was driving and the friend was killed. There was concern that Ted might have brain damage; his memory was gone. He was hospitalized for several months and had a long convalescent period at home. The accident pushed things, propelled our relationship along. I visited him daily and when he became conscious, he told me he loved me. Probably under ordinary circumstances he wouldn't have done that. He clung to me desperately and that's all I needed because I desperately needed someone too. As he got better he hinted that he wanted more breathing space, but I couldn't. I was terrified of losing him at that point.

After he recovered from the accident, we lived together for a year. We both went back to school and got our degrees. I went to Carleton University and he went to Algonquin College. In the midst of that we got married. That was in 1971. There were good times. We didn't have any money then but we used to travel a lot—just go to the States and go here and there. We visited his parents every Sunday.

But there were some very bad times too—when he was violent. Ted seemed to be agitated, stressed a fair amount of the time. He was still feeling guilty about the accident. Even though he wasn't the driver, he had fallen asleep and he felt responsible that he hadn't awakened his friend. Ted started to hit me during that first year, about once a month. He didn't use anything other than his hands or his fist. One time he used a belt. I had marks from that. Several times I left and stayed overnight with a friend. I didn't consider leaving him. I felt I needed to stand by him and see him through this. The doctors had said they'd need to observe him for five years before they could clear him from the possibility of brain damage, to make sure there were no lasting effects from the accident. His mother told me that he wasn't a violent person at all, that he'd be the one to break up fights rather than get involved. So I felt that this wasn't the way he was, really, that this was one of the effects of the accident.

Another reason why that situation persisted was because at first I felt that it wasn't really him. I had the sense then that there was something wrong within *me* that needed correction. I know in the early years I was very possessive. My jealousy was out of proportion. It would physically grip me. Sometimes I could hardly breathe. I went to the Royal Ottawa for group therapy and that helped.

Ted was everything to me at the time. We didn't really have friends. He wasn't interested in having friends. Actually my first real friends were in the group.

We both graduated and got jobs. Now we had enough money that we could travel and eat out and we both liked that. But we didn't really have much in common. I enjoyed my work and I got lots of positive feedback on what I was doing.

After the first three years, Ted's job required that he travel quite a bit and usually he was away for two or three weeks at a time. I really missed him and we had nice reunions.

We bought this house in 1976. The first year I felt extremely isolated and lonely. I didn't know anybody else in the village and Ted was away so much. We decided to have a child and our relationship improved.

But Ted was often inconsiderate—the little things. For example, when I was well on in my pregnancy, we attended a friend's wedding in Montreal. It was very hot and I was huge. Ted wouldn't *think* of carrying my suitcase. I'm not the type that needs doors held open for me but it wouldn't occur to him to be helpful. That evening we attended the reception. As the night wore on, I became very tired and uncomfortable. He refused to leave and we stayed right till the very end.

Around this time there was an episode that stands out in my mind. He was driving the car and he reached over, grabbed a chunk of my hair and pulled it out. It was extremely painful. I had a hair appointment the next week and I was very self-conscious and concerned that the hairdresser would notice and ask me questions.

I was toxic during the pregnancy and had to be hospitalized for the last month. Ted seemed to resent having to visit me but when Stephanie was born he was delighted. She was born by Caesarean. I stayed home full-time.

Before Stephanie's birth I was very unsure of myself, because I was worried that I would be jealous of Ted's attention to the baby. But it didn't turn out that way at all. In fact, Ted resented my attention to her and that caused lots of problems as well. She was colicky and she was a very demanding child. She didn't want to do things on her own. She wanted you involved with her.

Ted wanted sex a lot in the early years: in the morning and again at night. I found those years very, very difficult. After an argument or a beating he wanted to make love. I hated that. I just felt I wanted to shield myself from him, but if I didn't go along, that would infuriate him more. There was that feeling I'd be raped if I didn't consent. I started writing poetry secretly.

The Combatants

The battleground is strewn
with discarded clothing;
weapon unsheathed,
you require that I submit.
My fingers clench,
nipples stiffen in resistance
which you misinterpret
as delight.

Your bulk presses down,
ignorant of the danger below
as I plot my revenge,
capitulation only apparent
as you invade
my territory.

Unaware of the seething charnel
that threatens to overflow
you persist.

Breathing quickens,
sweat mingles,
pelvic muscles tighten
poised for the moment
when
I LOOSEN AND THE VORTEX OVERWHELMS.
Your eyes bulge in disbelief
as the surge sucks you in.

We did go a few times for marriage counselling but it always died off because of Ted's work schedule. The counselling was a little bit beneficial but I always had misgivings about it because it seemed to be just sort of scraping the surface. It made things smoother at the time but we never got to the root of our problems.

There were a lot of problems after Stephanie was born. Ted was under a lot of stress at work and he transferred it when he got home. I just hated to ask him to do anything. Any little request would set him off. Any involvement at home seemed to be an imposition on him. It seemed as if I was creating all the problems for him in his life. And I had to be so careful in what I said, the words I used. He always said I was putting him down if I used a word he didn't understand.

Ted put his job first, he definitely did. He really didn't need to be away so much. He was always available. He was at their beck and call.

After that first year of being at home with Stephanie, I started to meet people in the community. When she was two, I got a part-time job. I went through a lot of changes and I began to resent the way he treated me. I began to realize that I wasn't the cause of his problems.

Ted started to drink more. He couldn't seem to handle it. Anytime he'd drink I could count on it—he'd get really violent or nasty. He'd come home and I didn't have to say or do anything, he'd be in that mood.

He hated my family and he resented any involvement I had with them. I didn't want a lot of contact with them but they were still my family and I had a child. I couldn't have them here, that would cause a problem. My grandmother was very, very important to me. She was the most important person in my life, but I could hardly ever see her.

One evening in 1978, for some reason I can't remember, Ted pinned me down and was screaming at me and calling me by my father's name. He beat me and marked me up enough that I did have to leave him. I took the baby and stayed overnight at my next-door neighbour's. I did have to call the police because I was afraid to go back. I called his family and that was the first time I involved his family. His dad came the next day and talked with Ted. Ted was calm at that point. The police told me that they felt it was safe for me to return. Things sort of died down. I went back. He wanted to be very close right after: to make love. He may have apologized. That was something he ordinarily didn't do. Ordinarily it was as if it didn't happen. In my mind, it was almost as if I had imagined it.

I started running and I discovered this physical self that I wasn't in touch with before. It was a release. It was a renewal. I had to go out first thing in the morning when everyone was still in bed. Ted sure put up lots of barriers to prevent me from going, but once I was out the door he didn't have any control. I could breathe more easily.

SALVE-ATION

Under your stare, I methodically complete my stretches.
Grudgingly, you, jailor, permit me my allotted time of exercise.
As I stride from your grasp
You hurl out parting words,
powerless and frustrated by your inability
to follow as I close the door.
The sting of the winter storm outdoors
can be no more biting than your icy pellets.

I settle into a comfortable pace.
Renewal begins.
Muscles unwind:
the stomach unknots; diaphragm lifts;
bandages of tension loosen.
I am open to sensation
There is only me.

Music pulses through my veins.
The current licks through me
Cauterizing my wounds.
My pace quickens as I synchronize.
My spirit soars.

Prescribed course complete,
I slow to a walk,
stretching the remaining moments of freedom.

Salve of self-worth in place,
I return to serve out my sentence,
THIS TIME.

After a few years, I also started weight training at a health club. I became very strong and I liked that. I liked the strength. Ted was a very strong man but now I was more able to stand up to him and I wasn't so easily hurt.

Things sort of resolved for a while and in 1983 I got pregnant again. We both wanted the baby and the pregnancy went extremely well. I loved being pregnant, both times, and I was able to continue my physical activity right up to the last.

Michael was born by C-section which was okay and I arrived home one week later. It was in the summer and Stephanie was home from school. She was five years old. Michael was even more colicky than Stephanie. He threw up day and night. I tried to breast feed but that didn't work out. Ted had to go on a five-week course to the States and that caused a real upset because I felt it could have been postponed. A friend of Ted's told me he didn't really have to go, but Ted felt it was in his best interest to go, so he went. The baby did not sleep and he was losing weight. I couldn't get my sleep and I was just a nervous wreck. So we survived, the children and I, through that stretch, but it was awful, just awful. I felt very hurt that Ted had made the decision to go away at that point.

I went back to work after the maternity leave was up, part-time at Christmas.

The next summer things got really bad and the violence escalated again. So much would happen in the bed. Say I was in the bed first and he'd come in and he'd be angry about something. If I didn't want sex or if I didn't respond about something, he'd physically kick me out of my bed. I couldn't stay in my own bed! I'd be on the floor and I'd have to grab a pillow and blanket and go to the sofa.

I didn't always respond because I guess I was feeling strong about myself in some ways. At this point I was working part-time. I was also involved in the community and I loved that. I loved organizing this and that. Then I helped organize a political campaign and I just dived into it. I was getting lots of recognition, but anytime something good happened to me, Ted would turn it around into something negative. Most of the time he said I was sick, I was stupid, I was a drug addict (I'd tried LSD three times when I was a teenager). Or he would say I was dishonest, or sneaky and that nobody wanted me. When he really wanted to hurt me, he called me by my mother's name. He knew that really bothered me because I didn't want to be *anything* like my mother.

I was afraid of showing any signs of weakness because he would use it against me. I had to be super strong, so collected and so objective, even when he was being outrageous. I could not get upset. I would talk to him, try to calm him down. And then he'd say to me after, "I never thought of that, you know. You're right." But it got to be such a strain. He told me he hated me but other times he said he loved me. It was so confusing. He would say things in front of Stephanie. She heard so much, saw so much. Just sitting at the kitchen table and we'd be talking and something would make him mad and he'd throw the coffee at me. It was so childish, so infantile. It was as if he couldn't put any controls on his own behaviour. I really thought that I could be killed. For example, I would never go out in a boat with him. I can't swim and I was afraid that something might provoke him into staging an "accident."

I knew I had to pull myself out of the situation, but I couldn't see how I could provide for the children on my own. I really loved the baby and I wanted to be home with him like I had been with Stephanie. I had felt so positive and so strong and he was just a part of that. He seemed a symbol of the new me. He was bright and alert and so friendly. But he was so little. I felt trapped. I didn't know how I could manage alone. Also, if I was on my own, I wouldn't be able to run or have access to the other activities outside my home. And then there was Ted's family. I felt close to his family. I liked going down there. It was part of my life. If I left, I would be losing more than Ted.

Ted's violence escalated. It was now weekly and sometimes daily and wasn't connected to any bouts of drinking. In fact, he hardly drank at all.

For a while I was still having success in other areas (the recognition for my community work) and it balanced. What I had with Ted was awful but I had the other to make me feel better, to know that I was okay. But suddenly it didn't seem to count anymore and I was becoming depressed. So much of my energy was going into surviving that I felt I was closing myself off from my children. I was becoming a nervous wreck and it just didn't balance out anymore.

I went to see a lawyer because I wanted to be sure of what I was doing–to protect myself–because I knew he'd be absolutely furious with me for taking the children. I didn't say anything to Ted about it but that was the only way I could do it. It wasn't like me; I'm not a deceptive person. The lawyer felt my circumstances weren't safe and he recommended Interval House. I hadn't planned to leave right away but he said, "Do it." It was Thanksgiving weekend coming up and his parents were supposed to come for dinner you know. I went home, phoned Interval House and packed. I left a note saying that I couldn't live like this and that I was taking my lawyer's advice. The note wasn't nasty in any way.

I took the kids to Interval House. It was an anxious time. I was worried about what would happen. I called a couple of good friends. Somehow Ted found out where I was. He called the police and told them I was unstable, that I had a history of psychiatric problems. The police came to the house that first night and insisted on seeing that the children and I were safe.

I was at Interval House ten days and I only went back because Ted was absolutely devastated by the situation. It completely shook him up. He said he was sorry it happened and he would definitely move out. I felt the relationship was over. Too much had gone before and I couldn't bring it back.

He did not leave right away. There was something wrong with the well. There was no water. He worked on it for hours and hours, actually three days. He slept in the bed and I slept on the living-room floor in a sleeping bag. He told me he loved me and he wanted me. He seemed so sincere. Things did get better and we went for several counselling sessions.

And then we entered into a new commitment. We had to put in a new septic system as well as a new roof, so we took out a sizeable loan ($8,000 for three years). We didn't have extra money before. Now there'd be no way. We'd have to be together for this period as a unit.

Things weren't too bad. There were no real heavy physical episodes. There were isolated incidents (he choked me once) but it didn't go on for hours and hours which would have been the case before. I always had warning: he'd start to chew his bottom lip just before he lost control. But he was more cautious now. He was more aware of the consequences; after all, I'd been to a lawyer and to Interval House. He was more careful as to where he would hit—usually a knock on my head where it wouldn't leave marks. Sometimes months would go by without any physical action but I still didn't feel right.

I was very concerned about Stephanie, very much so. I'd gotten her into counselling for children. She didn't go very long. The counsellor wanted to talk to Ted and me and we saw him a few times, and then that fell through because of Ted's work situation. Stephanie sort of settled a bit more.

Ted continued to resent the other things in my life that I wanted to do, especially that I still wanted to run. There was an international race in the Rockies and my corporation wanted me to compete but Ted didn't want me to go. It was important to me. For me it was the chance of a lifetime. But it meant that he would have to stay home with the children. Of course that was a big thing as well—that I was neglecting the children. He told Stephanie, "Oh maybe we'll be lucky, and she'll run right off a cliff and that will be the end of her."

Two months before the run, my grandmother died. I sort of fell apart. She was very, very special to me. She was the only person in the world who loved me no matter what. But because Ted didn't like her, my visits had been limited. I couldn't even bring her home for supper. I could have done so much more for her had my circumstances been different. Now she was gone. The first night I came back from the wake, I was in the kitchen crying. Ted came in and said, "What the hell's the matter with you now." I felt so isolated from him.

The week before I left for the run, Ted put his hands around my neck as if to choke me.

The run was great and I was gone for a week. I had hoped I could make a decision about Ted and I but it didn't happen.

I met a man, Colin, at the run. He made me feel very positive about myself. I could be completely myself and I felt very alive, very attractive in all ways: physically, intellectually. I could talk to him, he understood, and I didn't have to translate. Ted always felt that I was trying to put him down, that I deliberately used words to confuse him or mislead him. I'd always think, Now how am I going to say this that he's not going to interpret something else. He'd always be confused with simple things. For years I thought that perhaps I was a cold person, but now I knew I wasn't. I felt so spontaneous, so connected. I was being myself and someone was liking me. I was learning about photography and Colin was interested in seeing my photos. He liked poetry and he was the first person that I showed my poems to. I didn't feel any real physical attraction to Colin at the time.

Colin's work was centred in Ottawa but he travelled a lot with his job. When I returned home, I met him for lunch. I told Ted and at first he was very angry but then he said it would be alright for me to see Colin again if he knew about it ahead of time. Well, the next time he knew, but he didn't want me to go. This platonic relationship continued until Colin had to go out west for six months. That really hit me hard because I was receiving reinforcement to be myself. But it was good in a way because I had to sort things things out for myself about my future. Would I go back to work, to school? I was completely uncertain. I did not know what way my life was going to go. I could see that there could be more to my life.

The children were having behavioural problems, especially Stephanie. If I was trying to discipline her, Ted would shift it away from her and onto me. Anytime I did something with her he'd say, "You're trying to run her life just the same way you're running my life." So then he would start in on me and of course she'd be shifted off to the side and she'd get off scot-free of everything. I felt that if I was able to get myself together, I would be able to deal with her and Michael properly.

During this period my nerves were really quite bad. I began having all these physical things happen to me and I just felt like I was wired you know. I had muscle spasms, my muscles would go. I had no control. I didn't know how I could make it on my own with the kids. I was thinking more and more of that.

I checked into the programs at Carleton and Algonquin and I took tests to see what I was suitable for. I got legal aid.

I told Ted we had to separate and he became violent one more time.

Ted could never seem to come to a decision. I got so tired of always having to be the strong one. Sure I am a leader as such but I don't like that in *all* situations. I really like it where the partners are equal.

I sorted it out how we could handle it financially. I figured that in a few months when our income tax came back, and if I scrounged, we could pay off the loan and then he could find a place and he finally agreed to that. I was terrified of having to sell the house because the children were very attached to their friends and they felt comfortable there. So was I. This was the only house I had known. I was the one who did the papering and the painting. I was involved in the community. I felt tied here and Ted didn't have that. The thought of losing those supports . . . But when I did reach the decision I sort of put it in perspective and actually felt I could handle it if the house had to be sold.

Even though he had three or four months to find one, when our deadline came, Ted didn't have an apartment. So, at his request, I actually had to help him find a place. That was ridiculous but it was the only way I could get him to leave.

He finally moved out a month later and I had to help him move. He ended up being very angry because the place was not what it seemed at first and then, of course, it was my fault, and I had everything and he had nothing and all this. That's the way it's gone.

That first month, August, was a very strange month. I just couldn't believe it. Do you know Kierkegaard (the philosopher), *The Dizziness of*

Freedom? That's just the way it felt. I was almost ecstatic that month. It was incredible—the weight that was lifted off me.

Later in August I called Colin and he came to visit. We had the most wonderful evening. We talked and talked and everything we did meshed perfectly. We lit a fire and had supper. It was really late and he was going to go and I didn't want him to go. We had a discussion about that. He didn't think it was a good idea to get involved at that point. My whole situation was just new and this would complicate it, but I persisted. He stayed the night and we made love. It was a very special experience. Everything felt so natural, so gentle. There was no force. The next day he had to go back west for six weeks.

I had a lot of difficulty with Ted. He was harassing me and I couldn't get him to stop. He'd phone six times in a row, within minutes, or stop in at my work place. A public display didn't seem to bother him but then the people around here didn't know him. It meant more to me to be humiliated and called names in public. He was supposed to take the children every second weekend but he wouldn't come on time or bring them back on time. When he came, he would always look around and make derogatory comments and call me names like "fuckin' slut," within earshot of the children. Before he left, he'd go to the basement and take something. Usually it was his tools, but I just wished he'd clear out all his possessions and be done with it. I felt my territory was being invaded. His visits were never smooth.

I had the locks changed and that infuriated him. I kept pushing my lawyer to get some sort of protection in place for me, but nothing happened. I called the police and they said there wasn't much they could do about Ted's harassment because it wasn't like an outside person bothering me at work. I was very nervous and very discouraged. As soon as I could see Ted coming into the drive, I started to shake. I just couldn't control it.

Then everything fell apart: the TV, the vacuum cleaner, the lawnmower, the plumbing and my car. I'm mechanically inept and Ted is just the opposite—he's very handy. The plumbing resulted in major repairs costing $1,000. At the time, one of my friends said, "Mark this down and when you look back, you'll be amazed you survived it."

But at this point I was really lucky. My boss decided to go ahead and have some surgery so I was given three months full-time work and this helped me break even financially. I was able to pay for everything except for the car. My Dad helped me out on that. I found that when something really bad happened to me, shortly after something good would come up unexpectedly.

Then there was a bad episode. One Saturday morning in November, Ted came to get the kids. He rang the doorbell (I had the door locked). He waited thirty seconds and then he broke the door in and punched me in the head. He said he was going to get the computer printer and I said he couldn't because I needed it for my work (I had just gotten a contract to edit a book for a local committee). He went to the basement anyway and when I tried to block his way, he shoved me against the walls and into the closet and started to choke me. Michael was nearby and had an awful look on his face. He didn't say anything. It was like he didn't know how to react. Ted went out with the printer and came back for the children. Stephanie didn't want to go.

I just felt like crawling into a hole. I went to my room and cried and cried for a while and then I thought, No, just don't let this go. This is something real. It *has* happened. You knew he was building up to something.

I called the police and they said, "Well, unless you have this piece of paper" . . . you know, nothing could be done.

I called Interval House and I think it was Joan who answered and she said I should have my injuries documented. So I went to a doctor who was on call and that was the best thing I ever did. She talked to me for about an hour and she understood the situation. She didn't discount it and she put me in touch with a counsellor at the Kanata Resource Centre [The Community Resource Centre of Goulbourne, Kanata and West Carleton]. The counsellor was wonderful and I still see her on an irregular basis.

That week I called my lawyer, the police and the Crown Attorney and was told by all three that if I laid charges against Ted it would take three months before the case actually reached court. I was going to be no further ahead than going through the regular process to get a restraining order that the lawyer had talked about. I felt so vulnerable. During this period, Ted would always threaten not to give me the money for the child support. Or he'd keep it till the very last minute when I was desperate for it. He held that over me so I was afraid to proceed. Ted had already ripped up my draft separation agreement before he moved out. We had nothing in writing at that point regarding protection, custody or separation.

Out of all that, I eventually got a restraining order but Ted got one against me at the same time—a mutual restraining order. It angered me that my lawyer agreed to that but she said that the order against me really didn't mean anything and she felt she needed to agree to certain things just so there'd be something in place. I checked with Legal Aid, and they said if I went to another lawyer, I'd have to go through the whole process again of applying for legal aid. I was really unhappy with my lawyer's attitude so I sent her some information I got from Interval House to educate her about women in my situation.

The separation agreement was eventually worked out and I was given exclusive possession of the house and $500-a-month child support. So I felt better at that point. But Ted still made it a point to come in when he came for the children, and every week it seemed he *still* had to go downstairs and get something from his workshop. And of course, each time he would say something of his was missing and I was supposed to be accountable for it you know: the chainsaw or something. I wouldn't even *touch* the thing. So what was the use of calling the police? How long would it take them to get here? He'd be gone by then.

Later, on one of Ted's visits, I went to bed with him. It was strictly to satisfy an animal urge and wasn't very pleasant.

I was having a lot of trouble with Stephanie over that period and she was making things worse. She was ten years old and she was just furious. She couldn't even look at me without being angry. She thought I was being very, very unfair to her father. She denied that he ever hit me. She called me names and wouldn't help with *anything*. It seemed as if she was assuming Ted's role. That got me down. I had thought that after Ted left I could focus on the kids and try to keep more discipline and be consistent and then things would settle down. But Stephanie didn't go along with that. She would purposely not be ready when Ted came to pick up the children so it would be an excuse for him to come in. And then she would say she wanted to show him something in the house.

My counsellor was really helpful. She was my lifeline. I don't like dealing with someone who is remote and she's not like that at all. She will offer experiences of her own you know. We really relate. She understands and she's got the practical information as well. She explained that children often deny what they don't want to believe. She put me in touch with the Ottawa Youth Services Bureau who came out and talked to Stephanie and me. But Stephanie refused to get involved in their group program and it was too far for them to come out to talk to her on a regular one-to-one basis.

Things sort of settled down for a while. There were instances of demonstrations of affection from Stephanie. There were still instances of the other but things were smoother.

Then I started getting calls from the junior kindergarten teacher about Michael. Ordinarily he was a real go-getter, a real active child. But for some time he had been lethargic and sad. He sat a lot with his blanket. Suddenly, right after Christmas, he switched and became this angry little mass. He was hitting other children and even kicked the teacher. He'd be sent to the office and I'd go to the school and try to control him and try not to react angrily back to him, even though he'd be kicking and punching and digging his nails into my hands.

The school helped me get counselling for Michael but there weren't any openings until May.

That winter was a very difficult period. I was accepted into a retraining program for a word-process operator. It was as if something had fallen into place again to save me. My full-time work just finished and this program paid a training allowance and they covered my babysitting as well. But I wasn't prepared for the stress involved in that they really crammed a lot into the course. It wasn't university, it was college and you had all these tests every night and assignments and homework. Most people had a commercial background and I didn't. And I have this thing where I like to do very well at whatever I do. So it was very difficult, plus the winter driving to the city and my old car. . . The temperature light was coming on, it was boiling over. There were so many problems with it.

So Michael was having these problems too at the same time. I'd get home and go and pick him up and as soon as he'd see me he'd run away. He wouldn't want to come home. It really looked as if I was mean to him.

Colin came back and we resumed our relationship, but it seemed to me that he was pulling back. He had trouble fitting me with the other elements of my life—the children, my dilapidated car, the endless house repairs. It made me very uncertain. I didn't want to push, but I needed more than he did at this point.

One Saturday in February, we severed our relationship. He was going away again. That was the start of a very bad period for me. I thought I had already gone through the worst, but this was the worst, really the worst. I had completely shared my real self with another person. There was a part of me that was being sustained by this relationship and now it was over. I came crashing down. It really frightened me. I kept a grip on myself because my children were coming back the next morning and I had to hang on. That night I went to see a very down-to-earth woman and shared a little of my situation. I knew that her matter-of-fact advice would get me through the night.

The next day I had a three-hour session with my counsellor. She had been trying to prepare me for this possibility. I had exams at the end of the week so that helped me to focus as well. When my course was finished I decided, Okay, you don't have to have someone else to reinforce you.

A few days later, I went out cross-country skiing. I had a bad fall and ripped a ligament in my knee. Running was out for three months. That was terrible for me, running was my outlet. I thought, This just isn't fair.

My counsellor suggested I register for a two-day conference on wife abuse. Previous to that I hadn't really thought of myself as an abused wife, but during the conference I kept connecting to what was being said. It opened my eyes to the years of abuse I had tolerated. It was a tearful day.

As for my life now, there are many positives. There's been accomplishments in my relationship with my children. Stephanie even comes and hugs me sometimes. Michael attends a summer program at CHEO and he enjoys it. The comments are very good from his teachers and it looks as though he'll be able to attend regular school in the fall. He's very eager to talk. He told them about me being choked and how he was scared and didn't know what to do. The staff feel that part of his problem stemmed from that event and that he may be confused about his male role. The doctor said he's definitely very bright and she feels that Michael is a workable situation.

Ted was in contact with the doctor and I guess he tried to give her a snow job—that he was concerned about me and my handling of the children. He told her I was unstable. She said she couldn't take sides in our situation. She prefered to deal with one parent only and she found no reason why she shouldn't continue to deal with me as the parent. I was very pleased with that.

I took a vacation with the kids, a vacation I couldn't afford, but we did it anyway. We spent one night in a motel and three nights with relatives. We saw Wonderland and then Stephanie and I had a special time by ourselves at the Shaw Festival. As we were driving back, we talked about our relationship and what we liked and didn't like about each other. Stephanie told me that she liked my laughter and the fact that I tend to find the humour in situations. She also said she liked our conversations because I listen to her and try to understand her. I was surprised to hear of her appreciation of my laughter. Ted always told me I was the most depressing person around.

I'm functioning at the poverty level. I have a $300 monthly deficit right now. I'm up-to-date with heating, hydro, phone and mortgage payments but when my car died, I had to get a loan for another and I can't afford the car insurance. I used to panic, especially about my financial situation, but now as long as I can see a way through, I feel alright. I know I'm resourceful. I've been able to supplement my income by selling photographs, editing and writing. I used my writing skills to barter for a full membership at a health club. My father is helping me out financially.

I don't like the way my finances put limitations on the children. Ted takes the children to lots of fun places and Stephanie can't understand why I can't afford things like swimming lessons. I paid $40 a month for her piano lessons and that was a real hardship.

It's ironic that Ted thinks I have everything and he has nothing. He's not rich by any means but he's managing on the same amount that the three of us are living on and he also has a company car. Even to this day he still does not have a telephone. He wears a pager and I have to buzz a certain signal and then he may call us. This means I have to be home when I call him, otherwise he wouldn't know where to call. For example, I couldn't call from a hospital. He phones home when he knows I'm at work and leaves messages with Stephanie—messages he should give directly to me. He moved, and for a period of time he would not even tell me where he moved to.

I'm still very aggravated when Ted comes for the kids. He now wants joint custody. He wants the status and the say but doesn't want any more time with the children. I don't prevent access but I don't want to be restricted by his indecision.

Something which I didn't know about until two years ago has really upset me and alienated me from Ted's mother. She has never forgiven me because I went to Interval House. She said even if she was being killed, she'd never take the children away from their house and their father. She said her husband used to beat her but she sort of stuck it out (Ted said he was never aware of that at all). She felt that I was at a halfway house with derelicts off the street or something. It really angered me you know.

I feel more comfortable with just being myself. I don't feel the gap that used to exist. I can see a normalcy to life now. I'm not conscious of my situation every day. Life goes on.

I have several women friends that I cherish. We share childcare and conversation and our community work.

I know I need a bonding with a male but I'm wary. I will never ever be involved in a situation where my personality is negated. The relationship has to be in reciprocal terms.

It was a Monday evening when Lauren and I met for the update. She was living in a house just down the road from her previous home. Michael, now twelve, smiled from his perch on the couch and talked comfortably about his summer plans.

Lauren's new husband of one month also greeted me warmly and went on with his work.

When we found a quiet corner, I set up the tape recorder and we began our task. Lauren openly shared her life over these past eight years. But, as the interview went on, I became concerned. There was a tone of futility in her voice and some of her statements were alarming. Finally I said, "Are you thinking of suicide?" She admitted that it was uppermost in her mind. At once the interview was over and now my focus was on her and the preservation of her life. I asked the necessary questions. "Where are you on a scale of one to ten?" She felt she was off the scale. "Do you have a plan?" Her vision was of her lying on a white sheet. There was red all around her.

Knowing that she had a long commute to work, I asked, "What about on the road. Have you thought of that?" Yes, she had, although it was more to do with running. But she had dismissed it somewhat. She was afraid that she wouldn't do it right and would be left maimed.

However, Michael was holding her back. She knew this would hurt him.

We discussed going to the hospital right then. I could drive her. Her husband could care for her son. But she brightened a bit and said no, she'd be alright tonight. So we made a plan. She would call her doctor first thing in the morning and explain to him that she had to see him that day. She would tell him that she was suicidal. I would phone her the next evening to see how she was.

Lauren called me in the morning from work to say she had made the appointment and would see the doctor that afternoon. I was relieved.

When I phoned that night, her husband said she had just been admitted to the Queensway Carleton Hospital.

I visited her on the Thursday evening of the same week. She had slashed her wrists that day, with a broken mirror, on the white sheet of her hospital bed. She had made her vision come true.

Fortunately, she was discovered before it was too late.

What brought her to this state? I replayed the taped interview and looked for clues.

First we talked about Stephanie. She's eighteen years old. It was a nightmare for quite a while. She's been on her own for two years. She's expecting in October. She's feeling pretty good about it. I feel less . . . positive. She called me the very same day she found out. I didn't want to put up any walls. I stopped before I spoke . . . thought . . . and said, "Well Stephanie, you do know I have some concerns, but first I want to tell you that I do believe that you will be a very good parent." And I do believe that. She is quite mature. She's very bright—a very caring person, and she's absolutely excellent with Michael.

It's been very hard because I've had to step back from her life, her situation. She's only got her grade ten. She had honors in her first semester at high school and I was so pleased. I thought, she's getting herself together. And then there was a teachers' strike. She got used to not being at school. She had a school phobia. It was real and it still is. She cannot handle any kind of stress. She gets migraines—like me. It was crisis after crisis at the high school. She just wouldn't respect anything or anyone at the school. She would just do her own thing. I'd be called at work and then I'd drive out the thirty miles to the school and take her back to the hospital or wherever and, of course, I'd have to make arrangements for Michael. She tried many programs—the hospital's day program, the alternate school. We'd get something set up and she'd get started and then she'd take off and they wouldn't take her back. She took pills—she had to have her stomach pumped. So, of course, after her doing that to herself, everybody was really nervous.

Stephanie has been seeing a psychiatrist for several years now and has hinted that she was abused. She doesn't remember anything of her childhood. The psychiatrist told Lauren that she is suspicious of Ted.

From the age of twelve, Stephanie has had a series of boyfriends, all much older. She ran away for a while and then brought home a fellow who was eight years older. She showed up with him. I wasn't going to make any judgements based on his appearance, even though he was straggly and unkempt. I gave him a chance. I was glad to have her home again at least.

But after a month, Lauren had to ask him to leave. When she came home that night, they were gone, and some of her possessions were also gone. Things that mattered: my only necklace, gold, a family ring, my dad's coin collection (I didn't know the value, but it turned out to be worth $5,000). That was one of the worst nights of my life. I felt betrayed.

Ten days later Stephanie contacted her and they met. She refused to implicate her boyfriend who had a record and a history of alcohol and drug abuse, and she refused to accept that she had done anything wrong. Rather, she blamed her mother saying it was Lauren's own fault for making her boyfriend leave. Lauren went to see the police and checked into what the consequences would most likely be if she had her daughter charged. Of course her dad sided with her. He got a lawyer for her and they went to court together. She did get probation and a community service order, but it wasn't what I would have hoped. It wasn't a supervised situation. I was really disappointed in that.

Where she's at now, I feel she's much more subdued. The relationship she's in now, she's taking the lesser role and she doesn't have the spark that she had. Although he's not abusive, he's in control. This fellow is also eight years older than she. She's his intellectual superior and I feel she will outgrow him in time.

On the other hand, she calls, she chats. She's a real chatterbox. She's quite interested in learning all she can about her pregnancy. She's doing all the right things.

Lauren was pleased about Michael. He is in a gifted program, and she gets many compliments on his behaviour. He's quiet and serious. He's close to me. He still likes to be hugged.

She recounted an event in which she received a significant award from work. Michael accompanied her as her escort. He was wonderful. He was on his best behaviour. I couldn't have been prouder to have anybody with me.

Later, Lauren observed him polishing her trophy and realized that he was proud of her too. It was such a wonderful feeling.

Michael and Stephanie have a good rapport, but Michael is not keen about his visits with his father. His dad is very harsh. Michael goes willingly, mostly, when it's his time, but he doesn't want to go extra. Ted pulls the guilt trip on him and makes him feel bad for time not spent with him, so Michael will generally back down and go.

I asked her if she was still running. I was until the winter. It was hard to keep up with it. I put in long hours at work—generally about fifty hours a week—and then there's two hours a day driving. I have very little time to do much else other than get the meal ready and collapse. I miss the running. It was one of the things that helped me. It was a good way to deal with depression.

Lauren has been quite successful at her job. I'm now a communications manager—I've got a lot on my plate. I thought it was stable there, but it's nothing of the sort. We've lost three of our staff. I've been given additional responsibility.

Five years ago, Lauren joined an abused women's support group in Kanata. She became the successful role model in the group. She was the one who did all the right things and was on her way. She is frustrated now that her emotional life hasn't improved. Two years ago it was so bad: the cracks were happening and I couldn't force them together any longer. I did see a doctor for almost a year and that did help at the time. But there was so much that I was dealing with then. I was so frustrated: Why am I at this point after trying so hard ? And I know *so* much. If I could just *see* the edge of something else, I would excavate it. I would deal with it. I couldn't find anything else, but there had to be more. Why was I always arriving at such a terrible, desperate point? Two years ago, I was no longer standing at the edge—I was *lying* on the edge, and I just didn't have the energy to move away from it.

Lauren has had a series of intense relationships over the years. Some of the men have broken up with her. In the last two, she initiated the severance. At a workshop on stress, she charted her highs and lows. Each new relationship was a high. Each breakup was a low—lower than before.

She was involved with one man for two years. They decided to live together. She entered into a financial contract with him in which she put the money up front for the house she's now in. They both signed the deed and he promised to pay her for his half as soon as he sold his house. He didn't put his house up for sale, and the relationship broke up. Although she has offered him an easy way out, he has become vindictive. It has already cost her more than $9,000 in legal fees. And now I'm married and I'm still stuck with this person's name on the deed and mortgage. But it got worse.

Lauren fell deeply in love with a married man. It was the best and the worst experience of my life. We didn't really become involved until after we made what I thought was a clean break in each of our existing relationships. It was magical, magical, magical. But he felt he owed his wife a second chance.

I've recognized certain patterns. I've sort of fed myself. I never went completely cold from one to the other. I've always had somebody else there that I could go to. I've had six men love me—like really, honestly love me. I seem to really need that. I'm at my best when I'm in a relationship. I don't give any less than what I get. I know I give more.

Her new husband of one month is an alcoholic. He is very bright. That was appealing. We do have common interests and backgrounds. His parents were rooting for me. Everyone was so open about liking me. But, basically, he drinks ninety-five per cent of the time. I find I can't be immune to it.

Lauren has been taking antidepressant medication for the past year.

It's got to the point that if one more person says to me, You're the strongest person I've ever known . . . I know I'm strong, but I think I'm like porcelain. There's almost no me. I'm handling what I have to and it's taking everything to do that.

I'm still stuck with this persistent sense that I will do it one day.

I asked her what she meant by "do it."

Take my life.

This is an update on the update. I've talked with Lauren several times and can see a marked improvement in her outlook on life. The suicide attempt, I think, was a necessary demonstration to herself and to others that she needed relief from all her responsibilities and concerns. She stayed at the hospital for two and a half weeks and then returned home. She is now on extended sick leave and has her psychiatrist's support to take as much time as she needs.

Some days I feel good. It's sort of like I'm in neutral. When I wake up, I don't feel this great weight, this dread. I said to the doctor, "I feel like this has given me a chance."

Lauren is assessing the toll her career has taken on her life. My job is hard because part of what I do is strategy and I don't like it. There's manipulation, a twisting of the truth.

Lauren was feeling very positive about Michael and particularly Stephanie's support. She is the one who truly understands all this. She was good when I came home. She stayed for a few days and took it upon herself to get Michael on board.

She was hopeful about her husband's reaction. At first he was bewildered and feeling hurt and angry. But it appears that he is trying to understand and be helpful. I really feel he's on the verge of taking a big step—accepting some responsibilities, doing some work. He wants to contribute to us. He says, "Your job is just killing you."

She's had visits from old friends and co-workers and is feeling positive about renewing those connections. I just want to be open about this. I'm not going to give details, but I'm not going to hide it.

Lauren's advice to other abused women is also positive. Basically, believe that there can be something else. No matter how bleak your future may seem, there is something better there for you. There is hope.

THE 'ISMS

F'ism

Feminism or feminist. It is the F word. Occasionally it is uttered with an accompanying hiss that you hear with the words communist or leftist. One friend thought he was defending me when he declared that I wasn't a feminist. But I am. And the women I work with are too.

Mind you, you will seldom hear the word uttered at the shelter. Although it is the foundation of the shelter's philosophy, it is rarely a topic of conversation. To espouse feminist counselling does not, contrary to popular opinion, mean trying to turn other women into feminists. Rather, it refers to counselling based on a belief that women are equal to men and should be given the same opportunities, responsibilities and privileges.

Feminism is a most difficult word to define. I rather like what English author Rebecca West said about it in 1913. "I myself have never been able to find out precisely what feminism is: I only know that people call me a feminist whenever I express sentiments that differentiate me from a doormat or a prostitute."

So what exactly is feminist counselling? It is counselling designed to empower the woman so that she can take control of her own destiny. In simple terms, when a woman talks about the abuse, the counsellor believes her and supports her in her quest to find the best way to deal with her reality.

This is a change from the past when victims were shunned or blamed by society for their abuse.

It may be easier to understand feminist counselling if I explain what it is not. It is not telling an abused woman that if she goes home and prepares a delicious meal and puts on a sexy dress, all will be well. It is not suggesting she get pills for depression and take up quilting. It is not telling her to buck up and be grateful for what she has. It is not telling her to pray for forgiveness.

Feminist counselling is about allowing women to speak their truths and deal with those truths.

Feminism is sometimes equated with man hating, but for me, it is a positive term. It has nothing to do with putting down men, but rather, everything to do with empowering women.

L'ism

Lesbian or lesbianism. What happens to you—physically, emotionally—when you see those words? Can you say the words comfortably?

Many years ago, a staff member had a button that read, Mother Nature is a Lesbian. She wanted to wear it on the job. Other staff disagreed on the grounds that the word lesbian could make some residents feel threatened. I reasoned that coming to Interval House was a big step for most women. Forcing them to deal with lesbian issues at this most stressful time in their lives simply wasn't fair. The button was removed, but I must say its message rather tickled my fancy.

I have been homophobic. I laughed at the jokes that ridiculed gay men or lesbian women, and I can distinctly recall my discomfort the first time I saw two women lovers kissing. It was at a women's conference in the late '70s. Although I would like to think otherwise, I know I am still not at ease with the demonstration of passion between two men or two women. I suppose it has to do with our culture and the overwhelming message that the only "normal" love relationship is between a man and a woman.

But I'm learning. And again, the women at Interval House have been my teachers. But even in a women's shelter, where tolerance and acceptance of others is the norm, women still feel reluctant to come out.

A dramatic example of this happened at a staff meeting. One woman, a vibrant and hard-working staff member, warned us that she had an announcement to make. But, she said, in order to find the courage to make the announcement, she had to stand up and show off her new knee-length bloomers. There was laughter of course, but also concern. Was she going to resign? She had so many talents and skills. How could she be replaced? It would be such a loss. When she finally said, her voice trembling, "I am a lesbian," you could hear the collective sigh of relief. Oh good, she's only a lesbian. She's not going to leave.

But I can still see her pain.

"They're all dykes," is a common accusation used by abusive men who think their wives might turn to a women's shelter for support. It is the most frightful threat they can think of. One abuser, who had just admitted to his wife that he was gay, questioned her reasons for going to Interval House. He said, "You know, seventy-five per cent of them are lesbians."

Fortunately, most women faced with the choice of possibly meeting a lesbian or of staying with an abuser are willing to take the chance. They are often amazed to find we shelter workers to be the ordinary people we are.

It is only in recent years that the shelter has begun to look closely at homophobia. Staff and board have taken a heterosexism workshop to raise our awareness and deal with any personal discomforts.

The shelter seeks to find a balance so that it is a comfortable place for all women, regardless of their sexuality. We raise the issue of abuse in lesbian relationships and have responded to lesbian women who have come to us for support.

There are other 'isms the shelter plans to explore—racism, ableism, ageism, etc. in order to increase our knowledge, understanding and tolerance and to become more inclusive. There is much work to be done.

MAY'S STORY

May left Interval House looking the same way she did upon her arrival there two months earlier—defeated. She had been married for more than thirty years to an abusive man who raped her shortly after their wedding and continued to be verbally, sexually and physically abusive for much of their marriage.

May had several nervous breakdowns during the relationship and was on the verge of another when she went to the shelter. She was wracked with guilt. Her husband accused her of having an affair and she felt totally responsible for his latest abuse.

May worked hard at the house, preparing delicious meals and sewing for her son and other residents. Although she appreciated our praise and encouragement, she worked without spirit. The only time she became animated was during a conversation about her childhood.

Her eyes sparkled as she related a harrowing experience that occurred when she was a grade eight pupil in a rural one-room school. A harsh substitute teacher had threatened May and made a peculiar reference to the "protection" she carried. While the teacher was in the outhouse, May searched and found a small revolver in the woman's coat. She immediately ran to the nearby general store and phoned a member of the school board. The teacher was subsequently fired.

I was elated to see this short-lived take-charge side of May. But, after telling the story, she retreated into her shell again and try as I might, I could not rekindle that enthusiasm.

May had several children. The last one, an eleven-year-old boy, was many years younger than the rest and lived at home with his father. May really missed her son so arrangements were made for her to visit him at school. Two shelter workers accompanied her because she knew her husband was aware of the plan. I was in the lead, and as I entered the school office, I realized that the enormous man sitting in the visitor's chair, talking to the principal, was May's husband. I quickly turned and mouthed to May, "He's in there." She hid behind a tall tropical plant in the hall. Feeling like a conspirator, I stepped back into the office and invited the principal into his private, adjoining office. When he complied, I closed the door and whispered, "His wife is here and she doesn't want to see him." Then I noticed another door that opened from his office into the hallway and said, "Can she come through there?" The principal was protesting that he didn't want to get involved when I, rather desperately, opened the hall door and May, who had been pressed against it, almost fell into the room.

The principal, observing the frightened look on her face, must have decided to get involved after all, and said, "I'll get rid of him." Back he went to the outer office. We could hear the principal's soothing voice gently encouraging May's husband to leave. The reunion with her son took place without further ado.

On another occasion, May was advised by her lawyer to retrieve her car which was parked outside her home. May loved the car, referring to it fondly as my Malibu. The police couldn't provide protection, so this time there were three staff members standing beside May as she took the ownership papers out of the glove compartment. Her husband came out of the house looking quite angry. She explained to him that it was her car and she needed the keys. After a long and heated conversation, he finally consented. We were all greatly relieved when the Malibu's engine came to life and May was on her way back to Interval House.

The time came in the custody negotiations when May's son had to choose between a father who would spend any money he had on the boy and was promising a trip to Florida, and a mother who provided for the family and insisted that her son do his homework and go to bed on time. May knew she wouldn't win so decided that the only way she could raise her son was to move back home. One evening, she quietly left the shelter. I entered the house the next morning to the words, "May went back." It was hard to be optimistic.

Three years later, May wrote a letter to the Interval House staff, thanking us for helping her and bringing us up to date on her activities. She offered to share her story, so off I went to visit her on a chilly November morning.

Eggs For Sale and Home Baking signs adorned her roadside home. I could see a huge garden in the back yard. She greeted me at the door with a big hug, and it was obvious that her enthusiasm had returned. She glowed as she proudly held up her new granddaughter for inspection and talked of her baking business. We joined her husband next to the wood stove in the sun-filled kitchen. Coffee made the rounds as they both enthused about recent events. May laughed often, and I couldn't imagine a happier, more contented woman.

May's story reinforces the shelter's philosophy that a woman's own decisions must be supported and that no one else is as expert as she when deciding which course to take.

Here's May's story.

I was born in a village in Lanark County in 1933. I was the only girl. There were three boys older and three boys younger. My father was part Indian. He was a wonderful jack of all trades. During the Depression he was able to do all kinds of jobs to support the family. He ran a sawmill; he did blacksmithing; he bought a threshing machine and travelled with it from farm to farm.

I finished school in grade eight. In those days most children, especially girls, didn't go beyond grade eight. If you wanted to go to high school you had to board with a family in town as well as buy all your own books. Our family simply didn't have the kind of money for to have me do that.

I got a job at the woollen mill in the village and at fifteen years of age I was a looper. That was like sewing the sweater sleeves onto the sweater.

My grandmother had a heart attack and father brought her home to live with us. She was no problem until she took a stroke and so, when I was seventeen years of age, I quit my job and stayed home to help my mother. Grandmother had no control and always wet the bed. We didn't have electricity and so it was an enormous job just to do the washing. I had to carry water from the creek, heat it on the wood stove, and then crank the handle of the washing machine to make it work.

How I met my husband is a very comical story. One night I was out with a cousin at a restaurant in town. A young man walked in with a bunch of girls and he sat down at a counter across from us. He looked directly at me and then he stood up and he pointed his finger at me and he said, "There's the girl I'm going to marry."

I was very embarrassed and my cousin and I left right away and went on to the Saturday night dance. I knew a lot of the guys and girls there so I was having a good time dancing, when all of a sudden I felt someone cut in and here was the same fellow. I said right away, "No I don't want to dance with you, I think you're a bit odd."

And he said, "Well, I just want to talk to you."

I said, "Alright," and so we sat down at the side of the hall. His name was Earl and he told me a big white lie that he needed my address for a mutual friend who was in Korea and wanted to write to me. But of course he was lying. All he wanted to do was get my address so he could come and hound me.

The very next Saturday night Earl came to the dance in my village. He walked over to me and didn't even ask, just reached out and caught my arm and pulled me up and we were dancing around the hall. I was lamenting about it and going on but he didn't listen. Later we went outside to talk to some friends and he picked me up and tossed me inside their car. I was going on and he said, "Would you shut your mouth," and he kissed me so hard that he put my tooth right through my lip. And so then I was really angry and I said that he was going to have to take me home right away because my lip was all bruised. I thought that would be the end of him because I gave him such a hard time. The next Saturday night he was back with flowers, chocolates—the whole bit—asking me to go to the dance again. And this is the way we started.

Earl came every weekend and helped with the washing. He would crank the handle of the washing machine while I did the rinsing and the sorting and hanging the clothes on the line. I don't know what I would have done without him.

What sold me on Earl was his way with children. He was an athlete and I went with him one day while he was training young boys and girls to run. He could run backwards faster than they could go forward. He was so good with those children. I thought, What a wonderful father that man will make.

We got married three months after we met. We had planned to have a big church wedding but my grandmother died two weeks before our date. I had walked down that aisle with grandmother's casket ahead of me. I was very upset because I loved my grandmother very much. I thought about having a wedding in two weeks time and walking up that aisle to be married and I just couldn't do it. I talked to the minister and we made arrangements to be married in the manse. That was in 1951. I was almost eighteen years old. Earl was twenty.

We lived in an apartment in town. We had only been married a few weeks when Earl lost his job. He was sort of upset, so we used our last little bit of money and took a bus to see a show in the next town. We went down on the bus and were coming back by train. After the show we went to the station, but the train wasn't in yet and so we went for a walk along the tracks. We were walking along, talking, and all of a sudden Earl grabbed ahold of me and he threw me to the ground. He started pulling up my clothes. He had intercourse with me there on the ground in the dirt and the cold. I was very, very embarrassed and I had to get up from there and go into the station and I realized my clothes were all dirty and that anybody looking at me would see what had happened. And this shook me up very, very much. It even shakes me up now talking about it. It was a new side of Earl that I had never seen before. Through the years, if a baby was cross or if he lost a night's sleep over a baby, I could expect this kind of treatment from my husband.

Earl got a job with the railroad in a village in Quebec and we lived there for four years. We had a small farm and a big garden and I looked after the hens and pigs and I loved it. We started our family one year after we married. I had four children in five years.

In 1957, Earl had an aneurysm. I think this was part of the reason why he was violent. He was operated on successfully but it left him with scar tissue and he developed epilepsy. He had to take drugs for to stop the epileptic seizures. It started out that he had about three seizures a week but it sort of slackened off to about two a month and gradually ceased altogether in fifteen years. Usually after coming out of a seizure, he would be very violent and ugly and "Get me—anything." I had to do it right on the spot no matter what condition the house was in or what else I needed to be doing at the time.

Earl lost his job when he had the aneurysm and we moved back to a village near Lanark County. We lived there for twenty-three years and during that time my husband joined the church and the children went to church and Sunday school and I was a Sunday-school teacher, and as far as outsiders knew, we were a very normal family. I was also a leader of the Messenger Group [a children's church group] and I found it a very good thing to be doing these things because I was with my own children. I knew what they were learning. Emotionally, I was getting more out of it than the children. It was my time away from the house. It was my social life.

Earl was very clever in how he abused me and generally he didn't leave any evidence. For example, in the pretense of hugging, he would squeeze me so hard that I couldn't breathe. I never knew whether I would get a loving hug or an abusive one. Sometimes I was left with bruise marks on my ribs.

At other times, Earl was a darling. He was his old self and this is why I continued to love him. I could not bring myself to leave him because he loved the children so much and he was never violent toward the children. I just couldn't tell the authorities that he was a partially violent man.

After Earl's violent episodes, I was very bitter and would take out my frustrations on the children. I would go into great tangents of cleaning the house and I'd put the children's toys away so they couldn't play. Or they'd bring home their artwork from school and I'd just throw it in the garbage.

Sometimes I wondered what reasons did I have for living. I loved looking after the children but I thought there should be more to life than being just a nursemaid. I also had to watch my husband to make sure he didn't fall and hurt himself and all the rest of it.

I got pregnant again. Our youngest was only two years old and I thought this was the last straw. I was so desperate I actually got a rope and hung a noose on the stairway. I must have gone up those stairs twenty times that day but I didn't have the nerve. I prayed for a miscarriage. We lived on mother's allowance and I felt I couldn't stretch it any further. I earned extra money by sewing for people and selling baking on the weekends at the flea market.

Earl did odd jobs and he helped with the children, but he spent most of his day at the pool room. He was a good player and sometimes he won money. I remember one day I sent the children to the pool room to fetch Earl because I needed him to carry water from the well to the house. He told the kids that they could do it themselves. They did. When he still hadn't come home for supper, I sent one of the children over again but he didn't come home then either. I was so angry I marched over to the pool room, grabbed a pool cue and broke it over his head. He came home later that evening after having won over $300 from a visiting pool shark. He picked me up and threw me across the room.

After the fifth child was born I felt guilty because I didn't want the baby.

When the seizures quit, Earl started a business with a partner, George. He lost weight and he got to be a nice-looking man again. He loved that business. George had just separated from his wife and was devastated. For a time I looked after George's son.

Several years later, I had linoleum flooring coming in to the train station. George and Earl came home for lunch. George had a car and a trailer on behind and he offered to help me get the flooring. So I jumped into the car with George. Earl stayed with the kids. When we got there, we found out the station was closed at lunchtime. So we waited. There was nobody around and it was back in a secluded area. George reached over and pressed a button and the seat went down. I had on wide-leg shorts and before I knew it, I was raped. I was devastated.

When the stationmaster came back, I didn't even get out of the car. George got the linoleum.

When we got home, Earl came out and helped George unload the linoleum. When Earl came into the house, I asked him to go into the bedroom with me and I told him what happened. Earl looked at me like he could have killed me. He told me that George had already told him the truth—that I was a slut, that I came on to him! Earl didn't believe me. He believed George! And then he just grabbed me and threw me on the bed and raped me again.

After that I just sat. I stared at the wall. I had my first nervous breakdown. I was hospitalized at the psychiatric hospital for two months. They gave me shock treatments.

With shock treatments you lose your memory and then gradually your memory comes back. I had flashbacks and I started to remember the rape again. I had a second nervous breakdown. I was hospitalized and given shock treatments again. I'm sure with each breakdown I had come to the point that I could no longer cope. My psychiatrist told me, "May, you either have to go out to work or you have to have another baby." I got a job in a hotel and three months later I found out I was pregnant. I was thrilled about both events. I worked till my eighth month and went back to work six months after our son Harry was born. Everything was fine. My older two girls were my babysitters and, while they were in school, I had a neighbour that took the baby.

We went off of mother's allowance. We were self-sufficient. My husband had things to occupy him; I had things to occupy me; the children were all in high school; the baby was spoiled rotten. We redecorated our home and fixed up a nursery. We were very happy.

I changed my job and became manager of a hotel. I did the cooking and worked behind the bar and I was very happy with this job. I loved meeting people. I worked there for six years. When the hotel was sold, I was looking for a job again.

But while I worked at the hotel, there was an episode that stands out in my mind. One night I invited friends for dinner. We were all gathered around the table and having a good time. Earl started flicking his lighter and turned it up to the highest point. I asked him to put it away. He reached behind me—my hair was really long—and he started my hair on fire. I ran to the bathroom to put it out. Everyone quickly left. I was devastated.

Soon I was hired as a homemaker with the VON [Victorian Order of Nurses], and I worked at that for about three years. I was very happy with the work. One case involved an elderly couple that lived in the States in the winter and came to a cottage near us for the summer. That fall the man had a heart attack and had to be hospitalized. I looked after the woman and helped her move back to the States. I packed up my Malibu and I stayed with her all that winter. I only got home for three days at Christmas. Earl and Harry came to visit me at Easter. I was very lonely down there. But one thing, while I was in the States, I established a homemaking service just like the one I worked for in Ontario.

On returning home I was faced with . . . for some reason, Earl didn't put my money towards making the payments on the house. Our house was being sold out from under us. It hurt me very deeply but I tried to manage. I got a job at a nursing home as a nurse's aid. I loved my work there but doing the job and trying to get my house back was too much for me and I had another nervous breakdown. The outcome of this was that we had to move out of our house.

In 1980 we moved to an apartment in a village in Lanark County. I was under doctor's care. The first week that we lived in the apartment my son Harry was hit by a truck on the busy highway in front of our home. Although he recovered from his serious injuries, the episode took it's toll on me and it was another year before I recovered from my nervous breakdown. My mother-in-law died during this time.

I didn't know what to do with myself. I was the sloppiest housekeeper you would ever see on the face of the earth. The dishes piled up, the laundry piled up. I would lay in the bed and cry. I would walk the floors. I would smoke one cigarette after another. I wouldn't talk to anybody. In fact, people scared me. I would hide from people. I didn't want them to know that I was looking and feeling the way I was. I spent a lot of my time in prayer. Eventually, with the doctor talking to me, I came out of this nervous breakdown.

I got a job in a sewing factory but I didn't like it. It was too impersonal and I didn't like the hectic pace. I got another job doing alterations and I loved it. I was my own boss, kept my own books, I was in business and it was wonderful.

Earl was getting crueller and crueller. He began accusing me of adultery. He would beat me and say, "You did this with so-and-so and why don't you admit it,"

And after a while I'd finally say, "Yes, yes, I did it." It got so that I started to believe him. I felt so guilty.

Earl didn't want me in his home. He was putting me out. I went into another nervous breakdown due to the shock that I had done so much for my family and now I wasn't wanted. It was very heartbreaking but by now I believed I deserved it. I still didn't want to leave and my husband became violent. I had nowhere to go.

At this time Earl had to quit his job due to his asthma and arthritis, so he applied for a disability pension. One day he took me along with him while he met with our provincial member of parliament, to discuss getting the pension. In my nervous state, I felt that everybody was on my husband's side including our MPP. It seemed that no one saw my difficulties or realized what a burden Earl could sometimes be when he wasn't well. I had to carry on and keep the household going and keep my job going and I felt it very heavy.

I was going to my doctor for psychiatric help and I told him what was happening and he was very kind and understanding. I tried to live at home but it became almost impossible. One day I was crying and very upset. Earl took me to the Emergency and the doctor suggested I stay at the hospital. It was at Christmas time and I was supposed to go home for Christmas dinner. I refused to go. I couldn't let my children see me in this condition because they would see the guilt on my face and the hurt in my heart. One day I was feeling good and I phoned Earl to bring Harry in for a visit. When they arrived, Earl came into my room and he grabbed my hand and he squeezed it so hard I thought it would break. He said, "Don't you think I have better things to do than to answer your phone calls?"

I wasn't smoking at the time and the cigarette smoke in the ward was really bothering me so I asked my doctor to move me somewhere else. He moved me to the children's ward which was a wonderful thing for me because I was able to get dressed every day and wander around the ward and I would help the nurses look after the babies. And me and babies just get along fine. This was a great boost for me. I started to get better.

I came back home in January but the violence was still there. Earl mostly yelled at me: I couldn't do anything right. I couldn't cook his breakfast right. I couldn't do any of the household chores to please him. I felt it was just as much my fault as it was his.

My father-in-law died. He and his wife had been my confidants. They had encouraged me to leave Earl. My father-in-law used to stick money in my pockets because he knew we were having trouble making ends meet. Now I had no one to turn to.

At this time I started calling Interval House. When things got bad, I would phone the house and say, "I'm coming, I'm on my way." But I couldn't bring myself to leave my son.

I was still seeing a psychiatrist and Judy, a mental-health counsellor. One day I finally told Judy, "I can't take it anymore. I need some place neutral where I can think things out or I'm never going to get better." And so she drove me to Interval House. It was the winter of 1984.

When I got to Interval House, the girls there welcomed me as though I was walking into my own home. I had bad nights and bad days but there was always someone to talk to and to help me. In my nervous condition I can remember all their faces but I cannot remember their names. It is their personalities that I remember.

During that time I started divorce proceedings and custody proceedings. Harry went to school in Carleton Place and I would make lunch for him and visit him during the lunch hour. I was so lonesome for my son. Earl was trying to turn Harry against me. One day during one of these visits Harry asked me, "Mom are you an old whore?"

I did sewing at the house and was beginning to feel happy again. After a couple of months, I decided to try it again. One of the workers lived near me so I asked for a lift and went back home.

I had my own key to the apartment. No one was there. I walked through the door and the mess that greeted me in the face just about knocked me down. The first thing I did was clean the oven 'cause I'm a stickler on food and ovens. I picked up dirty clothes which I found from one end of the apartment to the other. I did a washing, I vacuumed and I started supper. I had just sat down for a breather when I heard my family coming up the stairs. Harry was the first one through the door and he yelled, "Oh Mother." Earl wasn't quite so pleased. He mumbled away. He was very bitter because I had taken my car and I had started divorce proceedings and custody proceedings.

It was very bad that week and I don't know how I got through it. Earl and I tried to avoid meeting face to face. We ate our meals at different times. We tried to make a normal atmosphere for Harry but we spoke through our son and not to each other.

My daughter phoned and I broke down and cried. I couldn't talk. She said, "I'm coming for you and you can stay with me until things can be worked out."

I told my husband that I was going to start packing in order to go to my daughter's. I was still sobbing and crying. He jumped up from his chair and he pounded the back of my head with both his fists. He said, "You're not going anywhere but back to the hospital." He got my coat on and he dragged me down the stairs and he put me in the car and he took me to the hospital. The doctor took me right into his private office and asked me what happened. I told him. Then he phoned my daughter and told her to come to the hospital. I was very upset because this was another violent attack. I was very shaken. I was almost put back in the state I was in before I went to Interval House. The doctor occupied Earl, and I left with my daughter and went to her home in Ottawa.

There was very little room at my daughter's. She had two little children. I had to sleep on the couch. It wasn't a good situation. My daughter was on mother's allowance and she would get into trouble if she was keeping someone in her home other than her immediate family. I called Interval House to tell them where I was. A community worker came and brought food to help us out.

The next Sunday was Easter Sunday and we all went to church. It was a lovely church and there were lovely people. We were waving palm branches and singing the "Hallelujahs" and I was enjoying myself immensely. I heard the words that Christ had died for our sins and that we were all forgiven. These words went right to my heart and I knew for a fact that God had forgiven me for my supposed adultery and that I should never have to worry about it again. I was truly sorry and had repented. I was sort of in a state and at one point I didn't really know what I was doing but when I came to my senses again the people in the church had their arms around me and they were crying. I said, "What happened?" and they said, "May, you've been saved." I was laughing and crying at the same time. I said, "God has forgiven me."

We went back home and we put the Easter ham in the oven and then we got dressed in our bathing suits and we went to the community pool. I was trying to teach my grandchildren how to swim that day and I felt so happy. I felt that the water was washing my sins all away. I never knew such happiness before in my life. It was the most marvellous thing that ever happened in my life.

We came home to the apartment and I phoned Earl. I wanted to return home. He was agreeable and when he came to pick me up his attitude was completely different from the previous week. He took me in his arms and kissed me like a man in love. I have no explanation for it except that God must have gotten to him as well. He and Harry had just moved to town and so off we went to our new home. I felt such confidence.

I still continued to see my counsellor Judy, twice a week. One day Judy was visiting and Earl came home with a beautiful yellow rose bush and asked, "Where would you like me to plant your rose bush?"

Judy looked at our happy faces and she said, "I don't think you need me anymore."

We stayed in that house for a year and I babysat my niece's baby. But we didn't really like living in a big town. We went for drives in the country and one day we saw a house for sale in a small village near where I was born. We went on to a snowmobile dinner nearby and my brother and his wife were there. During our conversation we told him about the house and how we wished we could buy that house. Three weeks later my brother came to visit and he said, "May, you're going to kick my arse."

And I said, "Now why would I kick a dear brother's arse?" He told me that he had bought the house for us and we could rent it back at a rate we could afford. I was so happy that my brother would do such a wonderful thing for me 'cause he knew I wasn't happy living in a town. I am a countrified person.

We moved to our new home and the first thing we did was buy 100 laying hens. I supplied a restaurant with eggs and I sold the surplus from the house. Then in the spring we planted a large garden and I sold vegetables along with my eggs. This went over very well. This past summer I started selling home baking as well and it has snowballed. Now I am a very busy person. I'm planning to build a bake shop at the back of the house.

During this time, my daughter had a baby. She had separated from her boyfriend and she found herself very upset emotionally. She felt that she could not care for this baby. So she put the baby in a foster home. I prayed about this and it came to me: Why couldn't I take my little granddaughter and raise her? My health is good, I have everything going for me. I didn't want my little granddaughter lost to the family and so we applied to take her in. What a happy, wonderful day it was when we brought the little darling home. Now her mother visits one weekend and her natural father the next. He pays for the babysitter I hire while I do my baking.

Right now I feel wonderful about myself. I feel better than when I was a teenager.

I used to feel sorry for Earl but I don't anymore. And I don't fetch anymore. I still hear about it but I can live with that. I've accepted him as he is. I know he'd be a different person if he was in better health.

Our sex life and married life is A-one. When I need to be held, he's there. I went through so many years of him taking what he wanted, but now I decide when sex will happen.

Earl's a very intelligent person and I have learned a lot from him. He has a photographic memory and can remember everything he reads. If I need to know something, I just ask him.

I worry about one son: the oldest boy. When he was a child he saw his father not too active and yet getting what he wanted. He left home before Earl got a real job. Now this son sits in his home on welfare with his wife and children. I think he's very hard on his wife. He's picked up all the bad habits of his father.

My second youngest child just moved back and is living with us while he attends college. I love having him at home. He and Harry do a lot of work around the house and they are nice company.

I'm enjoying my religion. For a long time I was angry with God but now I have returned to my Christian roots and my involvement with the United Church and feel very happy indeed.

I want you to be sure to say how much Interval House meant to me. I don't know where I would have gone if it hadn't been there. I didn't want to stay with any of my children. I didn't want them to have to take sides.

I also want you to say that sometimes abusive men can change and the marriage can work out.

When I visited May seven years later, she had much to tell. She said that the first few years had gone well and that she and Earl had celebrated their fortieth wedding anniversary. They had actually renewed their vows in front of family and friends in a beautiful church ceremony.

However, shortly after this event, their daughter accused Earl of sexually abusing the granddaughter May had been caring for. The child was removed from their home. Although the charges were never proven, and May believes them to be false, the loss of the child was devastating for May. She was hospitalized for a month. When she returned home, she said Earl reverted back to his old personality: Demand, demand, demand. *And, even though he spent much of his time in a wheelchair, he also became physically abusive. The police were called once. They talked to Earl and suggested to May that she could leave. She decided to stay. Earl's behaviour improved for a short period. She lived this way for four years.*

It was May's sons who got her out. Two sons, Harry and Clark, were living at home at the time and were very aware of their father's abuse. One evening, Clark thought he heard May being hit with Earl's cane and her falling. He found a lump on her head, but when he asked his mother what had happened, she couldn't remember. Earl demanded to be driven somewhere and Harry complied, but shortly after their return, when Harry was out of the room, Earl roughly pushed

May into a closet, bruising her arm. Again, when asked, May could not remember the incident.

That evening, another of May's sons, Dennis, phoned to ask her to come to his home in Kingston—he said he needed her help. He insisted that she come right away. Clark drove her down. When they arrived, the two men talked to their mother about Earl's abuse and persuaded her to remain there. That night she went to bed and, Had the best sleep I've ever had in my life.

Within four months May found an apartment and got a job in a clothing store. On her days off, she went back to her home to get some of her possessions. Earl had assured her that he would help her and drive her back to Kingston. I will never get into a vehicle again that he is driving. He turned and went the wrong way in traffic. At first I thought it was a mistake, but now I'm inclined to believe that he was trying to kill us both. I left a lot of things there.

That was a year ago. Since then, she has experienced many revelations. She joined a group sponsored by a mental health agency called A Time For Me, whose focus was to help her remember her past. It was run by psychiatrists, but they didn't act like psychiatrists. They were just like one of us. They played a tape of running water and loons calling. We were to lie down on the floor and see how far back we could remember. You were to think about the trees in your life and your memories of those trees and of your memories at that time in your life. Actually, we would go into a sort of a trance. This was the greatest thing for me because I could sort out my childhood; I could sort out it all.

During the eight-week program, May started to remember the abuse of her past. The most dramatic new memory was of the rape by George and how the shock treatments served to blur the memory but not deal with the trauma. May also remembered that she had never committed adultery but only believed she did because of Earl's ongoing accusations and brainwashing. She learned how she had blocked out Earl's continuous abuse almost immediately after it happened, so that when her son questioned her about her bruises, she actually had no recollection. I had this ability to close my mind, and I lived that way for days and days.

May joined a speakers' group and has since become a spokesperson for the program.

It is with great pain that May talks about her relationship with her daughter. This woman now has four children and May is concerned about their welfare. Her daughter is very verbally abusive to the children and may be neglectful. She has since told May that she only accused her father of sexually abusing her daughter so she could get her daughter back and sue the child's father for child support. Her daughter has also accused one of May's friends of rape. The charge was ruled unfounded as the man was not in the area when she said the rape happened. I feel something has happened in her life but I don't know what. I'm sure my daughter is schizophrenic. What she heard my husband say over the years to me is what I think warped her mind. I think Earl is schizophrenic. One minute he was the sweetest person and the next minute he was off the wall.

May turned to the Church for support and became a born-again Christian. I knew I had to have help. I had to know. Being born again, I have more insight than I ever had before. My life is beautiful. The lord came to me. He gave me a picture of what life should be. Life is love, not harboring hate. I cannot hate my husband; I cannot hate my daughter or anybody else who would do injustice to me.

May is involved with several outreach groups through her church.

She went to her doctor because she was worried about her health. The doctor suggested that at sixty-two years of age she should not be working so hard. He also told her she didn't need to take drugs for depression. May has been off the pills for some time and feels great. So that's another healing that has taken place. I also attribute this to God.

With her doctor's encouragement, May has decided to apply for a spouse's allowance that she is eligible to receive. The paperwork for the divorce is complete and is awaiting Earl's signature.

When I was visiting with May, a friend dropped by. This woman used to hang out at May's home when she was a teenager and she had information to add for this book. She said, "I'd be there and talking with May and her kids and Earl would beckon to May that he wanted her in the bedroom. And then he'd rape her. This happened often. We knew what was going on. The things that woman put up with."

May added another image. She talked about the time she was dancing at a recent family gathering. Her nephews were astonished. They didn't know she could dance. They had only seen me sitting beside Earl and not looking at anyone too much. He never wanted me to get involved in a conversation with anyone, woman or man, that would take my attention away from him.

May had advice for other women who are being abused. Get out as fast as you can for a man can be cruel and will try to make you feel you have done wrong when you haven't. He may make you think he's changed, but it's not going to be permanent because he has a fixed opinion of who you are and what you are and he'll not let you be yourself, ever. He's going to make you like the little mushroom that's in his mind. He's not going to let you grow. Only by the grace of God, I'd still be under that thumb.

PILLS

Some women who come to Interval House bring along an arsenal of drugs—pills that have been prescribed by a family doctor or a psychiatrist to help the women deal with depression. In a few cases, a woman has assembled this arsenal by switching doctors and drug stores, but the majority of women get the drugs from their own doctor.

I often think that some doctors, in particular psychiatrists, are drug dependent. They do little to help a woman deal with the real reason for her depression or even investigate if she could be coping with incest, child abuse, rape or wife abuse. Instead, they turn to the prescription pad.

And what about the side effects? One night, when I was on shift at the shelter, the women were discussing their drugs and how they had been affected by them. It prompted me to get the drug book, which listed the common drugs prescribed for depression and which described the possible side effects. May (see previous chapter) asked about one particular drug that she was taking. I located it in the book and found a lengthy list of possible reactions. The last side effect listed was sudden and unexpected death. That's a side effect?

I remember another woman who had been recently released from the Royal Ottawa Hospital. She had left an abusive relationship but had been hospitalized for a long period of time for extreme depression. She was experiencing tremendous mood swings at the shelter and the counsellors suggested that she call her psychiatrist to see if her medication could be at fault. One staff member had already noted that two of her drugs were listed as incompatible. When she made the call and told her psychiatrist about the two drugs, he responded in an uninterested manner, "Oh yeah, I guess that's right." He did not apologize or even seem concerned about the repercussions of his mistake but simply told her to stop taking one of the drugs.

Dependence on prescription drugs has been a long-time problem for many in our society, especially women. Pharmaceutical ads in medical magazines used to target women as the gender in particular need of their antidepressant or anti-anxiety drugs. Doctors are still more likely to prescribe these drugs to women than to men with similar symptoms. Valium was the cure-all for anxiety. Prozac has become the wonder drug for depression.

Amethyst House in Ottawa is a treatment centre for women who are addicted to prescription drugs, over-the-counter drugs or illegal drugs, alcohol or any combination of substances. Women receive one-on-one counselling to help free their bodies from drugs so that they are ready to join a group and work on long-term recovery. It is a lengthy process to get the drug out of a woman's system and to help her recover from her emotional dependence.

Research by Amethyst has shown that a significant number of women turn to drugs because of some kind of loss—a miscarriage, the death of a child, the end of a relationship—or because of abuse—childhood sexual abuse, rape, wife assault. The women drink or take pills to dull the emotional and physical pain. The only way many abused and addicted women survived the abuse was to take drugs or alcohol.

Most women who go to the shelter have found that the best medicine for their emotional pain is the opportunity to talk to other women who have experienced similar difficulties.

A woman cannot concentrate on her healing until she is in a safe place. She needs time to deal with the past and to put it in some perspective. She needs to be believed and understood. She needs to talk out loud about the abuse, to cry, to be angry. She needs to talk about her loss, her grief, her guilt. She needs to forgive herself. All these activities are essential for real healing. Each woman deals with her pain in her own way and recovers in her own time.

There is no better cure.

CINDY'S STORY

Cindy has an appealing, cocky way about her. Her slight French accent and her direct and open way of speaking endear her to others. She accepts her past in a matter-of-fact manner, but she's not about to take any more abuse, I've had my share.

Cindy arrived at Lanark County Interval House within a month of its opening in 1979. Her large, dark eyes overwhelmed her tiny, frail frame. Sad eyes. She had escaped an abusive husband at the cost of leaving her two young sons behind. Her concern for their well-being, coupled with the lack of understanding or support from the legal system, finally robbed her of her will to fight back. She became severely depressed. She spent most of her time sleeping or crying. I remember the daily scene of trying to wake her and then tempting her to eat. She just wasn't interested—no matter how appetizing the food looked or smelled.

Cindy was the first and one of the few women to attempt suicide at Interval House. Since then, the counsellors have become very alert to the danger signs and take action if a woman talks seriously of taking her own life.

Cindy's situation also opened our eyes to the reality of sexual abuse within marriage. We were appalled to learn that Cindy's husband demanded intercourse at least four times a day and beat her if she didn't cooperate.

Cindy has only recently remembered the sexual abuse of her childhood. She had blocked out the memories of her first fourteen years of life until she was forty-five years old. At that time, for no apparent reason, she started to cry. She went to see a psychiatrist and he helped her to remember.

Here's Cindy's story.

I was born August 3, 1944, in the Ottawa General. I was given up when I was born. I lived in an orphanage till I was four months old and then I went to a foster home till I was fifteen.

There was a bunch of us in that house—twenty-four of us. There was the grandmother (she was my foster parent), the grandfather, two sons, two daughters, two sons-in-law and their families. There were three bedrooms in the attic and four bedrooms on the second floor. I slept in a room with eight of them—eight kids. You see, she took in kids that was from broken-up homes. The parents would come and get them on weekends. I was the only foster child.

I got beaten all the time. Whatever their kids did, I got the blame for it. A fly swatter across the bare back or a yardstick. They locked me in the basement for three or four days at a time.

My foster uncle used to get drunk all the time and then he'd wake me up in the middle of the night to go and get him some stuff from the restaurant. He raped me a couple of times. The first time I was six. The second time I was nine or ten. I was molested by another foster uncle. They both told me not to tell the Children's Aid or they would beat me up and they'd put me in jail. I was scared of going to jail.

I was scared of men for the longest time. I didn't even start dating till I was almost twenty. I wouldn't even look at men.

I was the oldest of all the kids so I had the responsibility of getting them all ready for school. The school was only a block away so we all came home at lunchtime. When I came home at lunchtime, if I didn't have all the breakfast dishes and lunch dishes done, then I didn't eat. I went to school till grade eight and then they took me out to babysit.

The grandmother was the only one who was nice to me. I used to call her Mom. She died when I was fifteen.

I was sent to another foster home in the country. I had to sit in the corner all the time (in a chair), but I wasn't raped. The mother beat me almost every night. She beat up the girls but she didn't beat up the boys. She locked me in the bedroom. She put a blanket in the window and took the lightbulb out and locked the door. I used to cry and she'd come in with a stick with that tape on it and beat my back. Her and her daughter beat me. Her daughter was twenty-five and retarded. The tape would make it hurt more. They fed us kids peanut butter or bologna while they were eating great big meals. I don't eat those things now. My kids do, but I don't.

I got lice in my hair. I had beautiful long hair. The mother cut it and then soaked my head in Javex and boiling water to kill the lice. She burned my scalp. The kids at school all laughed at my short hair. The teacher saw the marks on my head and called the Children's Aid. They took me away from there and the three little ones. One little girl was beaten up so much she had a brain tumour. They took us to Rideau Regional.

Rideau Regional wasn't too bad. The psychiatrist kept on saying, "What are you doing here?" How am I supposed to know? I was doing grade eight. There were a lot of other kids my age. I went to Brownies and Girl Guides. I was a Girl Guide captain.

A registered nurse took me out of there when I was sixteen. I lived with her to look after her little girl. But her husband raped me. She was working the midnight shift and I was sleeping. He came into my room and punched me in the mouth and knocked me out cold and then raped me while I was unconscious. When I came to, he was just getting off me. There was blood all over the sheets. He told me to wash the sheets before his wife came home. I didn't run away right away. I just told him if he ever did that again I'd report him to the cops. He got scared and he didn't touch me again. I told a friend of mine and she told the nurse. I guess her husband finally admitted it to her because she divorced him.

Children's Aid found me a job babysitting five kids in Ottawa. That was good. Both parents were nice people. I stayed there two years.

When I was eighteen, I got a job in an electrical store as a clerk. I was the manager's assistant because I spoke two languages. I liked it there. I lived with one of the boss's aunt and uncle. They were elderly people, in their seventies. They were very nice to me. They treated me like a little girl.

I started dating Ron when I was twenty. I met him through Lucy, a friend of mine. He was from a small town outside of Ottawa. We double dated with Lucy and her boyfriend. I thought Ron was very nice. Oh he treated me like a queen; everything I wanted, I got. If I wanted a new dress, he'd buy it for me. We dated for about two years and then he left home and moved in with me in my apartment. I was working and he was working and it was really nice. We used to walk a lot and go to the shows and stuff.

The first time I had intercourse with him, I got pregnant right away. I liked having sex with him, at first. We got married four months later.

That's when things started changing. We used to leave for work at the same time. But he wasn't bringing home any pay cheques. The way I found out: I called his boss one day and he told me he fired him three weeks before. Ron and I had a big fight about it. He said he was scared to tell me because I might get mad. We couldn't pay the rent because I wasn't making enough money so we got evicted from that place. We moved to a basement apartment.

I had a hard time with the pregnancy so I was in and out of the hospital a lot. Ron didn't get a job. He started drinking at the hotel with his friends.

I was in labour for two days before Teddy was born and Ron never came to the hospital. He and his friends were in the hotel, watching the strippers the day Teddy was born. He told me. I was so mad.

I was in the hospital eleven days. The thing is, when I got home I couldn't get into my apartment. There was a big lock on the door. The landlord had repossessed the apartment and everything in it—everything—the baby clothes, everything. I called Lucy and she came and took me and the baby to her home. I lived with her for a couple of months. Ron moved back to his mom's. I heard that he was going around telling people stories that I had left him.

Then his mom called me and told me I could come and live with them. She said Ron had a job. So I did. He was good because his mom and dad were there. Then we got an apartment of our own.

Our relationship wasn't very good. We weren't getting along at all.

When Teddy was nine months old he got really sick with bronchial pneumonia. He had a temperature of 106.8, so I rushed him to the hospital. When I came home I was crying 'cause I was worried about Teddy. Ron put me in the corner and started choking me and slapping my face at the same time. I can still feel it. I'd been slapped too much across the face when I was small. I felt like killing him then and there, I tell you. He never apologized, but right after, he told me he loved me. I lay on the couch and cried myself to sleep.

Teddy recovered, and the next month Ron got a good job in another town. We rented a big house beside his brother's house. Two months later we were evicted 'cause Ron was laid off work and we couldn't pay the rent. We moved in with Ron's brother and his wife and two kids. When Ron got a job, we got an apartment. He kept that job for three years.

We weren't getting along at all. There were lots of fights. Ron always wanted to have intercourse all the time. It didn't matter what I wanted. And we fought about money. He would buy things we didn't need and couldn't afford.

I had a miscarriage and then I got pregnant in 1971. I had pneumonia and I was hospitalized for two months before Tommy was born. The baby was only two weeks old when we were evicted again. We had to move back with Ron's brother. It wasn't too bad. His wife was nice and his brother was good to our boys.

We moved eleven times during our eleven-year marriage.

Ron favoured Tommy over Teddy. He never liked Teddy because he looked too much like me and Tommy looked like Ron's mother. If the boys ever got in trouble, Teddy would get punished and Tommy wouldn't.

I got a job at a Woolco store when Tommy was about a year and a half and Teddy was four. Ron wasn't working so he babysat the boys. One day I came home from work, sick. My next-door neighbour came and told me that she had the two boys because the police had came and picked Ron up: he was in jail. Ron had been arrested for molesting the seven-year-old daughter of my girlfriend. He had been babysitting the little girl. He got the neighbour to take our boys and then locked himself and the little girl in our house. One of her older brothers heard her crying and tried to get in and couldn't. So he climbed in through a bedroom window and caught my husband masturbating himself on top of the little girl.

It was my thirty-second birthday and I thought, What a birthday present this is! I called my sister-in-law and she came and got me and the kids. I cryed like anything. She took me to the hospital and I was put under heavy sedation. I stayed there for two weeks. When I went home the neighbours wouldn't let their kids play with mine.

Ron was sentenced to three years' probation. There was no counselling. I was going to leave him but I had no one to turn to. Everyone in his family talked me into staying with him. They said, "He's learned his lesson. Give him a chance."

We moved to another town. We were evicted four times in two years. He had a job but he got fed up and quit. For a while I babysat five other preschoolers. Then I got a job in a nursing home. I worked the midnight shift. I also babysat the three boys of another woman who worked the evening shift in the same nursing home. I got off work at 7 a.m. and if I was a bit late getting home, Ron would accuse me of sleeping with the fellow who drove me.

We fought a lot. Ron wanted to have sex every time I turned around: four or five times a day. He drove me crazy. He was lucky if he got it twice a week. He punched me when I didn't go along with him. He used to go to bed at eight o'clock and expect me to go too. The kids and I would watch TV and he'd say, "The kids and TV mean more to you than I do."

Our money problems didn't get any better either. When the mailman knocked on the door it usually meant that he had a garnishee notice or a summons for us. I hated to open the door. Lots of times I pretended I wasn't home. One Christmas, Ron bought an expensive floor model colour TV. It cost over $2,000. The payment was late and the store manager phoned and I told him to come and take the damn thing back. He did. If Ron answered the phone he'd always tell the store, "I'll pay you on Friday." I don't know what he was doing with his money. It sure wasn't coming home to us. The fridge was often empty. I think he was gambling, but I couldn't prove it.

That's when I started drinking. I figured if I was drunk I couldn't hear what he was saying. I drank anything I could get my hands on: rye, vodka, gin. I was drunk about every night when he came home. I could still cope with the children. I wasn't that bad that I didn't know what I was doing.

When Teddy was six years old we moved to another town. Ron got a job near to our house. He used to come home at lunchtime and expect me to have sex with him. The kids were there for lunch and I wouldn't do it.

He'd wake up at three in the morning and want sex. He'd yell at me and beat me. The boys still remember this you know. Even the neighbours could hear. I felt I was being used by him. I told him over and over, "I'm not a sex object; I'm a human being."

One day I was sitting, crying on my back step. My neighbour came over and asked me what was wrong. So I told her. She told me about the Children's Aid and she called them for me. That night a social worker came and had a session. She put Ron and I back to back on chairs and asked him questions and asked me questions. She came several times. If I told her too much, after she left, Ron would beat me up. I had to tell her to stop coming.

One day, Ron came home from work and beat me again because I wouldn't have sex with him. I ran out and got to the Children's Aid office. The workers came to the house with me. Ron wouldn't let the kids go, so they took me to a welfare hotel in another town. There was a drunk banging on my door; he wanted to come in. I was scared stiff. So after two days I called the social worker and said, "I've had enough of this. I'm going back to Ron."

Everything was fine for two months and then it started all over again. I went back to Children's Aid again and they told me that Interval House had just opened. Two social workers came that night to get me and the kids. Ron threatened us with a knife. He wouldn't let the boys go. The kids were crying and screaming. They took me on to Interval House. I was crying. I was afraid he might molest the boys.

It was horrible for me at Interval House. All the other women had their kids and I didn't have mine. I cried all the time and I wouldn't eat. I was there about a month and then I took an overdose of Gravol. I ended up in the Royal Ottawa. I was there two weeks and didn't get to see a psychiatrist. The nurses apologized. They said they had forgotten about me. I went back to Interval House for another month.

I got a lawyer and tried to get custody of the boys. Court was remanded a couple of times. When the hearing was finally held, I wasn't even allowed to speak. Just the two lawyers and the judge talked. They must have believed Ron's lies that I was an unfit mother. The judge said he was giving Ron custody because I left without the kids and because I had a nervous breakdown. My lawyer was no damn good. I cried all night.

Beth (she was a volunteer) took me to visit the boys. When we left, Ron called me all kinds of names and told me I'd never see the boys again. I was scared to go back. The lawyer told me I could visit the boys but I couldn't take them anywhere. Ron was supposed to leave for my visits but he wouldn't.

The next time I went, two or three women came with cars to help me get my personal things. The kids were at school and Ron was away. But his new girlfriend was there with her kid. I was shocked: she was only seventeen. I grabbed my stuff and got out of there.

I got a job at a nursing home and got myself a bachelor apartment. It was very lonely. I didn't have any transportation to visit the boys so I didn't see them for months, not even at Christmas. The first Christmas I was invited to Interval House for dinner. I cried the whole day.

I met Hans in January 1980, through my next-door neighbour. Hans was kind and I liked him right away. He took me to see the boys.

In March we got a two-bedroom apartment together. Now I could have the boys on weekends. I stopped drinking.

I worked at the nursing home for a year. The pay was very low, so I went to Manpower to see about getting a better job. They sent me to Algonquin College for upgrading and secretarial training. I really liked school. There were others my age and I got As in everything. I almost got my grade ten.

One day I got a phone call from my lawyer—he wanted to see me. He showed me a paper that said Ron wanted a divorce because I was committing adultery. I was mad. I told the lawyer that Ron was doing it long before I was. The lawyer said, "Do you want a divorce and get rid of the son of a bitch?"

I said, "Yes."

He said, "Then take the charge."

So Hans and I had to go to court. The judge made both of us swear that we were living together. Then Ron's lawyer asked if I wanted more visiting rights. They gave me every second weekend, one month in summer and March break. Ron never let them come for March break.

Hans and I took the boys camping in the summer and they loved it. They hated going back home, especially Teddy because his dad was still picking on him. Ron had another young girlfriend and the boys said that every time they came home from school, Ron and the girl were in bed. They also paraded around in the nude. The boys didn't like it. They were confused.

In 1982 Teddy called us from a payphone. He was crying; he was hysterical. His father and the girlfriend had beaten him with a belt and pulled his hair. We rushed to the town and took him to the police station. He was covered with marks from the belt buckle. The police told us to take him to our home. They said they'd had many complaints from Ron's neighbours that one kid was being beaten all the time.

The next day I took Teddy to see the lawyer. He told us to go to the hospital and have the injuries documented. In the afternoon, the lawyer asked Teddy who he wanted to live with. Teddy said me. I registered him in school and had to sign a form telling the teachers not to let Ron pick him up.

That summer Hans wanted to go to Scandinavia to see his family and go to his parents' fiftieth wedding anniversary. We decided to get married and then the trip would be our honeymoon. It was so much fun. It was my first time in an airplane and I didn't sleep at all. Hans' family was very nice. A woman in the next apartment looked after Teddy.

I got a sewing job and kept it for two years, but they were very pushy. I became a nervous wreck. I had to quit.

We moved to this house in 1984.

One night we got a phone call from the Children's Aid. They said Ron was in jail for molesting two young boys and a retarded girl and they wanted to know if we wanted to take Tommy. Of course we said yes. The worker brought him to our house. He was crying. He'd been doing his homework when the police walked in and arrested his father. I had been worried for a long time because every time we took Tommy back home, there were young kids in the house. I suspected something sexual was going on.

Tommy was quite upset because he loved his dad. He was only fourteen. We took him to the doctor and he was given sedatives. The next day I went to the lawyer. I was automatically given custody of Tommy because his father was in jail.

The next night we all went to get Tommy's clothes and Ron was there. He was going to hit me but Hans stood between the two of us. Ron started crying. He told Tommy he wanted to kill himself. When we finished packing up the truck Tommy said, "What a relief. I don't have to look at him anymore."

Now the only time the boys see their dad is when they visit their grandmother. Ron has to live with her as part of his probation. They enjoy visiting her but they hate seeing him. They come home and say, "Dad was bullshitting again."

We went to Scandinavia again in 1986. Teddy came with us. He really liked the trip.

I'm forty-four and I'm happier now than I've ever been. I have a good husband and I've got my kids. I've got a family. We go camping every summer; we've been so many places.

I want to be a bookkeeper. I'm taking correspondence courses in bookkeeping and the lowest mark I've gotten was a seventy-six.

I'm very proud of my sons. Both of them do well in school. The neighbours can't get over how nice our boys are. They don't smoke or take dope.

Teddy is a nice boy, a hard worker. He has two jobs. He's just finished high school (*graduated from grade twelve*) and he's going to college in the fall to be a policeman. He has a nice girlfriend, lots of friends. He's a real tease but he's fun to have around. I'm going to miss him when he leaves.

Tommy is always happy-go-lucky but sometimes he has depressing moods. When he's like that he gets mad easily. When you ask him to do something he gets mad. He and Hans wrestle every night but Hans can still beat him. Tommy also has jobs. He wants to be a bodyman.

The boys think the world of Hans. They never talk back to him, and they help him.

About two months ago I started crying a bit for no reason and I went to see a psychiatrist. That was when I started to remember the abuse of my childhood. Some memories are still coming back, especially when I have nothing to do. Sometimes I try to block them out. A mental health nurse visits every week and we talk. I have antidepressant pills. The doctor told me that it was normal to feel depressed because I've gone through so much. He tells me I must be a strong person to have survived it all.

Cindy's mental health nurse asked Cindy to make a list of the qualities that she liked about herself. Both Cindy and I thought it would be a good way to conclude her story.

- I am a good cook.
- I like to meet people.
- I like visiting my in-laws.
- I like to have fun.
- I am a good wife.
- I am making good progress with my counselling sessions.
- I like to help people.
- I am a good housekeeper.
- I am a good singer.
- I am independent.
- I am a good swimmer.
- I am proud of myself.
- I am a good mother.
- I am a good listener.

I knew when I went to visit Cindy for her update that she had a tragic story to tell. Five years ago her beloved Teddy was killed in a car accident. He was an honours student in the Law and Security program at Loyalist College in Belleville and was to graduate in the spring. He had gone home for the weekend. It was the first fall snowstorm. Hans answered the phone call at 12:30 at night. I just heard him give Teddy's birth date and I screamed, "What's wrong with Teddy?" We drove to the Civic. He was in a coma. I passed out when I saw him. He lived about twelve hours. He couldn't breathe on his own. I signed a paper to have them take him off the life-support. They did an autopsy—it was his brain that was damaged. If he'd lived, he would have been a vegetable.

I signed the paper to donate his organs. His heart was transferred right away to a ten-year-old boy at CHEO.

He had his seat belt on. His head hit the corner of the dashboard. The driver, his friend, had two broken legs.

I don't remember the wake. I just remember the four school buses of college students.

It was a closed casket. I had him cremated. The funeral director was really nice. He said, "I bet you don't have a suit for him because his clothes are in Belleville." He said, "Don't worry, I have a nice suit here. I'll fix him up nice." He never charged us to keep his ashes there the whole winter.

The thing that really got me was that my ex-husband and his mother were at our house. She was carrying on. She was mad because we didn't give her the cross that was on Teddy's casket. (We put it in the casket with him). She started screaming when she saw Teddy's friend (the driver). She said, "He killed Teddy."

In January, Cindy had a nervous breakdown and was taken to the Civic Hospital. I was just holding everything in. I was there for two weeks. I only saw the psychiatrist four times. They did nothing. They gave me four Prozac a day. I was on them for about six months. I surely wasn't right. I got my doctor to take me off them. He did it gradually.

What helped me was talking to people. I started going to meetings—to Survivors Bridge [a program for those who need support with mental-health issues], to the Interval House support group. I had to quit for a while because I was getting too upset on the way home. I had to pull off the road and cry.

There was more trauma. Cindy's landlord sexually assaulted her. He was eighty years old. He fondled my breasts and told me to go lay down on the bed. Stupid me did it. It wasn't the first time. He said if I ever told anybody, he'd kick us out of there. I got up and ran out of the house.

I told Hans and he said, "What the fuck were you doing over there?"

I said, "Well, I went over to keep him company because he was over there alone and you were sleeping and I was alone. I didn't have nobody to talk to."

Then Hans said, "I'm heading for work now. Don't you dare call Interval House. Don't you dare tell anybody."

After he left, I did. I called Interval House. I gave them permission to call the police. The next day, an officer came in plain clothes to talk to me and then he went to see the landlord. The landlord denied it. That was all.

I didn't bother with him after that. If he came near the house I'd hide. I was petrified.

A couple of weeks later, I set fire to his gazebo. Then I got scared and called the fire department.

I told the cops that I did it. I knew I had done it, but I didn't remember doing it. They took me to the hospital. The doctor told me I was going to Kingston (the psychiatric hospital). I didn't want to go, so they knocked me out with a needle and they put me in an ambulance. I was there for a week.

I told the women at the support group about the fire. They all laughed and clapped their hands. Hans had built the gazebo.

We moved out the following spring and bought this trailer. The landlord died last year. I was glad. Two years ago, my foster uncle died—the one that sexually assaulted me. I read it in the paper. I was so glad.

I got my driver's licence. I got tired of depending on Hans because he works nights and sleeps during the day. So I went to the driving school and I passed on my first test. Hans was so happy when I told him. He picked me up and he twirled me around.

Two years ago Cindy took a Health Care Aide course. She passed with flying colors. But during the course, she hurt her back lifting a heavy woman out of a bathtub and hasn't been able to work since. It took several months to find the cause of her pain—a protruding disc. There have been two operations and intensive rehabilitation to help her learn how to deal with chronic pain. Now there is something wrong with her hip. She's on a disability pension and walks with the help of a cane. She goes for physiotherapy twice a week, takes part in a therapeutic swimming program and has joined a Chronic Pain Support Group.

Hans has been so good to me since my hip. He made supper last night. Sometimes he pisses me off but, what the heck.

Cindy has little contact with her other son, Tommy. He graduated from Algonquin College as a body mechanic and works close by in a body shop. He lives with a young woman and they have a one-year-old boy. His wife is real snotty. It doesn't take her long to tell you off. We've offered, but we've never looked after that child. They came for Father's Day and they only stayed twenty minutes. We don't go to their house unless we're invited. I get upset sometimes, I really do. After all, he's the only thing I've got left.

Cindy and Hans donated money to Loyalist College for a scholarship in Teddy's name—for the student who gets the highest marks in second year Law and Security. Each November, they and Tommy attend the graduation. Tommy presents the cheque and a plaque. Last year we got a real nice thank-you letter from the student who won it. It was the first time.

Ex-husband Ron heard about the scholarship and tried to take credit for it. Word got back to Cindy. He was going around telling stories. Said he donated money to the school—for the scholarship. He's a liar 'cause he never donated a penny. He still lives with his mother as far as I know.

Cindy and Hans visited Scandinavia last year for Christmas and plan to go again next year during the summer.

Cindy is proud to say that she's been off nerve pills for the past two years.

Her advice? Get out of it. Don't stay in it. I was in my first marriage fourteen years. It's not worth it. They promise they'll change, but they don't.

SUPPORT GROUPS

To my knowledge, the first formalized peer support groups were formed by men—Alcoholics Anonymous. Begun in 1935, AA and its offshoots continue to provide support to individuals and families coping with addictions, such as drugs and gambling.

The women's consciousness-raising groups of the 60s and 70s were also peer support groups where women discovered the similarities of our lives and uncovered hidden truths.

An important support group in my life was the prenatal classes I attended during my first pregnancy. It was a relief to learn that others were also dealing with mood swings, depression, discomfort—all a normal part of being pregnant.

In the '80s and '90s, new support groups have been formed, usually by women, to deal with specific and difficult personal issues such as abuse, incest and sexual assault. Lanark County Interval House began holding weekly support groups for abused women in 1987. They continue to be a resounding success.

At the shelter, the groups have evolved from closed sessions, where only those women who attended the first two meetings were allowed to continue for the twelve-week term, to open sessions where women can join the group at any time. The term has been lengthened to eighteen weeks and the fall session continues over the Christmas period, which is often a particularly stressful time.

A Second Stage group has been added for women who want to maintain connections and continue their education, and an older women's group has begun. The evolution of this last group is particularly interesting. It was initiated by a woman in her sixties. She explained that her issues were often quite different from those of the younger women who were the majority in the group. She was no longer concerned about custody or dealing with young children, etc. Her issues had more to do with the particular shame felt by older women who grew up believing that divorce was a dirty word and who had vowed to 'love, honour and obey.'

The groups are open to all women in the community, those who are living in abusive relationships and those who left abusive relationships long ago but never had the opportunity to deal with the hurt. Funds for transportation and child care are provided.

Each group is facilitated by two women who are experienced group leaders and take responsibility to keep in touch with members who may need extra support between sessions.

When the shelter had extra funding, it ran several support groups for children who had witnessed abuse of their mothers. These, too, were very successful. The children ranged from age seven to eleven. Most were eager to have the opportunity to take part in the fun activities as well as share the horrors they had witnessed with others who had similar stories to tell. In one group, almost every child had observed their father threatening their mother with a knife.

One boy's story had a lasting impact on the facilitators. The year before, he and his family had come to the shelter on a cold winter night. His father, in a rage, had just demolished the inside of their home, all the time blaming the boy because he had been too tardy in bringing in the groceries. The boy never talked about this episode, even to experienced counsellors. Although it wasn't part of the plan for the first session of the children's support group, this child seized the opportunity and told his story. The words tumbled out: how afraid he had been, how guilty he felt, how he was made to stand outside in the cold, how he couldn't remember beyond that. It was at this point that his brother, who was also in the group, helped him to recall how he got in out of the cold. It was the first time the boy had told anybody his version of the events. He felt comfortable telling his peers. His relief was obvious.

Local schools have recently taken on the task of running groups for children who are experiencing difficulty in school. Many of those children come from homes where they have witnessed abuse.

Support-group night is often an essential lifeline for the women. There is an excitement and positive energy in the room as the women greet each other and settle in for a session. It is a powerful release for a woman to learn that she is not the only one, that others have survived, that she can break down and it will be okay, that it is safe for her to talk about her degradation and not feel further shame, and that others will truly understand. Even if she is not yet ready to share her own experience, she can gain a certain strength just by listening to the other women.

The group also gives the women an opportunity to develop friendships—often essential for those who have survived abusive relationships because their abusers have isolated them from family and friends. Watching these friendships develop is heart-warming and sometimes surprising. In one group, an older woman, well educated and quite dignified, befriended a young mother who had little education, was distant and not yet able to articulate her pain. The warmth between these two reinforced the facilitator's belief that group membership should be open to all, regardless of status or education.

As well as having time to share experiences, there is a particular topic discussed or exercises to be done each night. Women learn about anger, about the various types of abuse, about the effects of witnessing abuse on their children and how to help them cope, about the law and their rights, about the broader issues of abuse and how their particular experiences fit into a societal pattern, a pattern that many women are challenging.

Through it all, the women become stronger and less vulnerable to those who would abuse them again. Some go on to become group facilitators themselves.

RACHEL'S STORY

Rachel was a stunningly beautiful woman. When she walked into a room, heads turned, both male and female. But her beauty was more than skin deep. She was also a witty, intelligent and charming person who cared deeply for her children and others. She seemed to have it all. So why was she a resident at Interval House?

Rachel appeared so self-assured that it was difficult to imagine her in the role of victim. In fact, while she was at the house, other residents turned to her for advice and support. Peer counselling is a cornerstone of most shelters, but in Rachel's situation she was doing most of the giving, and because she appeared so capable, little attention was being focused on her needs. For these reasons, it was easy to have Rachel in the house—she didn't make waves and she was fun.

I waltzed into the house one day with a new joke to share with everyone.

Q: What's the difference between a cucumber and a Corvette?

A: With the cucumber, the prick is on the outside."

Rachel convulsed in laughter. She said, "Fern, you have no idea how fitting that joke is to my life."

Rachel shared little of her past. She told us her husband had been physically abusive and that she had charged him with assault. She also admitted to being an alcoholic and having taken street drugs and was now very conscientious about attending AA meetings. She had been straight for two years and was determined to get her life in order. Although we knew we didn't have the whole story, we didn't push her but helped her deal with the issues she presented.

An episode occurred at the shelter in which Rachel felt she was being manipulated by another resident. A staff member sat down with her and compared this conflict to other problems in Rachel's life. She gave Rachel tips on how to be more assertive. I remember Rachel's excitement when she successfully stood up for her personal rights, gaining a new self-respect.

When I went to interview Rachel for this book, the life she revealed was truly an eye-opener to me. She told me that she had not told her full story while living at Interval House because she was afraid the staff would then not have liked her and would have asked her to leave.

Rachel is one of several women from Ottawa who have come to our house because the city shelters were full.

Here is her story.

I was born in Ottawa in 1961. I was the sixth child in a family of nine children. My mother was Catholic, very much so, and my father was an alcoholic. I was about four when father started attending A.A. and stopped drinking. I can actually remember him changing from being a really fun person to a really grouchy person. I think when he became sober, reality struck—he had nine children and a really heavy-duty job. He had a lot of responsibility and he just was not coping with any of it. He was really diligent about going to A.A. meetings. I remember that he was very open and very generous with other people in the program. If someone was new he'd adopt them and bring them into the family.

My father always had a bad temper though, and I think we all sort of grew up fearing him. He was the authority figure, the tough guy. I think he only got physical a few times with mother (maybe pushing her, slapped her across the face once) but he was a yeller you know; he threatened. He was abusive in that way. My mother was always saying to us, "Keep quiet, don't get Daddy upset." My mother sort of enhanced that image. She really did. I think her children were everything to her. She huddled the children together. She was the buffer between my father and the children, but she also, I think maybe without realizing it, didn't stop us from turning against him. She had a lot of resentment. Guilt seemed to be everywhere.

When I was six or seven my oldest brother (he was about fourteen) made sexual advances to me. He tried intercourse and he would ask me to do things like take his penis in my mouth and things like that. Sexual encounters with him became a regular thing, as long as he could trap me. Now, since I was the quiet one, the love-everybody-so-much-one, I was very easy to manipulate. I promised not to tell anyone. Even at that age I was protecting others. I had this thing that my mother had so many children that she didn't need the hassle of knowing there was something wrong. And because the way my father was, I think he probably would have murdered my brother. Also, my oldest brother was everyone's hero, and mine too except for this little dark corner of him that I tried not to think about because he was so wonderful in every other aspect. He was the one who would take me to my ballet lessons on the back of his bicycle and he would buy me things. This went on for a few years until I was about twelve and he left home. And when he left home I thought he left because of me. I was convinced that somebody had found something out and I was feeling so guilty because I knew I hadn't told anybody like I promised I wouldn't, time and time again.

I was one of my father's favorites when I was younger. I was very much a daddy-pleaser you know. But once I hit puberty he turned against me. I was no longer his little girl. My sisters were very slight but here was Rachel developing into a 36C. I remember experimenting with make up and father would say, "You look like a whore. Go wash that stuff off your face." Sometimes he kicked me down the steps to my room in the basement and he slapped me across the face really hard. No one in the family talked about it. I felt that I was the cause of friction in the household.

At thirteen I had absolutely no self-esteem, no self-respect. I had so many deep, dark secrets and I really felt I didn't belong anywhere. I didn't feel normal.

I became a rebellious teen. All my friends were much older than I was so access to booze was really easy. When I was fourteen I could walk into a liquor store and buy booze, no problem. Nobody asked for ID or anything. That was in 1974. Drinking was a regular weekend thing. I had been a good student up to that time and then I started to let things slide.

That Christmas things were really shitty at home. My father was really nuts: violent. It seemed no matter what I did, it wasn't right. I told my girlfriend I was running away. That was my New Year's resolution. I think she came along as more of a lark; her parents had just split up. We figured we'd move to Montreal and work in a theatre and sell tickets, although we didn't get out of Ottawa. She had a big bank account and I had some money saved because I babysat a lot. We stayed at a nearby motel and we weren't found for two weeks. My parents were really upset about this.

They had me committed to the Royal Ottawa and they didn't come to see me for two weeks which was really sort of rough. My counsellor felt I shouldn't be there but father didn't want me at home. I felt totally rejected. I started going to school from the hospital. The staff were very good to me and gave me as much freedom as the rules would allow. After two months I was allowed to return home.

About that time my father was diagnosed as a manic depressive. Lithium was prescribed. Unfortunately, he is one of the few people who react adversely to that drug. In a suicide attempt, he took an overdose and was committed to the Royal Ottawa. I visited him when he came out of his coma. I just wanted to let him know that okay, he's been a total creep, but

I still loved him. I think he really appreciated that but it was really hard for him to say, "You're not nuts, I'm the one who's nuts." And that's basically what he said. And then we just sort of left things 'cause our relationship didn't improve much.

Along with the booze and drugs came boyfriends. My relationships were usually short and sweet because I was very shy and I was probably pretty boring. I would just be so thrilled that somebody thought I was worthy to be their girlfriend. I would go out with anyone. I think I had this M on my forehead for mark, and all these creeps could see it. I met a lot of creeps.

So when I was fifteen I fell in love with a country boy, Josh. Both his parents were drunks: nice people, but give them a few drinks and they start throwing furniture at each other. It was very acceptable in that family to show your feelings. As a result, Josh was like that when he drank. At first it wasn't against me.

I got pregnant. I had just turned sixteen and Josh was twenty. Needless to say, I was not exactly equipped for motherhood. But I always wanted to be a mother. Even when I was a kid and playing with the boys in the neighbourhood, I'd have my baby on my back and my gun in my holster. I was such a weird kid.

My parents asked me to leave so I went to a home for unwed mothers for a few months. I got rid of the drugs and alcohol and straightened myself out. I knew I had to do this for the baby's sake. I became enthused about school again and passed grade eleven with really good marks.

While I was pregnant, Josh had a bad car accident (he was drinking and driving) and spent a long time in the hospital. I would go to school in the morning and in the afternoon take the bus to sit by his side for six hours. I was so devoted to this guy: it was really pathetic. His leg wasn't healing properly and he had several operations. He was on crutches when I was in labour. He only got there for the last hour and I was really angry with him. He looked like he was going to faint so I said, "Oh just get out of here." The delivery went well and Sylvia was born a healthy baby.

I got a one-bedroom apartment. It was pretty sleazy but I kept it clean and made it cute. I started correspondence courses. I lived on welfare and I stayed at home with the baby. It was really hard. Josh stayed with me when he wasn't in the hospital, which was only about a week or so at a time. His leg was slow in healing. The doctors were trying everything. But the reason why he wasn't getting better was because of the alcohol and drug abuse, but of course his doctors didn't know about that. So the reaction to the drugs they were putting him on was just incredible.

When Josh got out of the hospital for good he had a hard time coping with the fact that we had a baby and that she cried and she woke up in the middle of the night—it interfered with his sleep and his social life. I was not a demanding person and I would be grateful if he occasionally babysat for an hour while I bought groceries. That was very exciting for me. Babysitting your own kid—God! She was a really good baby, but he didn't know that.

There was a lot of pressure that we should get married. But at least I was smart enough to know that I was not going to spend the rest of my life with this man. Josh's drinking really started to get silly. He'd drink, he'd black out, or he'd think I was someone else and start yelling at me. One time he was talking like he was a little kid and he thought I was his mother. He came at me with a knife. I hit him with a chair and he fell down the stairs. I thought I had killed him. He woke up about ten hours later and didn't remember what happened—good thing.

I called the police once but they said they couldn't do anything unless something drastic happened. Of course I didn't know enough about alcoholism at the time: I really thought maybe he had multiple personalities or something. I eventually kicked him out. I couldn't cope with being a mother and looking after him too. For a while he phoned and demanded to see Sylvia, but I refused if he was drinking.

One time Josh called and he was in a real rage. He said he was coming over and he was going to kill me if I didn't let him in. My little sister was visiting at the time (she was about twelve and she loved to play with the baby). We barricaded ourselves in the bedroom: she was really frightened. We could hear him going around banging at the doors and then we heard the door window break. I could hear him in the living room crying, "Rachel, I'm bleeding." I finally went out. He had flipped out of his rage and his arm was badly gashed and bleeding. I bandaged him up with cloth diapers and told him to leave or I would call the police. After that we pretty well went our separate ways. When he did call, he was straight, and I'd tell him I appreciated him being straight.

I was feeling very, very lonely, very separate from my friends. Now that I had a baby I had little in common with them. I'm sure it wasn't that exciting to visit me and hear me talk about the baby for two hours because I was just enthralled with her. Most of them gradually stopped visiting. I didn't drink because I couldn't afford to drink.

My parents didn't really accept Sylvia. Father would call and casually ask, "How's the little bastard today?" That really, really hurt.

One girlfriend, Julie, kept in touch and was always saying, "You have to get out more." So she'd pay for a babysitter and off we'd go or she'd bring a bottle over to the house and we'd invite others in. She was a drinker and it became a regular thing. I was young so if I stayed up all night, I could still cope with the baby during the day and sleep when she slept. I dropped my correspondence courses. I remember getting a few letters from the teacher saying, "You were doing so well, what happened?"

My older sister invited me to share a house with her and a girlfriend so we got a really cute place down by the Rideau River. Then one of my brothers (who was into dealing drugs) got into trouble with the law and he needed a respectable place to stay, so we let him and his girlfriend move in. This brother had the highest IQ in the family but he was also the other one that my father turned against. Now I had the family I so desperately wanted.

My brother was really into dealing and it was amazing the money this guy was making. He had a big Cadillac. He used to hire me to do things for him: ironing, cooking. He put me on salary to answer his phone. It was great.

So we're all living together and we're having some pretty wild parties because there's money—lots of money. If my brother is rich, everybody's rich in the family. He'd been an outcast since he was fifteen so it was really exciting for him to be living with his sisters.

I was getting seriously into drugs now because they were easily accessible and I didn't have to pay for them. I tried anything that was going: marijuana, heroin, speed. We did a lot of coke because it was the party drug. I didn't worry about Sylvia. I felt she was in a sheltered atmosphere and I made sure she was well looked after.

Around this time I met a man that I fell in love with. Bob told me he was separated. He used to bring his little boy over to play with Sylvia and it was great. He liked to drink but he was super straight and I didn't let him know how involved I was with the drugs. After about a year I realized that he was married and had no intention of giving up his wife. So I was pretty hurt but I continued to see him. I think I was totally addicted to him.

Our little home split up after a year. I think my brother was sent to jail and my sister moved. I broke off with Bob. I found my own apartment in the same building as my old drinking buddy, Julie. I got to know all the partiers in the building. There were a couple of retired firemen who liked to drink so they'd take me out for a beer and buy my daughter ice cream; and we'd sit in the restaurant for a few hours. It made them happy to have someone different in their drinking circle and so they were willing to buy my booze, so that was sort of the bargain for the friendship. And the poor kid is dying of boredom. It's funny, for years after that she wouldn't eat ice cream. Her subconscious must have been saying, No Sylvia, don't eat that ice cream or your mother is going to get drunk.

I always made sure that Sylvia was well cared for. She was either with me or I hired a good babysitter. She was everything to me. At this point, my parents wouldn't allow my younger brothers or sister to visit me. My brother and I were considered the black sheeps of the family. Everyone else was getting a good education or had a status job.

I started to realize that I couldn't control my drinking and I moved again. I always wanted to provide a good home and be the ideal mother for my daughter. I moved a lot and usually when I moved it was a geographical cure. I blamed my neighbours for my drinking. If I wasn't so close to them it wouldn't be so easy. But no matter where I moved, I met the people who partied every night. I would get drunk but I was never a slobbering drunk. I never fell off my high heels.

I had a whole succession of relationships. Most were well-to-do business men who would take me to fancy restaurants and help me out financially. Many of them were creeps but I felt that in order to have company and affection I'd have to accept that or forever be alone. After all, I only had my grade eleven; I wasn't getting any younger and the only marketable skill I had was sex. Here I am talking like this when I'm eighteen or nineteen years old! I wasn't thinking at the time that most of them were married men and I was their mistress. But it was the only way I could see getting by. I was getting so little money. I couldn't even fathom the idea of going out to work 'cause anything I'd found made so little money, you know, and I'd have to be dragging my kid out at dawn and picking her up from some stranger babysitter.

Most of the men were nice to me as long as they got their own way. I had the feeling they were the "wonderful husband" to the wife but the mistress was the sleazebag, so it was okay not to always be respectful. I had so little self-esteem; I took their emotional abuse. It was something I had learned to live with a long time ago. You tell me that you love me one minute and then you tell me I'm a whore. Well, you're probably right. Some of them tried physical violence and that's what usually ended the relationship. I had some self-respect, not a lot, but the little I had I was clinging to.

I lived for a while with a man who had just split up with his wife. At first he was a nice guy but he was very much a chauvinist and a heavy drinker. So here I am, nineteen years old, trying to be the perfect housekeeper that he expects me to be: the perfect cook, the perfect mother to his two school-age children as well as my own three-year-old, and be able to drink all night with the boys and get up in the morning to be the perfect wife to this thirty-nine-year-old. I'm having a nervous breakdown inside but nobody knows this, right? I plan to leave him and then I find out I'm pregnant. I knew if he knew I was having this baby he would never let me go. I felt so trapped. I didn't tell him about the pregnancy. I left him and had an abortion. Somehow word filtered back to him that I'd had the abortion. He came to my new place. He had been drinking. I let him in and he forced himself on me and he said, "That's what you get for taking away the son I always wanted." I didn't even know whether it was a boy or a girl! I felt numb. I just tried to put this episode out of my mind.

So I decided to straighten myself out. I got my daughter into day care and started grade twelve. My parents were pleased. The first month at school I was a really good girl. I didn't go out. The second month was a little bit tough. I finally went to a party and bumped into my old boyfriend Bob. I was so lonely—I slept with him that night. This was a one-night stand with a man I was still probably in love with. I became pregnant. Oh God, how could I be pregnant! I told Bob and he said, "It's not mine," and I said, "I'm sorry you're the only person I've slept with in months," and he said, "No, no, I had a vasectomy six months ago." Anyway he gave me $500 to have an abortion.

Although I didn't really want to have the abortion, I didn't know how I could raise two children by myself. There was a hospital strike on at the time in Ottawa so they were running weeks and weeks behind at all the abortion clinics. My brother who's the heroin addict, dropped by and said he'd drive me to Montreal in two days for the abortion. But the next morning I discovered the money was gone. I called my brother and he admitted he had "borrowed" it. He said, "Don't worry sis, I'm going to have it to you tonight, and I'll give you extra because there's this deal going down now." He got busted that night so I never got the money. By now I was ten weeks pregnant. I was in the midst of writing Christmas exams and I had extreme nausea. So that week I thought, I don't want to get rid of this kid. I figured if there were all these things in the way of having an abortion, it must mean I'm supposed to have this baby. And I could finish my school year before the baby was born.

So I'm going to school. Because I'm pregnant, I'm not drinking, I'm staying straight and I'm getting good marks. Sylvia's doing well in day care. I'm starting to feel like I have some control over my life.

I hid the pregnancy till my sixth month. I didn't tell my parents. They just sort of noticed after a while that this girl certainly looks pregnant. They just let it slide: "She did well in school you know."

The last six weeks of that pregnancy I found really hard because it struck home that I was going to have this baby and I was going to be all alone with two kids. I felt really, really lonely. I gave notice to my landlords so they wouldn't kick me out. They were a really nice Italian couple but I didn't think they'd understand. They thought I was a widow with this little girl, right?

My sister and I found a house to share again. We moved in on the first of August and I had the baby, Marie, on the sixth of August. The day I had my baby, my sister unexpectedly left Ottawa and moved out west with her new boyfriend. So that's fine. I figured I'd probably take in boarders or something to help with the rent and it would all work out.

I had my twenty-first birthday the next week. I was very depressed. My parents came to see me and I think they finally felt sorry for me. They took this baby good naturedly. Father was calming down at this point.

I babysat three other children so I could pay my rent.

After Marie was born, I attended a single parents' conference and made many contacts. I joined a housing committee and an advisory committee and made applications for cooperative housing. I was determined to find an affordable home for my family.

I was being really good—not drinking very much and I had no boyfriend except for Bob. He'd come over and keep me company once in a while. It wasn't a sexual thing, which was sort of neat. We'd share a pizza and Pepsi and watch TV for a couple of hours—except for one night. That time he brought a bottle of wine and we ended up in bed. I got pregnant! I couldn't believe it! I was even on the pill! I simply couldn't manage another child and I had an abortion.

I have to tell you about something I did that I'm not proud. At this time Social Services had been pressuring me to name the father of Marie so he could be forced to pay child support. I can't remember how much they were fining me but it was making things a little bit tough. There was no way I could approach Bob about this; he still wasn't admitting that she was his. I had a lot of feelings for the man. He was married and I didn't want to screw it up because he came first 'cause I loved him, right? It was sick. So around the time I got pregnant with Marie, a guy did stay over at my house. He was really drunk and nothing happened, right? He passed out on the couch and I slept with my daughter and that was all there was to it. So I bump into this guy and the only thing I could think was, This is my way out. He said to me, "What have you been doing?" and I said, "Well, nine months after you spent the night at my house, I had a baby. She's now six months old."

What a whore, you know. And he being an honourable man, and he was actually a really nice guy, said, "What do I have to do?" So he went to Social Services and filled out the papers and started paying $100 a month support. He had a good job so it was no big deal for him. He assumed he had slept with me because he had wanted to. Actually he said he had been in a real depression. He didn't know what he was going to do with his life, and since I told him about Marie, he said his whole life had changed. I'm thinking, Oh you poor, poor thing that you had to meet me. But he's just thrilled about this and that made me feel even worse. He'd come each month with the child support and we'd discuss Marie and it was really tacky. I'm feeling amazing guilt and remorse for this and I can not live with myself. I never pushed him for payments and gradually he quit coming around.

I started partying with the neighbours and doing everything I'm not supposed to be doing. I just don't want to be me.

There were three women sharing a house next door, really nice people, always having parties. They were white women and they had black boyfriends. So I met this man, a black man, who's a really nice guy. He's married but by this time in my life, who isn't? He assured me that the marriage was over. He treated me with amazing respect and I'm not used to this. He was really, really sweet and he adored my children. He didn't want to know my history; he just took me the way I was. We fell madly in love. The only problem was that he liked to drink. But he was a nice drunk. We just drank on weekends at the neighbourhood parties. I tried to control my drinking because I didn't want him to know that I was a lunch bucket, but gradually we found out that we were both lunch buckets. This crowd drank Demerara rum and drank it straight, right, because it was the cultural thing in this group.

My parents, who brought me up to be open-minded about race, let me know that they didn't approve. My mother would say things like, "You're not planning to have children with him are you?"

I really liked my social circle and they really liked my kids and everything was really nice but I couldn't control my drinking. I blacked out a few times. I was leading a double life. I was very active in the community and worked on various committees. The people I worked with didn't know about my drinking problem.

About this time I went to my doctor because I was feeling really ill. And while she's discovering I'm pregnant, she's also telling me that I'm very yellow looking and my liver is enlarged. I couldn't believe I was pregnant again. This time I had been using an IUD! She did all these tests for my liver enzymes and she said, "How much do you drink?" So here I am in trouble (pregnant again) and I don't know if I'm going to be able to get an abortion because they were really giving me a hard time about it. She sent me to a social worker. We had a really good talk and I let her know that I knew I was having problems with alcohol and I was ready to do something about it. I requested that my tubes be tied but the doctors refused. They felt I was too young for such an operation.

I joined AA and after a couple of weeks I told my boyfriend. He thought it was a great idea and he joined too. And now we're going through a lot of changes in our relationship because we're not drinking. Now I was having to face a lot of different things. In AA I was learning about how low my self-esteem was and that I was going to have to make changes to make it better. One of the things that was really bothering me was that this guy was married. Not just that he was married but that he was living with his wife and children. So I explained to him what it was doing to me and I ended the relationship. It was the hardest thing I've ever done. That was a Thursday night.

Friday night I was feeling desperate for a drink. I went to the AA meeting an hour early and met Keith, my future husband. At the time I didn't know that he was there by a court order. He'd assaulted a woman while he was under the influence of alcohol. Anyway, we really hit it off and we went for a coffee in his Corvette after the meeting. We talked and talked and talked. We saw each other frequently that weekend and one week later my children and I moved into his big house in suburbia.

Keith had everything: he was single, he was a successful businessman, he was white and he wanted me. My parents would love this man and my children needed a father and on and on. I thought Prince Charming had finally arrived. We started drinking together, but not a lot. AA basically ruined my drinking; there was no more bullshitting myself. I started going back to AA. At one point he said to me, "Well, it's either me or AA," and I said I was picking AA. So that power struggle didn't work. So he started going to AA again too.

The verbal abuse started right away. I was very vulnerable and could only agree with everything he said about me: that I was a bad person, an alcoholic, I had two illegitimate children and no one else would marry me. He was really funny about my family and friends and didn't want to get to know them. So we didn't tell anybody when we got married. I didn't even know one of the witnesses. You know, it was just really weird. I was twenty-two years old.

The morning after we were married, I brought breakfast to Keith in his basement office. He instructed me to sit down and he said, "Just remember you're my wife now. I'm the boss and you'll do things my way." It was a complete turn around and I was shocked. But nothing else happened so I concentrated on being a good wife.

Keith said we didn't have enough money so I started babysitting children in our home. I later learned that he had lots of money.

The first few months were pretty good but I wasn't paying attention to the little things that were happening. He was very critical of how I looked and of my housekeeping and cooking. The house was spotless: you could eat off the floors. One day we ran out of ketchup and he threw a temper tantrum, "You're so stupid. If we ever run out of ketchup again you'll be sorry." It was so ridiculous I laughed. That made him really angry. It was scary, and for the first time I felt trapped. After that I tried to make sure things were perfect all the time.

Keith's next ploy was to use the silent treatment. If we ran out of milk or I burned the muffins, he wouldn't speak to me, sometimes for two weeks!

I feel I must have been really sick to let myself end up in that kind of situation and not see it for what it was. I felt I had no control. I was at his mercy. Right before I met him, I'd gotten involved with a housing co-op. I was to have my own home in four months. I threw that away. The only good thing that came out of marrying Keith was I was able to let the guy who was paying support for Marie off the hook.

I'm an affectionate person, a physical person, but Keith would only touch me when he wanted sex and it didn't matter whether I wanted it or not. He started making me do things I didn't want to do, sexually.

He was always comparing me to other women. We'd be driving in one of his new cars down the street and he'd point out a woman and say, "Look at the ass on that one. I'd like to . . . up her ass," you know. If I objected, he just laughed—it was like it was a big joke, anything I had to say was a big joke. If I gained five pounds, all he'd talk about was my fat ass.

Other times he'd come home with gifts for me and tell me how much he loved me and he was taking us out for dinner and everything was happy that day.

After we'd been married for about six months, I told him I had to leave him, that I was afraid of him. He broke down and cried and said, "I'll never, never hurt you, I'll try to do better, I love you, I love you, I love you." And he actually said, "If you leave me, I'll kill myself."

It became a cycle. When I was down and it looked like I was going to leave, he'd come home with gifts for everybody. He'd be like that for a few days and then he'd be sort of indifferent for a couple of months and then he'd be down in the shitty stuff again. I thought I was going nuts.

Keith had me so convinced that I was the one with all the problems, I went to a psychiatrist. The psychiatrist thought that maybe I was a manic depressive which made sense to me because of my father's history. He was going to put me on Lithium. I thought about it for a while and did a little bit of self-examination. I didn't think I was a manic depressive, but I still had doubts. No man had ever married me before.

Keith pushed me around occasionally and he was verbally abusive to the girls but he was never really physically abusive.

One night we had a fight, or actually he had a fight (our fights were like that), and I finally told him, "I've had enough, I'm leaving." He said he'd kill me if I left and he threw the fireplace poker at me. It missed me but it hit the china cabinet and all my beautiful antique china came crashing down. The next day he bought me a T-bird. He acted like it was a perfectly normal thing to do. It always amazed me how he could pretend that yesterday never happened. I was supposed to gracefully accept his gift and not talk about his abuse.

One night an AA neighbour, Al, came to visit us. Keith had said to this guy, "Any time you want to drop in for a cup of coffee, come on over." But when Al arrived, Keith went up to his room and just plugged himself into the TV. I chatted with Al for maybe an hour or so. When I went to bed, Keith didn't look at me. This was always a signal that he was going to be in a shitty mood.

The next morning he was still ignoring me and I was fed up. I said, "No, you're not going to do this again. If you're jealous about Al, that's your problem. You invited him over. Grow up."

The words 'grow up' really infuriated him. He came at me and tried to push me down the stairs but I held onto the railing. He grabbed me by the throat and he was shaking me. He threw me down and pounded my head against the floor. The kids were at the bottom of the stairs just flipping out. So then I guess he snapped out of his rage and and went into the bedroom.

I got the girls dressed, put a turtleneck sweater on to hide the bruises on my neck and drove to a Sunday AA brunch that we had planned to attend. My parents and Al were there. I could hardly walk or turn my head because my back and neck were injured. Marie ran to my parents and said, "Do you know what happened this morning to my mother?" Oh God. I sort of fell apart. So I sat down and talked to Al and decided I should charge Keith with assault.

On the way home from the brunch, I stopped at the police station and asked what I should do. The officer took out Keith's record and informed me that Keith had been charged twice before with assaulting women. He was really helpful and agreed to wait until Monday night to serve the papers so that I could make arrangements for the children I babysat and prepare to leave. So I went home that day and Keith didn't look at me and I didn't look at him. I slept in the kids' room that night.

The next day I gave my day-care kids activities they could do by themselves so I could slowly pack essentials and put them in the trunk of the car. I called the Interval Houses in Ottawa and they were all booked. So they said try the one in Lanark County. I think Joan answered the phone and she said there was room for us.

Keith came home early that day and took my car as well as all the car keys. He's not stupid. He could read me like a book. I'm flipping out. I called my father and he drove us to Interval House. My father was eventually able to convince Keith to drop off my belongings.

My first visit to Interval House was okay. I felt ashamed that I had stayed in a relationship for so long with a creep—another failure in my life. It was far more comfortable to feel badly about myself than to work on my self-esteem. I was so agreeable. I didn't want to rock the boat so I was nice to everyone. I was such a people-pleaser. I was so ill-equipped to care for myself. I didn't tell the staff very much. I didn't think people would like me if they really knew what I had done.

I had no contact with Keith for about a month and during that time I was fine. I had charged him and was going to stick to it. Then he wrote me a note that I got via my father. Keith was so full of remorse: "I love you, please try again, I'll get help"—the whole bullshit. And all I could think was, 'I really do love this man, I just don't love him when he's that way. I'm going to give him another chance.' Sylvia didn't want to return.

I knew it was a mistake as soon as I got back. The first thing Keith talked about was getting me to drop the charges. I went to see the Crown Attorney, but he wouldn't allow it, and the police gave me absolutely no help whatsoever. I was secretly glad. A few days later I got a letter from the co-op housing. They had a unit for me and I had to respond within a week. I remember just crying and crying and sitting there thinking, You idiot, why did you go back? I felt like I was slamming doors on my future.

Keith was really nice to Sylvia, like she could do no wrong all of a sudden, and now Marie got it.

I knew Keith was scared about the charge of assault. With the first charge he got a fine and probation; the second time, he got a bigger fine and probation and was told to go to AA This third time he knew it would be no joke. I guess he had spoken to his lawyer and his lawyer said, "Get her to drop the charges or you're going to jail."

Keith actually had the nerve to get physical again. One time he held me against the wall and slapped my face and said, "You see, that's assault, Rachel." Another time he held a knife against my throat. About once a week he reminded me about what assault really is. He said, "I can't believe that you're my wife and you love me and you charge me with assault."

I said, 'Keith, I can't believe that you're my husband and you love me and then you assault me." Well, he birded out. It was like I did the criminal thing by charging him. Oh God.

I went back to Interval House and stayed two months. This time I started to learn about being assertive.

I kept up a friendship with Keith so I could get my things and ease out of his life. It was just easier that way than to say, "No, I'm never going to see you again," and then he'd want to kill me because I wasn't doing it his way.

He often threatened, "If you take these kids away from me, something may happen. I always get my revenge." I still felt guilty because I had charged him. He would probably lose his business if he had to go to jail.

My parents allowed me to stay with them until I could find a place of my own. The co-op said I could have a place in a few months. I enrolled at Carleton University in May and took a night class. I did it because court was that summer and it takes forever to get to court. It helped take my mind off it.

Keith was still making threats to keep me from testifying in court. One time he said, "If you don't know where your children are, I know you won't go to court." So I was really afraid for the children so I would walk them back and forth to school.

Finally court day came and there I was, sitting beside Keith and looking like the dutiful wife. He was holding my hand and he just about crushed it he was so angry. It was really sickening. I can't remember what the threat was but it was pretty serious so I promised to sit beside him in court. He was only sentenced to a twenty-one-day temporary-absence program which required him to stay at a halfway house overnight. He was also forced to attend a group for men who batter.

At first it sounded like he was taking the counselling program seriously. He would phone and say, "We talked about verbal abuse. You know I did that to you all the time." He was amazed at all he was learning and yet he didn't change his behaviour. He continued to emotionally abuse me. I wanted a divorce and he agreed to give me one if I didn't ask for anything. He had some other threat against me as well. Even though I had put a lot of money into the house, I didn't have any receipts. I agreed to everything just to be free of any more hassle. I didn't even get the car.

The only good news during this time was that I finally got a place to live in the cooperative housing project.

I continued to allow Keith to see the children even though he didn't pay any support. I was still trying to ease him out of our lives and preferred that we remain on friendly terms. When the divorce became final he called and invited me to go away for a weekend with him to the States to celebrate the divorce. I can hardly believe I went, but I was feeling more confident and I wasn't afraid of him anymore. It was a really stupid weekend. We hardly talked to each other. He laughed about all the threats he had made. When we got back he gave me a little car.

I got a joe-job that suited me just fine at the time. It wasn't a big job, but I did it well. I was never late and it helped me build up the self-confidence I needed. I quit after a year because it was time to move on, but also because the boss' son was sexually harassing me.

Sylvia had an especially hard time the first year we were on our own. I no longer had money and was working long hours. I had to get the children up at 4:30 a.m., and Sylvia had a lot of problems adjusting to all the changes. If Keith called wanting to see the girls, I felt I had to let him see them. After they returned from a visit I would have to debrief them. Keith sometimes helped with babysitting.

It all finally ended at Christmas. He came to visit Christmas morning, and over some petty reason, he went storming out an hour later and I was glad he was gone. I didn't feel anything for him anymore. He came back on Boxing Day and took the little car.

I started dating a really nice fellow in January. Keith was insanely jealous and drove by often or phoned and said, "Who are you fuckin' now?" He threatened to take me to court for custody of the girls but I reminded him that if he did, he might end up having to pay child support. He's in such a high income bracket he'd probably have to pay $300 per month per kid. He called a week later and said I was right and he wouldn't bother me anymore. So I think I'm finally rid of him.

I've done a lot of growing up in the past two years. Now I can say 'No' and it's okay. If I don't like something, I can say that too. I'm a lot more open. I have to be open or I'll have the problems I've had all my life. I'm feeling strong. I think I can handle just about anything.

I've celebrated four years of being straight and that's pretty exciting. I go to AA at least once a week, sometimes twice.

I started going to Carleton full-time. Although it's really hard to study and raise my family, I'm coping and my marks are pretty good. I'm there because I want to be. I expect to have my BA in three years.

I'm seeing a chiropractor for my neck from that assault. I really resent that two years later I still suffer from Keith's assault and all he got was twenty-one days.

I have a wonderful relationship with a really gentle, sweet man. Alex is so different. He was married to an abusive woman. She stabbed him in the arm and he sought shelter at my place. It was a big joke among my kids and I that we were running an Interval House for men. I was able to share with him what I learned at Interval House and I suggested that he see a counsellor to work these things out. You know, there's a reason why he was with a person like that. So he's really into self-actualization and so am I, and we're both really changing a lot and we're growing and it's really neat. I don't feel like I need him, I just enjoy his company. If he were to walk out tomorrow, my world would not fall apart.

Father and I now have a very special and close relationship. My oldest brother, the one who sexually abused me, came a year ago specially to visit me. All he said to me was, "I hope you've gotten some help with why you married someone like Keith and for anything else that may have happened in your life." He's very well educated and he's probably learned that there's a correlation between sexually abused little girls who marry creeps. Since then we've sort of been working on a friendship and it's nice. We haven't talked openly about it yet.

My druggie brother went to a recovery home three years ago and is now an addictions counsellor. He's going to school too, and is getting straight As.

Sylvia is still having some problems and I plan to get her some counselling so she can unload. I'm sure there are things she needs to talk about that she wouldn't feel comfortable saying in my presence.

I also want to talk to the man who thinks he is Marie's father. I need to tell him the truth.

It is a relief to share my story. It's the first time I have told anyone everything. A while ago I wrote it all down but when I finished I threw it out. I didn't want any reminders. I don't like my story but it's the truth and I have to accept it. I hope it helps others.

Eight years later, on a rainy summer night, I met with Rachel at her cosy home in Ottawa. She was living with Alex. Her two daughters, now fourteen and eighteen, had their bedrooms in the basement, and one of her brothers lived upstairs. It was a full house.

Although several pounds heavier, Rachel still demonstrated that beautiful warmth. There was so much I was dying to know. Did she get her degree?

Yes, I finished my degree—a combined major in sociology and psychology. It was brutal. Every term, after exams, I'd say I'm not going back. But I kept going back. I got exhausted. I had migraines. It was insanity. It took me three and a half years. I took courses in the summer. There was never a break. After graduation, I took it easy for a couple of months and then I started looking for a job. I really had no confidence whatever. I had no clue as to how to do it.

The first job I applied for was for a SSEP (Social Service Employment Program) position, and I got it. It was in the addictions field—with street people, addicts. It was pretty rough, but I really liked it. My boss, unfortunately, was a manic depressive. He ended up quite ill, and I ended up mopping up the mess, but from that—I think because things were mopped up quite nicely—I was offered two other jobs. I worked at a men's shelter. That was pretty rowdy. Looking back, I met some really neat people there and I got really close to a couple of them. One of them committed suicide—that was really rough.

Rachel obtained several other contracts and now has a permanent job with a community agency. I work as a support person basically. I have a caseload of adults who live in group homes. Most of them suffer from schizophrenia. It's a neat job because it's in line with my thinking. It's client-directed. I really agree with the values.

What about your sobriety? I've been sober twelve years now. I stopped celebrating after ten years.

Tell me about Alex. We have a very nice relationship. I don't think that he's ever actually yelled at me, personally, in eight and a half years and I'm always amazed at that. Because I'm not perfect. I do have my PMS days. He's a very good person. He's good to the girls. They drive him nuts and he drives them nuts, but deep down there's a lot of love and caring.

In the last couple of years, the girls have, on their own, changed his status. Instead of calling him my mother's boyfriend, they call him my step-dad.

He's worked in the same business for twenty-two years.

What about the guy who was paying support for Marie?

I tried to find him to tell him that he wasn't her father, but I couldn't find him.

Did Sylvia ever go for counselling? She balked on counselling all the way. She ended up leaving home at sixteen with the boyfriend from hell. I was willing to be open about it, but as soon as I met him, the alarm system happened. Sure enough, he was abusive. There was a lot of wierd stuff. It was on and off for over a year. All through her time away from home, we kept our relationship going. She asked to come back home. She was so upset. It was really hard for her. She decided she really wasn't ready for a relationship. At the time, I said I thought it would be really, really good to get counselling. She went a couple of times. I think she found it pretty eye-opening.

She sees her father, Josh, about twice a year. He took her out for lunch on her eighteenth birthday. It was a six-hour lunch. She ate and he drank.

He got pissed and she listened. She ended up driving him home because he had lost his licence due to drinking and driving.

Marie is fine. I guess Sylvia is the screw-up and Marie likes to be the perfect child. Mind you, they've always been very different in temperament. But they are a lot the same as well. They're really funny and they're really creative. So Marie is the more steady, the more common-sensical person—less impulsive than Sylvia. She's such a wonderful child—helpful, cooperative. She's going through the disapproving-of-me stage. Rolling her eyes, you know. She's an A student. She got accepted at an art school that she had to try out for. She hasn't come home drunk, yet. Sylvia does that once a year—comes home drunk, pukes for two days and says she'll never do it again.

What about your family—your parents?

Mom and Father are mellowing. He's still a bastard—just not as often because he doesn't have as much opportunity because his kids aren't around. He's not well, but he's also not willing to get help or take medication. My sister got married in June and he boycotted the wedding because she didn't want the ownership thing—him giving her away. He's never going to change.

Did you ever talk to your brother about his sexual abuse?

We never talked about it. I don't see him very often, I'm glad to say. My kids find him creepy—he leers. I told my daughters about my history because I wanted them to be aware that there was a danger. I talked to my parents and to some family members about it and then I found out that two other sisters had been abused by him as well. One was a year older. One day, my druggie brother said, in passing, something about sexual abuse stuff happening. It wasn't the place to talk about it. So maybe he was abused, too.

I've been lucky in that I have a good relationship with most of my siblings. I was the family peacekeeper—the smoother-over. I tried to advocate for everybody. But I don't want to do it anymore. This past summer, with the wedding, there were a lot of problems. I told my family, you've got to deal with it yourselves.

Now, what about you?

I think I'm okay. I'm still stuck very much in a rut where I have been for most of my life. I've taken care of everybody else and then if there's anything left . . . I'm reaching thirty-five this birthday and I've decided now that I have permission to take more time for me. I want to join a yoga school in September. It means I have to take resources from elsewhere—time, money. You don't always realize how spent you are. It's really hard to take care of yourself. It's really hard to learn to listen to your needs, to identify your needs, to ask for your needs to be met. I wasn't socialized that way.

What advice do you have for other women?

I have this girlfriend—she's wonderful, and she's married to this guy, and he's got a lot of problems. He comes from a very abusive family and unfortunately he's portraying this model towards her. For ten years, she's tried just about everything to make the relationship work. The bottom line is, it's his responsibility to change and he won't do anything unless she's holding his hand. I keep saying to her, he's responsible for his own behaviour and you don't deserve it. That's all I can say. I always try to encourage her to talk about it. I don't let her get away with pretending that everything is rosy. But it's tough.

I try not to be judgmental by saying she's stupid for staying. You don't need to hear that because you've probably been called stupid so many times and that's why you are still stuck with this guy. I know that one of these days she'll call the police, or whatever.

Some of my clients are in relationships that are really not good for them. I try to give them guidelines—like how to hang up the phone. One guy, I'm so proud of him. His stepmother would call and really give him a hard time. It's taken him eight months, but this week we went together to the phone centre and he got a Maestro phone, so now he can decide whether he'll pick up the phone when she calls.

You don't have to stick around, you don't have to listen. The things I used to let happen to me . . . but then, I really felt powerless.

HUMOUR

I love to laugh, and my sense of humour usually gets a daily workout, especially at Interval House. Many people are surprised to hear that laughter is such an integral part of the shelter, but I have come to learn that as well as being fun, laughter is an essential part of healing and health.

Sometimes the humour at a shelter is pretty morbid as women try to deal with the effects of long-term degradation, but more often the laughter is a genuine reaction to something that is said or done.

Day-to-day living is funny. You do a washing and the white socks come out pink; your dog walks by with an old boot sticking out of its mouth; you find a long-lost item in a most unexpected location; you turn quickly and bump into a child who trips over a toy, which scoots to the other side of the room and makes a screechy sound.

If you live with an abusive, angry man, none of the above is funny. It is something you hide. You can't admit to making a mistake. Everything and everyone has to be perfect. Women often talk about walking on eggs so as not to upset their partners. The household is always tense, always on edge, always concerned about the repercussions of any action.

It is a wonderful relief for a woman to be able to laugh at herself and at situations. She can even tease or be teased and not feel threatened.

It takes about three days for a woman to begin to feel comfortable at Interval House and to find her laughter. That laugh is a sure sign that she's on her way to recovering her self. Her head lifts up, she stands a little straighter, she makes eye contact, she smiles. She gets a twinkle in her eyes. And her children begin to laugh as well.

It is what makes working at Interval House so worthwhile.

ELIZABETH'S STORY

Elizabeth had the most delicious laugh and a marvelous twinkle in her eyes. She saw the humour in every situation, even when she talked about the abuse. Oh yeah, he hit me alright, but don't think I didn't get him back (laughter), in a place he won't soon forget (more laughter). I can hold my own.

Elizabeth was a very petite woman who took great care with her appearance. At the age of twenty-two, she was convinced that if she didn't land another man soon, it would be too late.

It was fun to have Elizabeth in the house. She and I often played horsey with the children, the rougher the better. But when the children were out of earshot, we talked dirty. That was when her laughter was at its best.

One day, after laughing at one of Elizabeth's quips, I asked her if she'd like to share her story for my weekly column. She readily agreed. I can still picture her curled up on the couch while she talked about her past.

As the horror of her life unfolded, her laugher gave way to tears. I was stunned by what I was hearing. Although she had previously alluded to many of the events, each was always couched in flippant laughter. I had no idea of the continuous cruelty she had endured. It sounds corny, but that evening my heart broke. A few months later, I took a three-month leave of absence in order to deal with the 'burn-out' that started that night.

I never printed her story—I thought it was too violent and shocking for readers. Also, there was a real possibility that her attackers would recognize themselves and take revenge.

That night, she spoke of two rapes. Several years later, I visited her and asked her to retell her story for this book. Again I was shocked. There was so much more.

You may find the following information particularly upsetting.

Here's Elizabeth's story.

I was born in a Lanark County town in 1962. I had two brothers, one a year older, the other a year younger.

Mother had four pregnancies, all close together. She had several nervous breakdowns as well. I know she's always been like that but it didn't help meeting a man like my father either, though. Mom would get pregnant, more or less break down and go into a mental institution—Kingston, Brockville or the Royal Ottawa—come out and have a kid, and last about two or three months and then go back to the institution.

I think what turned her off having kids was that last baby. It was the only baby she wanted, you know. She finally felt healthy enough to have the last one. Her labour started on Christmas Eve. Father was out drinking so she got someone else to look after us kids and she went to the hospital. She was alone in the labour room, having contractions, when she went into shock and couldn't call for help. I guess the staff were partying downstairs and they didn't pay attention to her because she was considered a nut, you know. She had the baby halfway and it choked on her muscles. She was trying to get the baby out and she couldn't. The baby died. It put her right back. She told me this after my children were born.

Mom and Dad really battled. I think it was over sex. Mom was very naive about sex (even after she had four kids), like she didn't know, and I think father made demands that she couldn't tolerate. I don't think she has had sex since she left him, you know. She's never had an orgasm or any sexual pleasure.

The day she left, my brothers and I came home from school and the door was locked. We sat on the front step and waited, but mother never showed up. We were still there when father came back at midnight from his evening shift. We were so cold. Mother told me later that she had to leave him, and she knew she couldn't support us financially. She also felt that she wasn't stable enough to cope with us. She had made arrangements with a neighbour to look after us that first day, but the neighbour had had an emergency of her own and couldn't come over.

I became the housekeeper for my father and brothers when I was seven years old.

My dad had a good job and we always had nice furniture and stuff like that, but I can't remember where he was when we were growing up. I can't picture my father in a daily routine with us—it's weird.

He taught us how to steal, well more or less. We'd be in a store and he'd tell us to open a bag of candy, take some and leave it there. He was really ignorant that way you know. He never fed us properly and he never punished us or grounded us. I have no respect for my father at all.

He always downgraded my grandmother, but I just found out that she bought him the first house to make sure we had a home. I was often left with her. She made me feel dumb. She'd slap me and say, "You stupid bitch. You're just like your mother."

I was a pretty little girl. I remember when I was around the age of seven, a man stuck his tongue in my mouth and put his hands up under my skirt. My uncles tried too. They'd have me sit on their laps and I'd feel their things get big and I'd get scared and run away. I never told anyone because I thought they wouldn't believe me.

One time I was playing in the park on the monkey bars and I fell right across the bar and ruptured myself. I was bleeding and swollen and I showed my dad. He freaked out. At that time we had a boy babysitter and Dad thought the boy had done something to me. He drilled me and drilled me with questions. I finally got on my knees and begged him to believe me. I'll never forgive him for that you know, for not believing me.

Dad drank all the time. He used to promise us he'd stop and then, as soon as we were all in bed, "pop," you'd hear the beer lid poppin'.

He got the girlfriend about two years after my mom left. He's still with the same woman. They lived separately all these years. She had two girls but she never really got involved with us.

The only other part was when I had to go to the Children's Aid with my brothers. They got into a lot of trouble. They started stealing cars when they were only ten and twelve. One day they shot out the school windows. That's when Children's Aid got involved. Everytime there was trouble, we'd be sent to live at my father's girlfriend's house for supervision. One time when we were there, I overheard the girlfriend's brothers telling her that Dad should get rid of the boys, "the little bastards."

I went downstairs and I said, "How can you say that about my brothers? Do you feel that way about me too?" and I started bawling. I said, "I don't feel my Dad even loves me. He'll probably ship me off too."

I heard her tell my dad what happened when he came back. He came upstairs and he told me that the boys were going to a foster home 'cause it was the only way to get them on the right track. But he still didn't tell me he loved me you know.

I was about twelve years old when I got my first period. I didn't know what it was and I phoned my dad. After that I was too embarassed to ask him for money for pads so I went to my next-door neighbour, and she took care of me that way, you know. Any time I had my period, I kept the evidence really hidden. There were only boys in my neighbourhood to play with and so we all played together and had fun. I guess Dad thought I was pregnant because I didn't ask him for money for pads. He took me to a doctor to be examined. When I finally figured it out I was so mad, especially at my father's girlfriend. She could have asked me you know.

I quit high school in grade ten. I never associated with any of the guys at school: I was so small back then. But some of the big guys always bugged me. They'd pick me up, or put dirty letters or stink bombs in my locker. One bomb ruined my new leather jacket. I went to the principal and I asked him to stop them but he was a male chauvinist pig and he told me to shrug it off. One day my period stained through my clothes. I was so embarrassed and I didn't tell anyone; I just went home to change. The principal caught me, and when I told him why I'd left, he gave me a hard time. I threw my books at him and I said, "You can eat this shit." That's when I left school.

I moved in with my mother when I was fifteen. I left my father because he didn't trust me with my first boyfriend at all and I still wasn't having sex. I got a job as a waitress.

The first time I had sex was in my father's bed you know, just to spite him. I was sixteen and Ralph was twenty-one. We were both virgins. I got pregnant. My father had given me a book about sex but I never connected that the sperm could get you pregnant—that it came out of the penis. I knew I was too young to have a baby so I trucked down to Ottawa and had an abortion. I have never regretted it, never. I knew I couldn't manage a baby.

I got a bachelor apartment and I fixed it up real cute. I was on my own for about six months. I worked in a restaurant bar. I was serving drinks at age sixteen and running the bar at times—it was a real charge you know.

I liked sex and Ralph and I had good sex together. He was gorgeous, really built. He lived on a farm with his father and brothers. They were very religious and I'm sure his brothers were all virgins.

We planned to get married. We had everything arranged. We got a bank loan and went out and bought a house trailer, and he gave me a truck. I drove it without a licence. I was stupid that way you know.

Ralph bought me a nice low-cut dress for a wedding reception we were going to. I put it on at the farm and modelled it for him. It made me feel like I was good looking. I was really proud. I weighed a hundred pounds and had long, long hair. Ralph's uncle was there too and he was staring at me and staring at me, and then he winked. Ralph saw the wink, and he slapped me right across the face and pushed me down and told me to get the fuck out of there. All of his brothers came running and pounded the shit right out of him. I went back to the house and grabbed my bags (and my bank book of course) and left. That was it—no more. That was the first time a man ever hit me.

Some months later, Ralph came into the bar. He was sweating and everything, and I knew . . . He was fuckin' weird. I was not shocked when the cops came in and arrested him for the attempted rape of a thirteen-year-old girl.

Dad told me I should go out with different guys, not get bogged down with one. So I went out with this Greek guy but all he wanted to do was screw and I didn't want to screw him. He had a Porsche and I liked driving with him and to be a friend. He had lots of money and he bought me gold jewellery. He was older and a real charmer that way. I used to share the stuff with friends.

I met Peter at the bar. I thought he was a real gentleman. I worked with his sister and sometimes he was at her place. Peter was always quiet and I figured he must be different. I should have known—quiet and dangerous. He had nice, nice big eyes. He asked me out. We always drank when we went out. I was quiet too, and shy, but when I drank I felt more sure of myself, and I talked. We went out for three weeks before I slept with him.

Peter was older (in his thirties), and I liked the way he talked to me, always giving me compliments and showing me off to his friends. He introduced me to charm. He'd hold my hand or brush my hair, things no one had ever done for me before you know. I only knew Peter about seven weeks when he asked me to marry him. I don't know why, but I said, "Yes." We were both drunk. We got married three days later. We were still drinking—had a mickey the morning of the ceremony. At the time I didn't know why it was such a rush to get married you know. I believed him. I fuckin' believed Peter when he said he loved me. But it was a bet (I didn't find out 'till years after) between Peter and his friend Frank. It was a bet to see who could marry me first. Maybe that is why they shared me all those years—because of the bet.

Frank was creepy. I never liked him. He was always watching me. Frank would be sleeping with a girl on the couch, and me and Peter going at it in bed, and I'd look up and he'd be watching us—fuck. I'd say to Peter, "Get off me now." Even though I was drunk, it bothered me.

About a week after we got married, I went out with my girlfriends. I was so drunk I couldn't walk home. Frank picked us up and I passed out in the back of his car. I woke up to find Frank going down for the count. He was trying to rape me. I bloody freaked out you know. We were out in the country somewhere. I got out of the car and walked home. I slowed down on my drinking after that.

About three months after we were married, Peter changed. He became very possessive and suspicious. If I wasn't home right after work, he got mad. One day after work I walked to Mac's Milk to get some groceries. It only took me twenty minutes extra, but Peter came looking for me and met me on the bridge. He slapped my face and threw the bread and milk into the river and told me to get the fuck home. When we got there, I threw the rest of the groceries at him and I went to my mother's. The next day he came over and apologized and begged me to come home. I stayed with my mother for eight days.

I never paid any attention when Peter went out to drink. I guess I was independent that way, you know—you can do what you want if you let me do what I want. I was so busy working that I never really noticed how much he was away. But the alcohol was beginning to affect his mind. One day I came home and the whole fuckin' kitchen was ripped apart. He tore all the panelling off the walls and our dishes were broken. There was a knife in the wall near the door. He was passed out in the bed. Another time he came home and hit me when I was sleeping. I don't know what he hit me with but I had such a shiner, I couldn't believe it. I snuck out of the house that night and went to sleep at my mom's. I think my mom was afraid of Peter; she didn't really want me to stay with her. I went back to Peter. He never said he was sorry.

About six months after I married Peter, I got pregnant. I didn't drink a drop when I was pregnant. I wanted the baby so badly that I figured everything would be alright once she was born.

Peter was a good worker. He had his own business and earned lots of money, but he spent most of it on booze. One weekend he spent over $800 on alcohol. Another time he lost $1,300 gambling when he was drunk. He was a really nice person when he was sober, and I kept hoping he would control his drinking. I thought he was still attractive then, you know.

One evening I gave Peter my pay cheque to be cashed. He wasn't drinking at the time. He was gone for several hours and I finally found him in the hotel. He called me a slut in front of everyone. This time I was so mad, I hit him and gave him a bloody nose. Three nights later he was gone again. I found him in the same hotel. On his way down the stairs, he kicked me in the face and started to beat me up. It took three of my girlfriends to pull him off me.

My parents wanted me to leave him you know, but I kept hoping that he would change and take on his responsibilities as a father.

He started bringing his friends home, and they'd all get drunk there. I was always very wary when they were around, especially if Peter was passed out. I could feel them eyeing me.

Two weeks after Brittany was born, I was invited to a make-up party. There wasn't much booze in the house and Peter was sober, so I left him babysitting our baby. When I got back home, his friends were there and they were all drunk. The house was a mess and there were holes punched in the wall. Brittany was on the couch burping stuff up, and there was plaster dust on her face and in her eyes. It almost drove me nuts. After that I never left her alone with Peter.

Peter's friends were always teasing me about sex you know. They'd remark on my body—how it recovered and went back to normal so quickly after Brittany was born. These guys fantasized openly about me, "You make nice-looking babies." About two months after she was born, they started pinching my ass. They'd praise me first, but the drunker they got, the more hand-happy they got. I'd ask them to leave but they'd never go. I hated that—trying to get a bunch of slobs to leave.

I got pregnant again. Peter's drinking got worse. In fact, he was drunk during most of this pregnancy. His friends were always around and when he was out of it they would want to fuck me. They knew that Peter and I weren't doing it you know. They would never try anything when they were sober; it was only when they were drunk. They'd stop me on the main street and talk about how they'd do it. I was really big with Brandon and they'd say, "Oh, you just have to bend her over."

I was four months pregnant the night Frank started in on me. Peter was passed out and Frank kept throwing lit cigarette butts at me through the bedroom door. He grabbed me and raped me for four hours. I couldn't believe it was happening. I didn't fight 'cause I was scared of losing the baby. I finally grabbed a knife and he left me alone. He warned me not to tell Peter. I wanted to so badly. I was pounding Peter under the sheets, pinching him, anything to get him up. I was scared that Frank would attack me again you know. I said, "The guy tried to pull my clothes off and he tried to stick his dick in me and, you know, I'm pregnant and you don't care." I was too scared to say that he raped me. Peter didn't react.

I guess I just went dead, into sort of a shock. It bothered me for a couple of years after. Really, it still bothers me. I hate Frank so much.

Frank didn't touch me for most of the rest of my pregnancy, but he was talking crap all the time: telling me I had nice boobs and that he was really pleased that I was still tight. He always wanted to touch my stomach and he said weird things—talked about the devil. He said the devil would scare me so badly I'd wish I was dead. I was always scared of the devil as a child and it really bothered me you know.

It was weird because I never figured that Peter had to be like Frank in order to hang around him so long. They did strange things, but I was never curious to find out what was going on. Like one night, I looked out my bedroom window and Peter and Frank were jumping around and kissing and like, "We're brother's, we're brothers." I couldn't believe my own husband would be acting like this.

The other guys were always bugging me. They figured Peter was away so much and I'd be lonely. They all lied. They'd say Peter was in the hospital and that he'd sent them over to keep me company. I'd put the dresser up against the bedroom door and stay there with the baby.

I used to think that Peter was really popular (had so many friends), but every time he got drunk they'd punch him. He was like a female to all those guys. They really hated him. I started to wake up and see what was going on. I'd tell Peter that they weren't good friends, but he didn't react. I started to think about leaving him. I decided to wait until the baby was born.

Brandon was a very big baby, and it was a very painful delivery. It took me a long while to recover you know. I found getting raped while I carried Brandon made it more difficult to accept him. As soon as Brittany came to visit, I started bawling. I was so happy to see her. She got up on the bed and she said, "This is our baby, right Mom?" That helped me.

At this time, I met a woman and she became my best friend. She told me that Peter was sleeping around. She said she had screwed both Peter and Frank. I felt really close to her because she was the only one who told me the truth. Her daughter would babysit and she and I went out. Peter was very jealous of her. He accused us of being lesbians.

Peter would get in a real fit if I didn't screw when he wanted to screw. He'd say to his friends, "Why don't you fuck the bitch because I don't want to fuck her."

Peter got a real hate on for Brandon. He threatened that he was going to, "throw the little bastard through the window." One night he came home drunk. He banged into the crib and he was going to throw the baby against the wall. I woke up in time to stop him. I hit him with a glass baby bottle.

I always fought back after Brandon was born. I started standing up for my kids. I breastfed Brandon, so I guess I felt like a real mother.

It was about two weeks after Brandon was born that the guy upstairs come down and raped me. He opened the door, threw me on the couch, and raped me. Brittany was in the bedroom and I remember being quiet so she wouldn't wake up. When he was finished I said, "I hope you feel like a man now." I couldn't look at him again. I used to visit his wife. I liked her so much, and I knew she was planning to leave him, so I didn't tell her. I had to go to the hospital and get my stitches repaired.

Every day I was always looking for Peter. I wanted to catch him doing something so I would have a reason to leave him. Isn't that strange? I would beg him to get help, to go to AA before he ruined his mind. I talked about leaving, but he told me that if I left, he would find me and kill the children.

Peter started selling drugs. He didn't take any himself but he made lots of money to support his drinking. He was hardly ever home.

Frank would always end up at my place. For about two months he came quite often, and he raped me about once a week. Even if I had my period he still did it—pushed my tampon way up inside me. I was still too scared to tell anybody.

When Peter was away, the other guys kept coming around, fuckin' me too. Every second or third day they would show up. Three of them stayed three nights in a row. I'd always get these phone calls before they came. I was so scared; my nerves got so bad. I'd wake up before they got to my door and I'd let them in. I was afraid they would attack Brittany so I let them fuck me, get it over with, and then they'd usually leave. I would lock the children in their bedroom so they couldn't see what was going on.

I was like virgin material to these guys: I was always quiet then. They would go on about how much better looking I was than their wives—how I was so much tighter.

I guess I somehow put what was really happening out of my mind. I would try to do normal things with my kids: read to them, take them for walks, and I kept my house clean.

One night, Peter and his friends were in the kitchen. They had been drinking all night. Peter was so drunk he was talking to the table. The guys were talking about going out and fuckin' someone. Then they started pitchin' bottles. They threw seven or eight cases of empty twenty-fours against the kitchen wall. I had just carpeted my kitchen. There was one new guy. I liked him and I never expected him to do it. I couldn't sleep that night. The next day I went to this guy's house. He was sitting at the table, hung over. I said to his girlfriend, "I'm really sorry for doing this to you but my children didn't deserve what happened." I really started standing up for my kids, you know? I threw four glasses of water against the wall. Two weeks later that same guy offered me money to sleep with him. He said it really turned him on to see me throwing the glasses. I was so shocked. I couldn't look him in the eye.

Frank felt that since he went in me when I was pregnant with Brandon that Brandon was his baby. And (his sick mind) he said, because Brittany was so beautiful, that she was his too. At that time I was so confused. I didn't know anything else but to sit down and have coffee with the man, you know and talk with him. I wasn't scared of him when he was sober. It was the only way I could deal with it. You think a lot of weird things I tell you.

One day Peter and Frank were there. Frank picked up Brittany and he started talking about her beautiful satin-blonde hair. I grabbed Brittany and I said, "If you ever touch my daughter, I'll fuckin' kill you. I'll cut your fuckin' nuts off and I'll kill you both. I'll haunt you for the rest of your life." I was really stressed, I really freaked out. It was the first time I stood up to them. They left in a hurry.

Peter beat me only once in front of the children. I always tried to make sure that they didn't see his violence, but one day Brittany was sleeping beside me on the couch and he couldn't see her. He came home and started beating me and made my nose bleed. Ever since then she has been afraid of blood. One day I cut my leg and it was bleeding, and she asked if Daddy was home.

My nerves were shot and I couldn't sleep. I was always afraid that Frank or his friends would come over. He continued to harass me. One night Frank snuck into the basement and made animal noises that terrified me. He was always weird, said weird things. He thought he was the devil. He told me that someday he would take Peter away and come back for me and the kids.

I was too frightened to charge any of them with assault. I found it was easier to smile and agree than to fight back. I just hoped that somehow they would all kill themselves.

One night when Peter was away, his friends were cruising around our house. I was scared, so I took the children to my girlfriend's home. Later, Peter came to her door, grabbed me by the hair and dragged me home—by my hair! It was so painful. I ran back to my girlfriend's home. He came again and pounded the piss out of both of us. I started fighting back. I grabbed a bottle and I was going to kill him. My girlfriend stopped me, and she kicked him. He left, but before she could call the police, he came back and started beating us again. The fight went on for five or six hours. Someone must have called the police. When they arrived, I was coughing blood.

The police arrested him and charged him with assault. He was released and we lived together for the three months before the court hearing. He still beat me, but now I fought back. We fought all the time.

Peter was sentenced to nine months in jail. The police said that he had more than fifty charges of assault laid against him since he was a teen. They said I was a nice girl and what was I doing with a prick like Peter?

As soon as he was in jail, his friends started bugging me. I was really scared because Frank said he'd take care of me. I went to Interval House for the first time. I stayed for three weeks. I wasn't ready to accept any help because I wanted to rebel—fuck who I wanted to fuck.

I found an apartment in the next town. I really enjoyed being on my own with the kids you know. I was getting to know Brittany and Brandon. Before, I never had the opportunity to dress them up because somebody would always be over and interfering. Everything was fine for a couple of months and then it started all over again. Peter's friends kept coming over or phoning to check up on me. One night, five of the guys raped me. I think someone put something in my drink. One guy told me, "The only reason I'm doing this to you is because Peter did this to my wife." Another fellow came back the next day and apologized for his behaviour. I guess I sort of forgave him. He always paid attention to my kids. He thrilled me that way. After that, I gave up drinking. I didn't want to be like them you know. I felt like a slut.

I never cheated on Peter during our marriage, but now I felt the marriage was over so I started dating. One day I was at a restaurant just having a coffee with Phil, and Peter's friends arrived. They interrupted our meal to remind me that I was a married woman.

Some days the children and I would come home to find the men there. One of the guys had some sense. He always talked the others out of harming me. But one day my mother babysat and I went uptown to shop. Frank showed up and he dragged me into his car and we ended up at his house. He raped me all night. I wasn't able to call my mother.

I knew they never had the opportunity, but the guys started talking about molesting Brittany. I had to get away. I rented two VCRs and sold them to get money. I took a bus to a friend's home in southern Ontario. Peter's friends traced me there and they kept calling, saying they had guns and they were coming down to kill me. Peter called the city police from jail and told them I was going to be killed. The police came to see me and they told me I should leave because they couldn't protect me. So I moved again to another girlfriend's home.

When Peter was released from jail, he traced me. He begged me to meet him in Kingston. We stayed there together as a family for two weeks. He didn't drink, and he promised to be a good father. He was going to AA and seeing a psychiatrist.

We moved to his sister's home in Ottawa. I found an apartment and Ottawa Social Services gave me a cheque for the first and last month's rent. Peter got the cheque and took off. He phoned and threatened to come back to get the children.

I moved to another girlfriend's place. She was a bodybuilder and she had lots of muscular friends using the body-building equipment in her apartment. I felt safe there. Peter came around, but he was obviously intimidated by all the muscles you know. He left for Calgary.

The children and I came back to Interval House for the second time. We stayed three months. This time I found it a lot different. I was more ready to accept help. I was exhausted, ready to sleep. I met Rachel there, and we've become best friends. She would babysit. It was a real boost to get out and figure some things out for myself.

The staff persuaded me to go to the police about the VCR theft because it was really hanging over me. The cop was very understanding. He told me he'd do the same thing in my situation. He drove me to the magistrate, and went out of his way to help me get it straightened out. I was sentenced to a year's probation and had to pay back the store.

It was very hard to find an apartment in my home town. I think that Peter's reputation didn't help you know, but many landlords don't want to rent to a single woman with children.

I moved to Ottawa. Peter came to visit the kids and I took him back. We talked like we never talked before. He said, "I'm sorry. I can't change the past. I'm sorry for whatever happened." I felt he was sincere. I guess I was old-fashioned that way. I didn't want to share the kids with anybody else. He knew all this and he played on that. He didn't drink for a year. He was into hash, but I didn't mind because it kept him calm.

I started having trouble with my hormones. I bled a lot and I was really bitchy. I took it out on Brittany. One day I held her up by her hair and slapped her across the face. I guess she reminded me of me, and at that time I hated myself you know. I hugged her for an hour after that. I went to CAS and I said, "I can't control myself; I'm taking it out on my daughter."

I had to have a hysterectomy, and Peter agreed to care for the kids while I was in the hospital. I was so scared to leave them. I'd never left them before for that length of time. Peter really abused them during the week I was away. When I got home, I was so disgusted. Brittany was walking around with shit between the crack of her ass and Brandon was six pounds lighter. I was only home an hour and I had to clean the house.

That week, I found out Peter had thrown Brandon against the wall a couple of times. I confronted him and he started threatening: he was going to burn us out, he was going to kill us. But what really bothered me, was when he told me I wasn't a woman anymore. That's when I ended our relationship. I closed my door to him.

I told Brittany and Brandon to stay in the living room and watch TV and I went to the kitchen and got a knife and I told Peter to get out. He barricaded himself in the bedroom and I fuckin' hit the door a couple of times, and then I realized I couldn't go through with it. So I said to him, "I'm leaving with the kids and by the time I get back you'd better be out of here." I was completely calm. I felt so strong. He left. One of my brothers moved in to protect us.

I waited four months till I called Phil. I figured I needed the break. I didn't want to make another mistake with the kids you know. I met Phil after I left Interval House the first time. He thought I was too young for him (he was thirty-seven, I was twenty-two) but he liked my kids. He really got a charge out of them. He was the first man who didn't look at me like I was a piece of meat. He told me that he had served time for murder. He said he wasn't like that, that it was a situation of self-defense. I called his parole officer and found out that he was telling the truth.

We went out for four months before we had sex. Afterwards Phil said, "I don't want to embarrass you, but you don't know what sex is—you've never come before." He helped me to feel comfortable about my body and about sex. We talked and it turned out that I was ashamed of my body. Peter always said, when I was pregnant, "Oh, you look gross." He never said one nice word to me. My small breasts didn't help and I hated my bum. I couldn't stand to see my ass. So I really didn't feel like I was meant for sex, you know.

Frank came over a couple of times and Phil was there. After Frank left, Phil said, "You're really scared of him aren't you? You're trying not to look scared but deep down inside . . ." Then one day Phil was visiting, and Frank and about four other guys barged in. The guys were talking dirty and one of them asked Phil if he'd fucked me yet. Then he told him about how good I was to fuck. Phil took me into the next room and he said, "There's something going on here that I don't approve of." He goes, "Even if I'm not going to be here tomorrow, Elizabeth, I have to do this or I couldn't live with myself." He said he'd pay for any damage. He beat the shit out of Frank and threw him and the other guys out the door and he said, "If you ever come back near here, I'll kill you." I think they were scared of Phil because they'd heard of his past. I never had anybody do this for me and I was embarrassed to thank him. I don't remember ever being put in a spot where I had to say thank you to anybody.

Phil convinced me to move and he paid for the truck.

Peter didn't bug me until Phil moved in. He'd phone and say that Phil was probably sucking Brittany off, or that my brother was fuckin' her. He'd say like, "Are you and your brother fuckin' now?" or "Are you a lesbian now?"

I got a lawyer. The first time I went to meet her I took my kids with me. I said, "I'm not using my kids looks for this but you need to talk to my kids for a few minutes to know where I'm coming from."

She goes, "You're a very direct person, aren't you?"

I've been to court twenty-three times in the last fourteen months because of Peter. He accused Phil of molestation and Children's Aid has done their investigation. Peter wanted to get partial welfare. He'd get extra money if he got custody of the kids on the weekends. He doesn't really care for the kids; he only wanted the money to buy booze. He's never bought them Christmas gifts or even remembered their birthdays. When I was at Interval House, I had to send gifts with the kids for Peter to give them so they'd at least have that, so they wouldn't get hurt.

The last time I was in court, I really got mad. Peter told the judge, "She never lets me see my kids, she's always hanging the phone up on me."

I said, "You lying bastard." I said, "You've never even bothered to phone." I said, "You only use them kids to get to lay me, don't you Peter?' Oh yah, in the courtroom.

The judge called Peter an asshole. He says, "Why can't you just leave her alone?" I got custody, and Peter got visiting rights as long as he shows up sober. He got visitation rights because of his girlfriend. She runs a foster home. I don't know why they allow it because she takes punishment from Peter too you know.

Peter didn't see the kids for six months. He broke his visitation rights by not coming or getting others to pick them up. When he did come to get the kids, Brandon wouldn't go. Brittany went because she liked the attention she got from Peter's girlfriend. She never wanted to see Peter you know—he tried to turn her against Phil.

The custody agreement has been rewritten. Peter was to pay $450 a month child support. He's never been back to get them and he hasn't paid any child support.

Phil and I have been living together for four years now. I know Phil wants to get married in a year or two, but I don't know if I'll get married again. He tolerates a lot of crap from me. I'm stubborn. I'm selfish. I have a hard time saying, "I'm sorry." I don't give Phil what he needs, and I've never told him I love him.

I asked him about that, and he said I shouldn't worry about it. He said, "When you feel safe, you'll say it." I've told him every damn dark secret about myself and he understands you know. I could write pages about all the nice things he does for me; he leaves me love notes on the fridge. All my friends envy our relationship. But when I'm mad, I can't see any of his good. I hate myself for that. I have flashbacks and nightmares. Phil puts up with me; he goes around my moods. He says, "I know you don't mean that." When we're being nice, we cook for each other. I'm starting to leave little notes for him, too. I have no threat of Phil coming home drunk, and he's never lived off of me. Every time in bed with Phil is nice. We've got plenty of spark.

If I'm down, I call Rachael. She's really smart. She's going through for a psychologist you know and she's helped me understand my nightmares and dreams. One night we talked for five hours. She said that whenever I feel scared or insecure about something in my life, I dream that Frank is trying to rape me again. She said you dream the worst thing that's ever happened to you. That's why I keep dreaming about him.

I've finally figured out Peter's control over me you know. He was so sick, and he loved me in a sick way. He wanted to bring me down with him. I still can't figure some of it yet and maybe I won't for a couple of years. I know now that when Phil and I fight, I'm reliving the past.

I still don't trust that many people, but the friends I do have, I trust for life. I trust Phil. But it's hard. One day he was lying on his back on the couch and Brittany climbed up on top of his chest and she was squirming around; she was just getting comfortable. I almost wanted to kill myself for my thoughts. I wanted to put my hand on his prick to see if it was hard. I told him after, and he said, "I don't know what I can do to reassure you."

Brittany is doing good but she's immature a little bit. She has to have stability you know. If some man flirts with me, she grabs my hand and says, "My mommy, my mommy." It makes me wonder if she seen anything with all those men around.

She started talking like a baby the second time I left Peter. So I took her to the Children's Hospital to see if she had a speech problem, and they said it was emotional. I think she didn't trust me for a while because I went back to Peter you know. I spoil her by having her around me all the time. She's very particular about her friends.

Brandon, he's smart. He's doing really well in school. He says, "You don't have to yell at me, Mom. I know what you're going to say." But he can be hateful. When he doesn't want to do something, he can be awful. I was punishing Brittany for things he did, until one day I overheard him. He had lied to me.

I think that by hiding Peter's behaviour from the kids, they didn't really know what was going on, you know, why I left. I think Brandon blames me for things that happened.

I never regretted having Brittany and Brandon, but when I was with Peter I couldn't put them first. I'm so scared that something will happen to them. I still don't let anyone else babysit them, but I'm starting to change. I let them go to the neighbourhood park. I can see it out my living-room window.

I feel much stronger. I don't lie to anybody and I don't take anybody's bullshit. I don't want to hurt another female (especially a single mother), but I don't care whether I hurt a man. I do a lot of babysitting. There are a lot of single mothers in this area.

I don't talk to my father hardly anymore at all. I don't feel I need to. You know how you always go back and get your parents approval? And then I said, "Why am I doing this? The man doesn't appreciate it." You can't do nothing to change that person so you have to accept that.

I do more for my mother. I know she has a mental illness; she's schizophrenic. I have patience for her. I understand why she gave us up. I know she regrets it, but she makes up for it with Brittany.

I have a good relationship with one brother. He plays with the kids, takes them out. The other brother has mental problems. I don't have much to do with him.

I can't hug anyone right now, except Phil. A friend came over the other day. She was really upset, but I just couldn't hug her. I don't like the body contact.

I'm taking art classes now; I can do the work at home. I've always been artistic. When I was little, I had a Big Sister and she noticed I had a good talent for art. All during public school I was let go to the gym and design the murals. Soon I'll have my grade twelve Art, and then I'll get my upgrading. After that I plan to take Architectural Technology. As soon as Brandon's in grade one, I'll call welfare and I'll say, "Thank you for the years you helped me but goodbye now," you know. I've promised myself that.

Oh God, I could tell you about two hours more details about the things Frank did. There was a lot of mental rape. That still bothers me. I try to forget about it. I don't dwell on it. It's not like I don't feel sorry for myself but I don't live to feel sorry for myself.

Postscript: Over the years, several women sought shelter at Interval House due to assaults by Frank and his gang. None of these women would report the abuse to the police for fear of reprisal.

In 1988, a woman, a victim like Elizabeth, shot and killed Frank.

Elizabeth and I met for the update at a picnic table under a marvelous home-made, vine-filled arbour in her tiny backyard. She was living in a housing project in Ottawa. Her children appeared often, curious about what we were saying. Elizabeth's delicious laugh and the twinkle in her eyes were thoroughly intact.

We talked about Frank. I was very glad when I heard he was killed. About fifty people called me that day to let me know he was dead. I was angry that I didn't have enough guts to do it myself. I did feel more relief—I didn't have to worry anymore. He was a sick, sick man.

Then we talked about Peter. Peter doesn't bother me at all. He finally just saw that he couldn't control me anymore. He only comes around at Christmas time—brings gifts. He only just gave the kids his phone number six months ago—after nine years of not seeing them. They don't call him.

He's nice to me now. When I see him, I feel sorry for him. He still lives with other people and he still parties.

The children? I've had hell with Brittany for two years. She's going to be thirteen. Now she's not too bad—she's calmed down. You couldn't say something to her or she'd say, "Oh, you love Brandon more than you love me."

I just told her, "I don't care if you hate me for a while. I don't have to be perfect." I started getting her to go to other people's homes more. I'd make sure somebody was in a bad mood and I'd send her over to their house and she'd see for herself that other people are like this. It's not just because they're separated or divorced. I have her going to a group, too—the Youth Services Bureau—just so she'll recognize that I'm not a mean person. I really don't blame Brittany for being how she is sometimes. I'd always hold her away from people, especially men. I'd just keep my eye on her a little bit more and I guess she'd feel that tension.

Brandon's the lovable one. He's eleven. He's the one that's bad, but he's so lovable. He's very sensitive. He's the type that, if you're upset about something, he'll come up to you and show compassion and sensitivity. He's so good that way. On the other hand, if you say no to him, he's still stubborn. He goes upstairs and screams his head off. He's moody that way. He hasn't done anything bad, yet, and he's not very chauvinistic, yet. Living in a project, and at his age, I tell him, "Brandon, I don't care what the other kids do, as long as you always come home and tell the truth about the situation," and he always does. I tell him, "I won't squeal on the other kids," because I noticed I was squealing at first and then he stopped talking to me. You still can't outthink him, you can't outwit him. He's always been like that—just very good common sense. He says he's not going to drink or use drugs when he gets old. He says it just hurts people. And that's not you persuading him, it's really him saying that. So he's a very deep person.

My father's in the hospital right now. He's in there because of the booze. His body is letting go—brain damage, the whole bit. Brandon really doesn't know my father. We visited him and Brandon was crying when we went outside. He's at the stage where he can't tell you exactly everything he's thinking, but at least he feels it.

When I had arrived at Elizabeth's home, she introduced me to her husband, Alan, before he left for the evening. I asked, "What happened to Phil?" We got along well together, but we got along too well. I think I got too bored. I guess the age difference did make a difference. He was nineteen years older. He made me feel protected. I guess I needed that at the time. After a while, once I got more self-esteem, I became really bored of him. It just wasn't going anywhere, you know? I just told him to leave. He went out once, drinking, with the kids in the car. I just told him goodbye.

Elizabeth started to drink heavily. She got into cocaine. Although she made sure the children were taken care of, she was losing it. It's funny, you leave a drunk and you become something like that yourself.

Alan came into her life. I'd been by myself for about eight months and I said to a girlfriend, "I need a real good fuck."

She goes, "I know this guy who's single and he's pretty good at it."

Alan had survived his own addictions and he pushed Elizabeth to get help. He told me to go to AA or something and I said, "Fuck you." I had a real bad attitude. I figured no man was going to tell me what to do again.

They shared their pasts and he understood Elizabeth's fears. But she continued drinking, and after three months, he left her. He told me, "You can't get drunk or I won't see you anymore."

At about this time, a girlfriend of Elizabeth's killed herself. She had twin girls and a little boy. She kept drinking her life away. I thought, Wow, what am I doing?

She quit drinking on her own. The first year of being straight—I started seeing shadows coming up the stairs—all of these nerve reactions were coming back. I started getting very angry in conversations—a lot of anger. I was very selfish and cold and blamed everybody else for my problems. Alan said, "You need to do something about your temper." I started going to a group, Naranon, at the Royal Ottawa. It was a very good group. It makes you stop and realize how you're responsible for a situation—not other people. It doesn't matter what you go through, it's somewhat your responsibility. I was scared. I didn't want Brittany to get . . . like we already had a nit-pick relationship anyways, and I didn't want her to get older and her to think I hated her. So I said, fuck, I better do something with myself, you know.

I went to the Rape Crisis Centre for counselling for three years and the lady down there helped me a lot. You don't realize all the damage. I guess I had a real hard exterior because, since I've been five, I've had to be my own person. She told me that I protected myself all those years by using my dolls. When I was a child, I had twenty dolls, all around my bedroom. I'd play out my problems with the dolls.

I like going there. I can tell somebody how I feel, even if it's stupid.

After eight months, Alan came back. They lived together for three years, and three years ago they got married. I do like the title. The kids were after me to get married. Brandon has always accepted Alan. Brittany had a real hard time believing that Alan liked her. I tried to explain to her that women are different from men. Women are more affectionate in some areas, and men—you know—very few men are.

It's more of a real relationship with Alan. The last two years have been the best. I'm not affectionate towards touching and stuff like that. That died a long time ago, and it's never going to come back. But he's a man and he can decide if he wants an affectionate person or whatever. I'm glad I'm not like that with the kids.

He's on a disability and he works part-time. He's got a chemical unbalance because of his drug abuse. He's never called me a nasty name. He never once swore at me even after I swore at him and called him everything. I guess he's in touch with his woman's side (laughter). He slapped me once, but I slapped him first.

Alan's eighteen-year-old son moved into the household six months ago. He really likes it here because I talk to him. I spend a lot of time with him.

Elizabeth's mother comes to visit every three weeks. She stays overnight. That's all I can handle. She comes and sits on the couch and she follows me around. She's very heavily medicated. She lives in the country and she drives. I don't know how she drives, her reflexes are slowed down. She's no support. It's like I'm the mother and she's the child. I watched a program on TV about the bonding of a parent to a child. I cried the whole day after.

While we were talking, a young girl dropped by. Elizabeth invited her to get a snack from the refrigerator. I'm bad for taking in kids who don't get much attention at home. I guess I'm giving what I didn't get.

Elizabeth is attending school two mornings a week to get her grade eleven. In the afternoons, she works with autistic children. She became excited as she described her work and her successes. I'm hoping, by the time I'm forty, I'll have enough credentials that I can work in a community centre 'cause I like the work. I know I'm a good worker. I pick up fast. A lot of the parents can't get past the disability [autism]. I don't see it as a disability. I see it as something you have to get over—get past it.

Elizabeth has a very positive frame of mind and is excited about the new her. I've learned a lot in the past five years. I think I'm normal now. I feel a lot different now. I don't put up with any bullshit and I don't hide in myself. I think about things now instead of not bothering. Before I wouldn't even bother and I'd get lost. Now I think about everything—sometimes too much. I know I'm a good mother. That area I'm quite confident about.

She plans to have some physical repairs done. I hadn't noticed, but Elizabeth drew my attention to her skin. After my birthday, I want to get rid of the scars on my face and my chest—the broken blood vessels from all the beatings. They'll just laser them.

Elizabeth had lots of advice for other women. The biggest thing, I think, is they should be honest with themselves. To recognize how they made themselves victims. It could be a lack of self-confidence, a lack of parenting skills, growing up—any dysfunction. There are still a lot of women out there—they didn't get any affection growing up so they go look for a man who gives them no affection. They defeat themselves that way.

Once you've been abused, you overlook it. You think, oh well, it won't happen again, and you go out and you sabotage yourself again and you find some other asshole who just replaced the asshole you got rid of.

 I do believe women should get a lot of help before they go looking for another partner. They should know who they are and what they're going to stand for. I just think women should stop conning themselves, especially in between a situation. They should just stay by themselves—not be scared to stay by themselves—enjoy what they gave birth too.

I think I've been lucky. I've never wanted that for my kids. I think when I had kids, I really wanted them—for me. So when I saw them growing up, I don't want to do that to them. I've left a few scars on my kids, but none that can't be repaired. I imagine it makes up for itself somewhere along the line.

BURN-OUT

The popular term burn-out refers to a condition in which an individual is no longer able to function at work. Shelter workers often talk of burn-out. It has happened to me twice.

My first burn-out began in 1984, the night I listened to Elizabeth tell her story. I really admired Elizabeth. She was gutsy and sharp and gave the appearance of being in control of her life. But, as her story unfolded, it was clear that she had no control in her life at all. That night, she described two rapes. You'll see in her story that she was raped many times, but that night she only described two of those incidents. When she finished talking, I actually felt my heart break. It was a physical thing. It felt like a string had broken within my heart. After that, I deteriorated. I didn't want to face the cruelty of human beings. I couldn't accept that one person or several people could do such things to another person; that it would even cross their minds to do it; and then that they would actually carry it out. And to such a strong, defiant, fun woman. This little person who got through it all, somehow.

I felt a great sadness. I think her story awakened me to the fact that we were only getting superficial information about the cruelty towards women, that there was something much deeper going on in women's lives. It was like a loss of innocence for me. The women rarely told the shelter workers everything; they gave their stories in dribs and drabs. They shielded us from the full truth. Perhaps they did this because of the shame, because of the idea that if anyone could do such terrible things to them, then it must mean that somehow they deserved it. Maybe the women were protecting us from feeling the hurt.

I felt sad and depressed because I couldn't figure out how to fix this. I suppose I like to study a problem, find a solution, fix it and go on to the next. But there was no simple solution to this problem, and I felt insignificant. I also felt the insignificance of the shelter.

In the days after that night with Elizabeth, I observed her children. She had a quiet, reserved, baby-doll girl and a rough-and-tumble boy who, at two years of age, strutted his stuff and got his own way. And, I thought, it's not going to change. That was depressing, too. This problem can't be fixed in a few years. It is going to take generations.

Eventually I found that I couldn't listen to the other women. I didn't want to know what had happened to them. I felt emotionless, numb. Sometimes I hid in the office.

I took a leave of absence for three months.

The second burn-out took place several years later. A week before it happened, I was congratulating myself on how I had become more objective. I could listen to the stories of abuse, give genuine care and yet not feel the hurt. I reasoned I had learned how to leave my work at the shelter. I had even listened to a woman describe bestiality and how her husband beat her if she refused to have sex with his dog. But I *was* affected by that experience.

This woman had asked me if I would help her to tell her story. She warned me it would be difficult for both of us. We set up a time when another person was on shift so we wouldn't be interrupted. I held her and we rocked together as she sobbed and shook and, for the first time, spoke of the horrors she had experienced. Several days later she confided in another staff person that she couldn't understand how I had seemingly been unaffected by her story. I hadn't cried with her and she figured I must be very strong. She didn't know that after I had left her side that evening, I walked into the main part of the house, spied a volunteer who was learning about the job and beckoned her to follow me into the office. I told her I needed her to hold me and to listen. I gave her a condensed version of what I had just heard and then I cried my eyes dry.

Shortly after that episode, I told my husband that I hated men; I hated all men and I had to find a way to change that. I knew I couldn't continue to work at the shelter and deal with that anger. And I couldn't continue in my marriage without resolving it.

I quit working at Interval House and started interviewing women for this book as well as taking a university course. Eighteen months later, I went back to the shelter filling in for people who were on holidays. I gradually eased back into the job. I'm still there and I love it, although now, I focus on public education and have less direct contact with the women who come for shelter.

During it's sixteen-year history, there have been other sorts of burn-outs at Interval House.

Our first director, a woman who had expended a great deal of energy in getting the house established, gradually developed an ownership of the shelter. So much so that she spent most of her time there, not trusting others to make the right decisions and showing signs of exhaustion. A committee of the board asked her to take a two-week vacation just to give her a break from the heavy responsibilities of the job. She simply couldn't and wouldn't go and eventually had to be fired. Her burn-out affected everyone involved.

After she left, the staff evolved into a collective. This meant that each person had equal responsibility for the management of the shelter. It worked well for a while. But staff meetings were long and arduous as every issue was debated until there was unanimous agreement. Although all of the staff were idealists to some degree and strongly believed in women achieving equal rights with men, some had very strong ideals or, in today's jargon, were more 'politically correct.' And they experienced the greatest frustration because they could not compromise. Several of these women, although excellent counsellors, became victims of burn-out as well.

From the beginning, staff members were particularly vulnerable to burn-out because they did almost everything. They were involved in every aspect of the shelter's operation including fund-raising, house maintenance, personnel issues, public education, follow-up, etc. They helped women to move, they attended board meetings and they worked shift work besides. It was exhausting. Any large or small issue could be the final straw that would prompt one to quit. And then the repercussions of one person quitting would affect the rest. Everyone had to do extra work until the process of hiring someone else was complete.

In the early days of the shelter's history, board members experienced burn-out. Treasurers seemed particularly vulnerable as they tried to find ways to stretch too few dollars to cover the basic expenses, or when they worked on fund-raising projects which often had disappointing results. Some developed management plans which usually required staff to take a cut in pay. This would result in an uproar, causing people to take sides, and the treasurer, in complete frustration, would quit.

Recognizing the reality of burn-out, the Board of Directors has put measures in place to lessen the risk. A coordinator was hired to provide support to both staff and board and to be the one who has an understanding of the overall program as well as day-to-day issues. A strong board/staff structure was established in which representatives of both groups share committee work. The staff developed a modified collective structure, with a separation of duties outlined in clear job descriptions. The personnel committee established a realistic leave-of-absence policy and developed a policy that allows staff to take 'mental health days' as part of sick leave. This became possible because funding stabilized somewhat, allowing staff members to feel more secure in their jobs and comfortable in working reduced hours when necessary. The policy is also made possible by the existence of several on-call workers who are available to fill in for regular staff members. It is also helpful that there is a terrific contingent of volunteers whose work lightens the load.

All of these changes have contributed to better working conditions, better staff morale, and a better service for abused women. No one has left Lanark County Interval House due to burn-out since 1987.

But what of the future? Drastic cuts to government funding are having an impact on the financial stability of the shelter, which, in turn, affects the board, the staff and the service. Because of this, it can be predicted that burn-out will once again become a hazard of the shelter.

LOIS' STORY

Lois was a go-getter and had many appealing qualities. She wasn't at Interval House very long before she found an apartment and a job. This ability to make quick decisions and take action helped her survive—it also got her into lots of hot water.

Lois was a whiz at money management. Somehow, throughout a harrowing life, she managed to provide a home—usually a house—for her family. She worked hard to give her children the stability she had never experienced.

I was on shift the day after Lois arrived at Interval House. When she finished telling me of the incident that brought her to the shelter, I asked her if the police had laid charges against her common-law husband. Her eyes widened and she asked, Can they do that? *When I explained that it was now their duty, she became very distraught. Why hadn't they charged him, and even if there weren't any bruises, why hadn't they noticed her torn dress? We phoned the officers, and during the conversation, Lois recalled that she had minimized the abuse. Based on her information, the officers had little reason to pursue the case.*

Lois' children, Kathleen, eleven, and Jimmy, nine, were bright, inquisitive and adventurous, and always ready to take part in whatever activities were available during their stay at Interval House.

After Lois and her children moved to their apartment, she phoned occasionally to keep in touch. One evening she called to recount an escapade that clearly reflected her children's ability to find adventure anywhere. Earlier in the day, she couldn't find either of them in the apartment. Then she noticed the open window, the fire escape and the ledge that led to a flat rooftop. All the roofs of the neighbouring apartment buildings were joined, so the children had the run of the whole block. I relished the Mary Poppins image of them dancing around the chimneys.

As you read Lois' story you will see that she did not "brag herself up." She made choices that she has regretted, but the results of those choices are a part of her life and she is not one to hide from the truth. This absolute honesty is another one of her qualities that I found especially endearing.

Here's Lois' story.

I was born in Lanark County in a rural town in 1946. My brother was born four years later, the same year my parents separated. I rarely saw my father, even when he was with the family. He worked for Bell Canada and only came home on weekends. Mother was hardly ever at home. She worked at two jobs, both for lousy pay. I became the housekeeper and babysitter.

Mother was schizophrenic with a fair bit of paranoia thrown in. She was pretty strange when I was a kid. She fantasized a lot about evil: about people being unworthy and evil. The day father left, she was hallucinating. She thought he was the devil and she went after him with a knife. She told me afterwards that she wanted to kill him. She was often violent. She's gotten worse over the years. When I was a teenager, I remember her out on the main street waving a tin can with the lid partly off, trying to slice people. She was hospitalized several times. When this happened my brother and I would stay with our grandmother or the neighbours. A lot of my childhood is a total blank. I assume there's a good reason for it to be blank. I've got enough problems right now.

I had a lousy relationship with my brother. I always had to babysit him and I resented it. I was awful to him. I'd beat him up.

I always knew where my father was, but mother discouraged us from having any contact with him. He sent support payments faithfully every month throughout my childhood. When I was twenty-one, I wrote him a letter and he wrote back. He came to my kids' baptisms. About ten years ago, he called to say he'd been putting money into a special savings plan, and now he was dividing it between my brother and me. We each got $5,000. I used it to buy a new furnace and pay off a second mortgage. When I went to Interval House, I called him and he sent me $2,000 to see me through.

When I was thirteen, we moved to Ottawa. I was an emotional mess. Although I had been fairly bright in public school, I blew it when I went to high school. I started to smoke and hang out in the streets with deadbeats. Mom sent me to a shrink at the Royal Ottawa. He interviewed both of us and then told Mom that I was fine but she was a serious problem. So she didn't allow me to go back to see him.

I did some shoplifting—stole large brassieres, wishful thinking. I did the most mediocre things. I took off with one of the men who worked at the Ottawa Ex and stayed with him for four days. I left home when I was fifteen. I'd met this guy whose father worked at an embassy. I moved into his mother's place and became the housekeeper. I was also his girlfriend.

His mother was the same as mine. She used to break out in a rash and say it was because the communists were putting Javex in the water. There are a lot of crazy people around. We had to leave because she decided I was working for the communists and I was putting the Javex in the water. She was a carbon copy of what I had left—the same kind of violence and paranoia. I had walked from one totally insane situation to another.

We ended up getting married—marvellous. I just turned seventeen and he was twenty-four. We were two very lost people. He was as screwed up as I was. All we were doing was keeping each other company. We found two single rooms in a boarding house. I did housekeeping jobs in Rockcliffe Park and I was really well paid. My husband wasn't terribly useful. He did a bit of landscaping. I got pregnant and Andrea was born shortly after I turned eighteen.

Andrea didn't have a chance. I was a borderline mother. I kept her fed and clothed, but I didn't have enough emotional energy to love her and care for her. I didn't regard her as something that had feelings. She was an object.

When Andrea was a baby, I taught myself how to sew.

I still wanted a relationship with my mother and so Andrea and I visited her every weekend.

Mother hated men. She put my husband down so much that she convinced me he wasn't worth having around. I could see her point of view even though it was off-centre. I just got caught up in the whole thing. I got her approval by making him leave. One weekend, I phoned him up and told him I wasn't interested in him anymore, and that I wasn't coming home. I was really vicious to him. So that was cute. I never saw him again. I went back to our rooms about a week later. He had already taken his personal stuff. I took what I needed and I returned the furniture to the stores where we were still making payments.

It was cute because when I did what my mother wanted, then she kicked me out. I got a small apartment in a Lanark County town and worked in a snack bar for a few months. I hired a teenager to babysit.

I heard about an adult upgrading program they'd started at Algonquin College so I enrolled in that and moved back to Ottawa. I was about twenty. I got through most of my grade twelve and then I went off the deep end: started drinking and screwing around. Andrea practically lived at the babysitter's.

When I was about twenty-two, I got myself straightened around. I went to a regular high school and got my grade twelve. After that, I got a job with the Board of Education in the film library and worked for a year. I was fairly stable at that time. I managed to hold down the job and pay the rent, but Andrea was still being ignored. She was about six.

Andrea was really well behaved (she wasn't rebellious at all), but she had some health problems. She was badly cross-eyed. I took her for an operation to get her eyes straightened, but it didn't work and she started having seizures as well. She ended up having four eye operations and had to take medication for the seizures until she eventually grew out of them at age twelve. I think the first operation was screwed up. If I'd been older or a little more together, I would have sued.

I decided to go back to school and took a brand-new course that was being offered for social service workers. During that time, I met my second husband. He was a really nice man and had a very good government job. We rented a house together and got married when I finished school. It was his second marriage too. He had a son the same age as Andrea. He used to visit on weekends.

My husband received a promotion to head a department for the whole province of Newfoundland. We lived there for two years. I started my own dressmaking business. I ordered piles of material from Montreal and hired a girl to do the hems and finishing. I opened up a shop. It was a total disaster. It didn't go well at all. My husband wasn't terribly upset because it was a tax loss for him.

During this time, I got pregnant. Andrea was now ten years old. Six weeks after Kathleen was born, my husband was transferred again, this time to his home town out west. All his family lived there. We bought a house.

I really hated his mother. She was condescending. We did nothing but fight. The first Christmas we were there, she kept saying what a lovely first wife her son had, that it was too bad he split up with her. Anytime I cooked her a meal, she'd call the next morning to report that she'd had indigestion all night and couldn't sleep. She was a very small woman and she would say things like, "Your feet are two sizes larger than mine." I felt like a big clunker. I'm sure I contributed to the friction, but I was really angry with my husband for not taking my side.

At this point, I didn't like myself very much. I was always tense and feeling very weird. I wanted to be married partly because society tells us it's the ideal, but I didn't like sharing my life with someone else. I felt like I was being intruded upon. I invented problems, made mountains out of molehills. I think the only thing I was comfortable with at the time was rejection. I decided I would leave him, but I wanted another baby so I stayed on until Jimmy was born two years later. We went to marriage counselling but it didn't help.

Now I feel really sorry for playing with these people's emotions and affection. I wanted what I didn't have, and when I got it, I didn't know what to do with it.

I got a fair settlement. We sold the house and I got half the equity. The kids and I flew to Ottawa and stayed with a friend until I found a townhouse. My husband rented a U-Haul and drove my half of the furniture east for me. He's still supporting the kids—sends me $500 a month.

We lived in Ottawa for six months. I supported us by taking in sewing.

My mother convinced me the thing to do would be to move back to her town and be near her. Then the kids would have a grandmother. So that's what I did.

I bought a house with the equity from the first house and got a job in a nursing home nearby. At this time, Andrea was about thirteen, Kathleen was three and Jimmy was one. My mom was babysitting. But within a couple of months, I found out that Mother favoured Andrea and was physically abusing Kathleen and Jimmy. She told me that Kathleen was sent by the devil. She had been firing her against the wall.

To get around this, I worked evenings for a couple of years and Andrea had to babysit. She got as resentful about it as I did. She was totally unsupervised, and she was as emotionally screwed up as I had been at that age. And she felt degraded by always having to wear second-hand clothes. We used to get into knock-down, drag-out, physical brawls. When she was about fifteen, she moved in with my mother.

I was no kind of a mother to Andrea. I never had been. You don't see it at the time, but looking back, it was so glaring.

I got a neighbour to babysit. By this time I was doing fairly well in my job. I got good raises and I was working days.

Life went on fairly well for a couple of years until I got a severe case of burn-out and had to leave the job. Working in a nursing home, especially on the day shift, is physically very tiring. You are continually lifting people. There's emotional exhaustion too. People keep dying on you, people you get attached to. I got worn down. I was continually sick. I got a highly contagious infection from one of the patients and couldn't get rid of it. I was on sick benefits for six months. It turned out I was allergic to my thyroid medication. I'd been taking it for seven years.

Andrea moved in with a guy when she was eighteen and got pregnant. She split up with him and went to the Salvation Army home. They kicked her out because she was impossible to handle. Her behaviour was antagonistic and disruptive. She didn't know where to go so I brought her home. The deal was she was to babysit. By this time, Kathleen and Jimmy were in school so it wasn't asking very much. But Andrea totally undermined my authority with the kids. She told them I was a terrible, rotten mother. She said I kept my money for myself and that they should not do anything I said. She wouldn't back down from it, so I had to kick her out. She wound up in another Salvation Army home where her son was born.

Before he was born, she said that she was giving her child up for adoption, but I said he was part of our family, and if she gave him up I'd go for custody. At that point I had a good job, a home and I was only thirty-six years old. She decided to keep him.

When the baby was a year old, I saw him and talked with him. She wouldn't let me touch the baby. A few months ago I called her and she told me to fuck off.

It doesn't hurt to talk about it. It's just there. It's dead. If I allowed it, it would make me very sad. I don't miss Andrea because I never had any kind of relationship with her. I do feel sad because of what could have been. She was born in the days when mothers were knocked out cold. I think that helped—no bonding. And I started off with nothing. I had no support.

While I was on sick leave, I became basically self-sufficient. I used to go to the bush and cut wood with three or four men and then we shared the wood.

When the doctor said I could, I found a part-time job in a grocery store. Fred was the manager and he hired me. He had been separated for four years and his wife had just died. He was always telling everybody he was looking for a girlfriend. I was lonely too, so anyway, I ended up going out with Fred.

It was a terrible relationship right from the beginning, but I was so lonely I would accept anything. We went out together for about six months, getting along good half the time and having horrendous fights the rest of the time. At this point, Fred was fired from his job and he moved to a nearby town to open a store of his own.

I felt the relationship was really sick. I knew Fred had another girlfriend and I wanted to get away from him. After one of our fights, I put my house up for sale and sold it—bang.

I guess someone told Fred about my sale. He came banging on the door, I think mostly because he knew the house was three-quarters paid for and I would have a nice chunk of money. I had already put an offer on a house in another town which had been accepted. He talked me into walking away from it. He said he left his girlfriend and he loved me and that we would be such a good team together in his new store. We would share it. It would be ours. He was sure it would be a gold mine. We'd be set for life.

I put my furniture in storage and moved into Fred's three-room apartment with my two kids and two cats. His twenty year-old son lived there as well. The son worked at his father's store during the night and slept all day. Fred said that the apartment was only temporary. We would use my money to buy a very nice house and we'd all work at the store, a total family affair, and we'd all get rich.

Fred found a house that was way beyond anything I'd intended or expected and he made an offer on it with my money as a down payment. I overheard him talking on the phone with his former girlfriend, telling her that he'd met this awful woman with money and that he was going to use her money to buy a house, but that he'd have to live with her. God, I was so stupid. I didn't do anything about it. I felt totally trapped—nowhere else to go. Somehow I didn't realize that my money gave me all kinds of options. Really, I was lonely. I wanted a relationship.

We all moved into the house, including his son and the son's new girlfriend and her two-year-old son.

Two weeks after we moved in, Fred told me, "Thank you very much. Now you can leave. I'll help you sometimes with the rent on a cheap apartment and I will allow you to work in my store since you're too stupid for anyone else to hire. But in order to help with the rent, I expect a blow job a couple of times a week since that's the only thing you do well."

So there I was. I couldn't believe this was really happening. I stayed there for ten months, putting up with every kind of abuse that you listed in your columns and more *(see Seven Types of Abuse in appendix)*.

He only started beating me toward the end, before I finally left. The rest was intimidation and threats. He'd come home and say he'd spent $1,000 on a whore and he didn't know why he did because it was better at home. Or he'd come home and insist on a blow job, then tell me that he'd been with another woman an hour before and hadn't washed.

He encouraged me to drink. He'd bring home a bottle of my favourite drink, Tia Maria, and say, "You look tense and tired. Here have a drink—just one and you'll feel better." I get drunk very easily and as soon as I get drunk, I get horny. Then he'd call me a whore.

He was terrible to the kids (particularly Jimmy), nasty and cruel.

He put our house up for collateral and held me up against the wall with his fist in my face and made me sign for a $50,000 loan.

I was nearly crazy. I had to work seven days a week, twelve hours a day, and whenever I did get off, he'd send a bum home to mow the grass or whatever so I never got a chance to be alone. I was never allowed near the till in the store. He had everyone convinced I was a thief.

I told him I was taking two weeks off to visit a girlfriend in Kitchener. He said if I went, I wasn't to come back. The kids and I went and I spent the time trying to get myself pulled together. I couldn't stay there forever, so after the two weeks, I went back home.

He wasn't there and the house was a garbage dump. I cleaned it up right away. When he arrived, I could hear him downstairs talking in a loud voice that I knew was meant for me to hear, "The fuckin' bitch is back. I thought she'd stay away. She's nothing but a tramp and a whore. Now I'll have to take Valium." I ignored him.

The next day before he went to work, he was muttering and going on that I was ugly and scrawny and he didn't want me in the store. I knew a woman who needed a job, so I called her to replace me. I took her over to the store for an interview. As soon as she had gone, Fred said, "Well, we won't be needing you anymore. I know that woman. She gives blow jobs all over town." When I got home, I phoned the woman and warned her not to work there and I told her what he had said. She called her brother, who called Fred and said he was coming over with a baseball bat.

Fred was terrified. He phoned me and said, "I'll be home in five minutes. You'd better not be there." When he arrived he said, "Why did you do that? This sort of thing we keep in our family." Then the siege began. He waved a knife in my face and tore my dress to shreds and proceeded to torture me for three hours. He threw me on the floor and I stayed there until he picked me up and threw me on the chair. I was limp. I wasn't going to fight him. He was six feet tall and weighed 250 pounds. I tried to leave, but he wouldn't let me. The kids were outside, looking in the windows and I told them to call the police. The police phoned and asked if he had a gun. I said no. They said they'd be there when they got there. They arrived one and a half hours later.

When the police arrived, they separated us. I talked to one and Fred was in the other end of the house talking calmly to the other officer. I was in a state of shock and I did not describe what had actually happened for the three hours previous. I just said we weren't getting along and Fred would probably settle down tomorrow. My bruises didn't show yet.

The police suggested that I go to Interval House. At that point, I was the ninety-per-cent owner of that property, but it was never suggested that Fred leave. That really pissed me off.

I went to Interval House and stayed there for two weeks. The staff were incredibly supportive. I lost ten pounds, which I didn't need to lose, but that's what happens when I'm under stress. When the staff told me that the police or I could have laid charges, I stood in that office and screamed and cried.

I went back to our house, with police accompaniment, and took all my furniture and put it in storage.

I found a terrible apartment in a neighbouring town, but it was a place to live. I got two part-time jobs. Within a month, I found a larger apartment and got a full-time job. I worked six days a week, ten to twelve hours a day. That was all I wanted to do: work, so I couldn't think.

This is the part I don't understand. After I'd been gone six or seven weeks, I phoned Fred. I don't know why: somehow, there was this incredible attraction. He could be really charming when he wanted to be. I would take the kids and go back there and spend the night. Sometimes he'd be really nice to me and sometimes he'd be awful. If he was awful, I'd just pick up my purse and walk out the door and not talk to him for a few days. He phoned often. It was ridiculous. This went on for months and months.

Fred was afraid to stay in the house by himself. He never paid the hydro bills or the phone bills and he never cleaned the house. The place was filthy: dead animals floating in the pool, the lawn never got cut. There was garbage from one end of the house to the other. The place stunk. His employees were stealing from the store. In the winter, he started living with me in my little apartment. I paid his $1,800 hydro bill. By spring, I decided this was ridiculous. Why were we living over a bar when we had a $200,000 house? In spring we all moved back. He wanted me to quit my job.

Fred had a partner in some other business dealings. This partner got Fred to make him the first creditor on the store so that I couldn't put a lien on the business. One day, the sheriff came and told Fred that the store was being taken over by the partner. So there we were, with no way to pay off the mortgage, so we lost the house as well.

I rented a house in another town. We all moved in, but fifty per cent of the furniture had to be left in the big house because I couldn't afford to move it.

Fred went on a horrendous drunk and I had to put him in the hospital. When he recovered, he got a sales job and did very well. He was making piles of money. He became a saint. He stopped being verbally abusive. Sometimes he even told me I looked nice. Once he even got me a cup of coffee when I asked for one. He felt guilty and contrite. I had lost all my money. He was nice at Christmas too. He actually bought everyone a present. But three weeks later, he told me he'd bought them on credit. I'd have to pay for them. But even though I had to pay, it was a great improvement. Other Christmases he'd told us all that we weren't worth presents. His sainthood didn't last and I eventually kicked him out. As far as I know, he lives in motel rooms and his car.

The finances of the store and house were a mess. There were hefty lawyers' bills and a lot of other creditors, but I persevered and recovered some of my money.

I didn't hear from Fred for about three months and then he called to tell me about this great store that we simply had to buy. Another gold mine and he wouldn't screw it up this time. We'd work together as a team. The only problem was his credit rating. All the loans would have to be in my name. He saw it as a way for me to earn my lost money back. That was pretty easy to refuse. I couldn't believe his nerve and was totally insulted that he would think I would consider it.

The final straw was just before I moved. He told me his sales were incredible, that he had saved up a lot of my money and I could have it back a bit at a time, if he could live with me; otherwise I would get nothing. That made me angry. What he was saying was that I had to be a prostitute for my own money.

I heard about a CMHC [Canada Mortgage and Housing Corporation] program to help low-income people buy a house. They buy the house and resell it to you for twenty-five per cent of your earned income. I found a house that met their standards in this village. I appreciate the program incredibly, but here I am, starting over again, fifteen years later, with no equity in the house.

I like my house and my lovely, private backyard. I can have my morning coffee on the patio, wearing only my nightie. But I'm still a mess. I thought I had my revenge when I threw Fred out. After all, he has no friends or family or home, and no ability to get it together. However, I'm still angry. I feel that I've robbed the children of their innocence. They've had four years of horror. They didn't even have decent clothes.

Kathleen is fairly withdrawn; she doesn't make friends easily. She thinks she's fat and ugly. That's what Fred told her. She's doing really well in school; she's one of the gifted kids. But the weirdest thing happened. As soon as we moved here, she started having nightmares. She went to a counsellor and found out she had a fear of losing her mother. She was concerned about what would happen to her if something happened to me. So we worked out where she would go if something did happen to me and she has a copy of my will.

Jimmy wants to pretend that the four years never happened. He pretends to be four years younger at times. He tries to please me and will do anything I ask. He does well in school.

Neither blame me for what happened.

I've discovered I'm great in a crisis, but when things slow down, I don't do too well. I've got a job, but I'm barely coping with life. I'm close to the edge, but I'm not that close. I'm going for counselling soon. I know I need help.

I visited Lois for the update and met a changed person. Her voice was softer and she seemed calmer, gentler. When she finished reading her story, she was appalled. She said, I sound hard and vulgar and self-pitying. But mostly vulgar.

We began talking about her new life. Her eyes shone as she told me of her recent marriage to a man with three young children. Their wedding photos were lovely and showed that all the children were very much a part of the celebration. Jimmy's girlfriend with her brilliant red (and I mean fire engine red) hair added a delightful touch to the photographs.

But Lois' update contains many sad events.

When they lived in the CMHC house, Kathleen was sexually assaulted by a group of boys from the village. The police felt that going to court would be upsetting to Kathleen and that since the boys were juveniles not much would come of any charges. Kathleen was talked into letting the matter drop on condition that the boys went for counselling. But it didn't drop for her. The boys harassed her unmercifully, called her a double-crosser, beat her up and pelted the family home with rotten vegetables. Kathleen became suicidal and was taken to CHEO for three weeks. The psychiatrist recommended that the family move.

Lois rented an apartment in Picton and found a part-time job. But Kathleen's problems got worse. She started staying out all night and doing drugs. Counselling didn't help. Kathleen left, called CAS and moved to a foster home.

After six months, Lois still couldn't find a full-time job so she phoned her former employer in Lanark County and was offered her old position. She and Jimmy moved back to the area (to a different community), and Kathleen joined them six months later. But she was an emotional mess. She hit the streets in Ottawa and now has convulsions as a result of terrible drug use. She has been destroyed. She's not as bright as she used to be. She's living on a disability pension, she's on Prozac—an antidepressant.

She's really trying hard, she's really straightened out. She's going for counselling and she's taking courses at Ottawa U. It makes me sad. She was really positive, going places. When I think about it too much it really fills me with a sense of rage. Kathleen is tweny-one.

Jimmy, now nineteen, is doing well. He and his red-haired girlfriend live together in Ottawa and work in the same establishment. They are really happy. He's still really protective of his mom, but he's asserting his own identity. He still holds everything in. I can sense his suppressed rage. Initially, it was directed at Fred. Now it's directed at anyone who tries to push him around or make him do something that isn't right.

Lois re-established the family finances by buying a house that was being foreclosed. Since then she has bought and sold a few houses and has two rentals that give her a good return.

She works six days a week. I love working.

A very important part of Lois' recent life began while she was at work. A friend dropped by and asked her if she was interested in going to a small church. Lois had been a born-again Christian, but left the church when she was with George. The sermon was so well done—I was just intrigued. I think I haven't missed half a dozen Sundays since that time. Most of my friends are from that church. There's only about 100 in the congregation and half of them are kids. I've always had a tendency to fly off the handle and those guys (the congregation) put up with it.

I hadn't expected to get married again. I was making my own future as an older, single woman. Between my job, the church, my kids and the wheeling and dealing in houses—that was my life for several years.

Every Sunday this man sat behind me with his kids. We were friends for five years. Strangely enough, I just got this notion that, you know, I saw him struggling with his kids, and it's so embarrassing to admit it, but I phoned him up and I suggested that we could do each other a lot of good. Would you consider getting married? Oh, the poor guy. I suggested that we could take some time and get to know each other and see if it could work. On one level it was a very practical, sensible thing to do. And he did agree with that.

It started off as a business deal, but it didn't stay that way at all. The more time we spent together, the more we realized how much we were alike. We felt as though we were the other half of each other. We dated about a year and just got married two and a half months ago.

I heard a pastor say that when choosing a partner, 'It's not the person you could live with, but the person you cannot live without.'

I feel wonderful. I feel really good. I feel loved and cared for and protected. It's a major change, really. Lots of times I feel pretty, and that's a change for me. He is really good to me. We're really careful with each other—we've learned to value the positive.

We share now and we both feel that that's a really positive thing. We share the cooking, the dishes, the child care because we've both done it singly. So he finds it a benefit that I help him and I feel it's a real break that someone's helping me. It doesn't feel the same kind of stress and drudgery.

I love being part of a family. My husband has brothers and sisters and parents and they've all welcomed me and Kathleen and Jimmy, totally. The children have really been good to me. They haven't rejected me as their stepmother at all. It's been half my life coming, but it's been worth it.

Having been given this family is being given a whole opportunity. It's like a gift.

My advice?

You don't have to have the last word—just leave. Just walk away, forget it. Just write it off.

And then, after you leave, take your time. Just wait. Don't try to force your life.

THE "STRANGE" WOMEN

From time to time we have had to refuse to admit certain women to the shelter because it was determined that they were too dangerous or so unstable that they could not care for themselves. It is very difficult for most of us to refuse admission to a woman. Even more difficult is asking her to leave once she has been admitted.

Once, on the overnight shift, I answered the doorbell at midnight and welcomed a woman to the shelter. Her hair was stringy and her clothes a jumble. I escorted her into the office and brought her a cup of coffee. Initiating the conversation, I asked her where she had come from, had she eaten, how could I help her? Her answers were often incoherent or lost in her constant movement—up and down, pacing, crossing her legs. But it was her eyes that caused me the most concern. Wide open and wild, they never seemed to blink. This one's risky, I thought as I started to read her the house rules—no alcohol or illegal drugs, curfew of 11:00 p.m. on weekdays and 1 a.m. on weekends, no violence. I put the paper down and started to explain what those rules meant, but she was already heading for the door. She said she'd find another place, she had friends, she'd be fine.

She was my first runner. Perhaps she'd been in a psychiatric hospital, but now she was fending for herself, probably eating at soup kitchens and sleeping in doorways. A target for a rapist as she hitches rides in the Montreal/Ottawa/Toronto triangle.

On another overnight shift, police officers brought a woman to the door. They'd found her walking along the highway and she refused to speak to them. They drove her to the shelter in hopes that she might open up to another woman.

She sat on the couch and twisted her body so that she faced the wall behind. I was only able to get her name and, breaking all confidentiality regulations, phoned the Royal Ottawa Hospital to find out if she was a former patient and if she presented any danger to the other residents. They knew her and said she was a non-violent schizophrenic with relatives living in Lanark County. The next day, again breaking the usually tight confidentiality code, staff called the relatives because, by then, it was obvious that the shelter was not the appropriate place for her. The relatives said that she had an apartment in Ottawa, but she often took off, and it was not unusual for them to receive phone calls about her.

She was beautiful, well-educated and had been working in her profession until recent years. I often wonder about her.

In the sixteen-year history of Lanark County Interval House, there have been two women who presented a particular difficulty. Each took an intense dislike to one of the staff. Within the first year of opening the shelter, one woman accused a staff member of poisoning her food. This woman appeared to be perfectly normal with all the other staff members but became very agitated when Lynnette came on shift. Lynnette decided it was best to stay off work until alternate accommodation could be found for the woman.

Several years later, I learned how it felt to be singled out for another's anger. A woman had come to our shelter with her two children, and right from the start, there were puzzling inconsistencies in her story. Also, some days, Fran (not her real name) would take her children for a drive and end up miles away from her destination and then wonder how she had gotten there.

Fran's children were delightful, and one evening I praised their good behaviour and innocently said that I'd love to take them home with me. It was a common Interval House tease and usually caused a mother to beam with pride. Not this time. It was as if I had pulled the plug on a volcano. Fran erupted with screams and raged that she hated me and that I was the cause of all her problems. She quickly whisked the children upstairs and stayed there until the next counsellor came on shift. I recorded the incident. The woman remained calm and acted more normally (except that she constantly rearranged her bedroom furniture) until my next shift three days later.

When I arrived at Interval House, Ella was working. She warned me that Fran had become increasingly agitated as my shift time approached. Fran had decided that she couldn't live under the same roof with me and was in the process of packing. Ella offered to stay on.

Fran walked into the office, saw me and once again became instantly enraged. Ella was astonished at the change. We held a hurried conference in the hallway while the woman paced and raged about my presence. We decided to call the police to help us stall Fran until a Children's Aid Society worker could come and make an assessment (as to whether Fran was capable of looking after her children). The police officer arrived in two minutes, and as I let him in the door, Fran stopped raving in mid-sentence and said in a pleasant sing-song voice, "Hello officer. Are you here to help me?"

Fran eventually left that day with her children.

Then there were the women referred by the psychiatric hospitals—women who were not yet ready to live alone and who needed the support of others. Some of them were still heavily medicated. The galling point was that the hospitals had never sent anyone to assess whether the shelter's services could meet their basic needs. These women were being dumped and once they settled into the shelter, the hospital refused to take them back. Even though each woman had come from an abusive background, it was sometimes more than staff could handle. The women often required constant care and someone to ensure that they took the appropriate medication at the right time. Staff meetings went on and on with agonizing over What-to-do-with-Mary decisions. How would such a woman cope on her own? The shelter's services were inappropriate, but where else could she go?

Before long, it became obvious that all women's shelters were facing the same issue. Workers from the twelve Eastern Ontario shelters got together and set stringent guidelines. Women who were being released from psychiatric hospitals wouldn't be accepted until the hospital guaranteed, in writing, that they were capable of looking after themselves.

With increased knowledge and experience, shelter workers are less afraid of or threatened by the "strange" women. We do our best to ensure that the shelter is a place of safety for women and children. At the same time, we try to accommodate those who need extra support to find normalcy in their lives.

Some women are working to establish healing centres for those recovering from incest and ritual abuse so that they can deal with these traumas in an appropriate setting. It is a hopeful sign.

JACKIE'S STORY

I was on holidays when Jackie and her son, Danny, were residents at Interval House, but on my return to the shelter, her situation was still a topic of conversation. Whenever my co-workers discussed Jackie's complicated court case, her name would be uttered with a special warmth, often accompanied by a smile. It seemed that she had left a positive impression on all who met her.

She affected me in the same way. She has a delightful musical lilt in her voice that enhances her gentleness and grace. Her little son Danny is a beautiful child. He inherited his mother's ready smile and his father's dark colouring and curly black hair.

I interviewed Jackie in her tidy apartment on a hot muggy eastern Ontario summer evening. We positioned ourselves so the fan would swing from one to the other. Danny had already been put to bed with little fuss.

You may find parts of this story particularly disturbing. It contains information about unusual sexual abuse.

Here's Jackie's story.

You know, when I watched *The Burning Bed*, the film where the abused wife burned her husband, I thought to myself, What is the matter with her? Why doesn't she leave him and get some help? And yet, about one year later when I was living with Jonas, I was there too. Why didn't I leave? What was wrong with me? I loved him.

I was born in 1955 in a small village in northern Ontario. I was the second child and the only girl of four in a French Canadian family. Our family was very well-to-do and we never had need of anything. I was very close to my parents, especially my mother. I was never abused, but there was a lot of injustice towards the brother that came after me. He was born with a hearing disability and he spent most of the first year of his life in hospital. My mother never accepted him, this not-normal child. She didn't love him. Many times she would give him the lickin' when it was my other brother that had done the trouble. He went to special schools in Belleville and Montreal so he was away for most of the time. It was as though he wasn't part of the family. We had love, he didn't, so I always compensated for him. We were very close. We still are.

I was raped when I was seven by a sixteen-year-old boy. I never told my parents, never. I felt guilty. When you are a child you have an interest in your body and a couple of times a little girl and I (we were the same age) got caught looking or playing with each other's bodies and I got lickins for that. So when I was raped I never said anything. That little girl saw it. This man had me on the floor in the garage and she was looking for me. She peeked into the garage and she saw what happened. And I saw her see, and then I saw her run. We moved from that little village shortly after. I met her again in high school and she mentioned it. She didn't tell anyone, either. I don't remember any pain or injury. But to me, that incident has no bearing on the rest of my life. It just happened.

I did my grade thirteen and left home when I was eighteen. There was no work for women in the north. So I came to Ottawa and found a job as a bank teller.

I was married two years later to another French Canadian. We were married for ten years. There was no abuse, no arguments, nothing. We just grew apart. Today, he and I are best friends. We call one another regularly, but there can never be marriage between us because we don't feel that way about each other.

During my marriage, I got a government job and worked my way up to a responsible position. I worked with men only: carpenters, plumbers, electricians, and I had a very close rapport with them. I used to meet them early in the morning to take their orders. There were often lunch meetings where I would negotiate contracts and I would do site visits to make sure the warehouses were large enough for our needs. I did a lot of overtime. I loved my work.

Before I met Jonas, I went out a lot in the evenings. All my socializing was with people from my office. I drank quite heavily then, and I even had an affair with a married man for three years. I felt very guilty about that. I was born a Catholic and my guilt was so great that I stopped going to church. I prayed to God that he send me a man who would be religious and who would love me as much as I loved him.

Four years after my separation, I met Jonas. I thought he was my gift. He was a devout churchgoer, handsome, charming, soft spoken and very attentive. He would quote the Bible and seemed quite knowledgeable about his religion. This was very appealing to me. Finally, I could go to a different church that accepted and forgave me. I really became involved in Jonas' church.

Jonas came from a Caribbean island and was applying for refugee status. He had been involved in a revolution in his country and went to prison for three years for his part in planting a bomb at an embassy. Three people were killed. He was tortured mercilessly while incarcerated. The American government intervened and all political prisoners were released and offered political asylum in the States. Jonas chose to come to Canada. He started his own business and seemed to be working hard to become a Canadian.

Jonas was very thoughtful. He would call me every day. I felt very flattered. Even though his work involved manual labour, he was clean and always wore three-piece suits when he came to see me. We dated for four months. He often invited me to his home where several other people, men and women, lived and shared expenses. However, he never told me that one of the women, Emma, was his common-law wife and that she was pregnant with his child. Shortly thereafter, Emma moved out—disappeared. She contacted me and asked me to meet her. She warned me then that Jonas was violent and that I should beware of him. Of course, I ignored her warning. She was jealous, and besides, he wouldn't dare do anything to me. I wouldn't allow it. I could change him.

Eventually everyone left his home. He seemed so sad and depressed. He was worried about being able to afford the rent. I stayed with him that night. Jonas suggested that I move in with him right away, so I packed a suitcase. But, remembering Emma's warning, I decided to maintain my own apartment as well. I wouldn't be trapped with nowhere to go. At this point, I was thirty years old and he was thirty-five.

About two weeks later, I began to have second thoughts. I told Jonas that I needed time to think and that I wished to go back to my own home. I went to the bedroom to gather my clothes. Five or ten minutes later he came into the room with a Mona Lisa smile on his face. I honestly thought he was going to tell me that he understood and that he would call me in a few days. Instead, he pushed me so hard I flew into the closet and my body broke the plaster in the wall. He grabbed me by the collar and threw me against another wall, breaking it as well. He had me by the throat and dragged me from room to room and choked me. Then he let go of me and told me to follow him to the bathroom where he proceeded to have a shit, which he later made me eat while he took pictures. Then he told me to undress and he took pictures of me in embarrassing poses. Again he told me to follow him, naked, this time to the garage, where he took more pictures—all the while telling me to stop crying and to smile for the camera. He then took me back inside, told me to take a bath and shave my pubic hair. He forced me to masturbate with a cucumber and other items while he pretended to be a peeping Tom, looking through a crack in the door. Over and over again he raped me both anally and vaginally. When he was finished he said, "So you want to leave. I'll make sure no one wants you." He was trying to get a blade free from a 'Track II' but fortunately it wouldn't come apart. The whole ordeal lasted from 8 p.m. to 6 a.m. To make him happy, I promised not to leave, I promised to move in my furniture and to become pregnant. I then washed myself up and went to work for the day.

I got a rash as a result of that night. There was one week of intense pain. I went to a clinic and they said it was herpes, but it wasn't. It lasted two weeks. It never reoccured. Of course, Jonas accused me of fooling around and risking him with the rash.

From that moment on I became somebody else. I never gave him any reason to be angry with me. I became his slave: obedient, subservient, unimposing, not Jackie, no more. Jonas controlled me totally. I never voiced my thoughts, my fears. He never beat me again, but he hurt me in so many other ways: verbally, morally, psychologically and financially. I stayed with him for almost two years. I didn't know I was in an abusive situation. I loved him so much that to me it was the price I had to pay to be with him.

I didn't tell anyone. I couldn't tell my father. He wasn't happy about Jonas from the beginning because he was black. He told me to leave him. When someone tells you to do something, it's all the more reason to try harder just to prove them wrong. My friends were acquaintances from work and they never knew. They did see a big change in me, but they couldn't put their finger on it.

Jonas even controlled me at work. He'd find a reason in the morning for me not to leave. I started going to work for 9 a.m. instead of 7 and then it got worse. He always made me late, five minutes, ten minutes, just a little late, but it was enough to annoy my boss. I got two warnings and when I told Jonas, he smartened up. He didn't want me to lose my job. I wasn't even allowed to have a lunch hour. I was to eat my lunch in the office so he could phone me and talk to me. Of course, he never told me that I couldn't go out for lunch. But he would say, "I called you at noon."

And I would say, "Oh yes, I was out for lunch. What did you want?"

And he would say, "Well, if you weren't there to answer my call, then obviously you weren't interested in talking to me." And then he wouldn't tell me why he had called in the first place. So I *wanted* to talk to him and I *wanted* to be there for him so that's how it started. It came to the point where I would never leave my office.

Jonas would twist all my words. If I told him about something that happened at work, that I negotiated a contract with Mr. So-and-So then, weeks or months later, he would bring it back up and twist it around and accuse me of flirting with that man. He accused me of fooling around all the time.

He manipulated my whole schedule: my days at work and my nights at home. When I came home from my office job, I'd have to help him in his shop until 10 or 11 p.m. Then I'd make supper. At first it made me feel good that he wanted me around, but it ended up that I was doing a lot of the work.

The sabbath day was a whole-day event and so I only had one day left to clean the house, do the laundry, and bake cakes so he'd have cakes for the rest of the week. For almost a year, I never had time to watch even a little TV.

I gave Jonas all my pay cheques and he gave me back $50 a week. He made me sign over all my possessions: the car, TV, fridge, stove, VCR, etc.

He was fascinated with pornography and took videos of our love making as well as photos of me in the nude. He intimidated me into having sex with a dog on numerous occasions. He didn't tie me. He didn't force me. He *convinced* me. And I didn't dare say, No.

Our sex life was very good, but only at the beginning. He wanted me to become pregnant so there was a lot of sex, you know, two or three times a day. Once I became pregnant, everything changed. He had sex to pleasure himself which was very rough, so much so that the doctor told me no more sex because I could lose the baby. Jonas was very angry, "What does the doctor know," and continued to pleasure himself.

So that's when I said, "If you have to have sex, go in the back way and that way you can't hurt the baby." So then he really had his go at anal sex—very rough. I don't know how I felt. I never thought of myself at all. Do what you have to do and get it over with. I had no self.

About once or twice a week, Jonas would pick a fight—for any reason, just so he would have an excuse to leave the house. The least thing I would say, like, "I went for lunch with the girls," would trigger an argument. One day my car was sideswiped while it was parked and he got angry at that. He'd leave the house banging the door, and he wouldn't come back until late that night or the next day. One of the first times this happened, I was angry and hurt, and I asked him, "Where did you go. Why didn't you call?"

And he said, "Don't you ever ask me those questions. When I come home I want you to be smiling and be happy to see me."

And that's what I did. He would go for a day or two days and when he came home I would greet him at the door with a smile and his slippers and I would say, "Welcome home, I'm so happy to see you." There was a lot of "I'm sorry" from my side.

I was not Jackie anymore. I was not myself at all.

Many times, when Jonas would be angry with me he'd say, "I know how to hurt you and no one will ever know. You can never prove that I hurt you in these places." He was trained as a prison guard in his country and he said he had been trained how to torture so there was no evidence.

I was allowed only one friend, Isabel, and I met Isabel through Jonas. He often brought her to the house and I had suspicions that she and Jonas were having an affair. I'd ask her and she'd say, "But I already have a boyfriend." Isabel's visits were very good for me. She helped with the dishes and other chores. I was so lonely—no friends or family. She was a good distraction and she was a fair person. It turned out that she was as caught as I was. Three weeks before my baby was born, I found Jonas having sex with Isabel in the basement.

Still I tried to make our relationship work. I stayed with him because I loved him so much. Looking back, I really can't explain why I loved him. I guess the lies that he told me were what I wanted and needed to hear. When he was being nice to me, I was in heaven. I couldn't ask for better. After an abuse session or after giving me the silent treatment for a week, he turned ever loving, so that I would completely forget, because I needed to forget.

Jonas had his own ideas about Christmas. It was a day like any other: there was no acknowledgement of it being special and there were no gifts. I think that a distinct effort was made to ignore it; to make it dull and miserable for me. Mind you, when he was invited to a party on Christmas Day, he went, leaving me at home alone. I was pregnant then.

He promised he would take me out on New Year's Day. But, of course, he never did and I was too afraid to mention it.

Danny was born two months premature. In fact, I had to have an emergency Caesarean to save the baby. Jonas did not come to the hospital until much later, and then he was furious with me for authorizing the operation. He said I had no right. When it was time for me to leave, he refused to pick me up and sent a friend over instead.

Danny and I never lived with Jonas after that. While I was in the hospital, our house burned down. Jonas told me he found a house in the country for us, but it had to be renovated. He sent the baby and I to live with a very religious lady from the church. After two months, she asked us to leave, not because she was angry with us, but I think she saw through Jonas. She couldn't take him anymore and she didn't want him in her house. She knew that his religion was false.

I moved in with my brother and his family and stayed there for six months. Their apartment was very small and I didn't feel comfortable. I tried to be invisible and keep the baby quiet. I begged Jonas to get the house done so we could be a family. I took out loans for him to pay for the renovations and continued to give him my pay cheques. I don't know what he did with the money. I didn't ask any questions then. I would wait for him to tell me. He didn't drink or do drugs and it certainly didn't go into the house. It's a mystery.

While I was on maternity leave, Jonas demanded that I suntan every day only wearing a G-string. "I only ask one thing of you, that you sit outside and get colour." I hate the sun and I don't tan. There wasn't much privacy at my brother's house. I'd hang a sheet on the clothes line and I'd lie on a blanket and hope it wouldn't get windy.

I was able to get day care for Danny and I returned to work. I would take my lunch hour at the day care to nurse the baby. It seemed to me that Jonas always phoned my office while I was there. The secretary would tell me that he said he'd call back later and I'd be sitting on the edge of my chair waiting for his call, which never came.

In the meantime, Jonas "boarded" with another woman, a widow. He borrowed $60,000 from her. Her family made such a fuss about him that after three months he had to leave. He lived in my camper trailer—parked it in the driveway of another woman (a friend of his) about two blocks away from my brother's.

Jonas would come to visit only late at night. Most times he would park across the street and wait until I saw him. I would go out to his car and there we would talk. I had a baby monitor so, when Danny awoke, I would run to the house and bring him back to the car. I would breastfeed him and then return him to bed.

As Danny got older, the doctor was telling me that I had to feed him Pablum because he was underweight. Women in Jonas' country only breastfeed until the children are walking and that was what Jonas wanted me to do. My milk started to dry up and that was when I started to sneak food for him. There was no immunization in Jonas' country either, so he didn't allow me to take the baby for his needles.

If Danny cried while Jonas was visiting, I wasn't allowed to pick him up. Jonas would say I was spoiling him, that I should let him cry. He wouldn't allow me to get any toys or a soother for the baby either and he insisted that I tell the day-care staff that he not be given any toys, ever. That was fine when Danny was four months old but a few months later the day-care staff were insisting that this be changed. I bought two little toys, put Danny's name on them and took them to the day care, and I didn't tell Jonas.

Jonas wanted to make sure Danny had regular erections and told me to masturbate him or put my mouth on his little penis. I *never* did. He also told me that when he bathed little girls he always inserted his finger inside their vagina to feel their hymen.

Isabel phoned me at work to persuade me not to move back with Jonas. She told me about his abuse towards her. He had started beating her after Danny was born. The beatings were planned and very sadistic. One time he took her for a drive to an isolated place and cut her with a blade—her private parts. Another time he burned her private parts with incense sticks. A third time he beat her face with a tortoiseshell comb. Her face was totally swollen and bruised. She went to work and broke down when her co-workers asked questions. They took her to the hospital and to the police station. She made a full report which included pictures and a medical examination. She wouldn't press charges. She and I talked all that week. She's the one that made me realize that it wasn't safe for me to move to that isolated house in the country.

But I wasn't ready to accept it, not yet. I still didn't see that I was being abused. I thought I was fine. But I thought about it: what he had done to Isabel and how he was fooling around on me while I was waiting patiently for him to finish the house, raising his child, giving him all my pay cheques. I guess it all came to a peak when I went to church that weekend and spoke to a friend there. I opened up to this woman, told her everything. She knew Jonas a lot more than I did and she knew of Interval

House. Her mother lived near it. But I was sure they wouldn't take me in because I had no bruises. She phoned the house and Donna, one of the counsellors, asked to speak to me. She told me that I was indeed eligible.

I still insisted on going back to my brother's that night. Jonas came over. I was somehow hoping that we could sit down and have a nice romantic evening, so I would change my mind. Well, it wasn't to be. He just came to the door, gave me $50 so I could pay my room and board and left. I stayed awake all night because sometimes Jonas would drop by again in the middle of the night and knock at my window.

As soon as Danny woke up, I started packing like mad. I was afraid to go to Interval House by day; I thought Jonas might follow. So I went to my church friend's home and stayed there all day and then she drove me to Interval House at night.

Interval House was very, very good for me. The whole time I stayed there I never went out. But this was no prison for me. This was freedom. I had need of nothing; everything was supplied. There was good food, good company, the house was paying me money (a comfort allowance of $2.00 per day). I had need of nothing else. When I arrived there, the house was full, but about a week later, the other women left, so for a while there was just me and Danny. It was like having a home of my own, finally.

After a few days, I knew Jonas was watching the house. Several residents told me that a man matching his description was parked on a side street. He even stopped one of them and showed her a picture of me and asked if I was in the house. The police were called and they told him to move on. Looking back on it, that was probably a dead giveaway. I assume Jonas went to every Interval House and watched. When he found one he was being chased away from, then he knew I was there. Or perhaps Isabel betrayed me. She was one of the few who knew.

Another resident and I set up a plan. She had spunk like you wouldn't believe. I never answered the residents' private phone and so the next time Isabel phoned, my spunky friend answered and said, "Oh, she didn't tell you? Jackie has been transferred. I don't know where she's gone." And that's when I 'disappeared.' I didn't leave the house and I didn't answer the phone. Isabel didn't call again and Jonas wasn't seen after that.

I spent Christmas at Interval House and it was very excellent. There were lovely gifts for Danny and me. Oh yes, I have good memories of the house. I found subsidized housing and moved out of Interval House after two months. I was ready to move. Some of the other women at the house were starting to get on my nerves.

I was very, very lonely when I left Interval House because my friends were the counsellors and I didn't want to phone and bug them. But I went to every Lanark County Interval House potluck and support group meeting.

While I was at the House, I started legal proceedings to get custody of Danny. My first lawyer told me to get out of the province. She said there was no way that Jonas would ever respect the law. So I went to another lawyer and she was more enthusiastic. I told her *everything*. Some I even hadn't told the staff at Interval House because I was too ashamed.

The lawyer made sure my name was cleared of all Jonas' financial responsibilities and then she tried to contact the other women in Jonas' life. Emma was too afraid to swear an affidavit, but the day before the case was to go to court, Yvette phoned my lawyer and offered to testify.

Locating Yvette was like a miracle. Emma was taking a night class and, one night, she was showing photos of her daughter to another classmate who turned out to be Yvette's sister-in-law. The child in the photos so closely resembled Yvette's child that the woman asked, "By any chance would the child's father's name be Jonas?" Emma was shocked and became cautious, but she eventually opened up and told this woman about me and that Jonas was fighting me to get access to Danny and that I needed help.

Yvette's testimony corroborated mine: pornography and horrendous sexual and physical abuse. My lawyer was really ready for Jonas. He came to the courthouse but when he saw Yvette and Isabel, he left. My lawyer put in a request for Jonas and I to have our parenting skills assessed at the Family Court Clinic with the idea that she would then apply to the court to have him undergo an assessment at the Sexual Behaviours Clinic, but he didn't show up. Legal Aid refused to represent him so the case was dropped.

Yvette was the one to suggest trying to deport Jonas. At that time, I was contemplating changing my name and the baby's name and moving to Brockville or Kingston. Yvette said, "Don't run away. You're a Canadian. You have every right to your happiness and freedom."

We went to Immigration, but they had no other complaints about Jonas. Then I remembered a name he once used, and when the immigration official entered that name into the computer, we learned that Jonas had been deported from Toronto several years ago for physical abuse, gross indecency, buggery and making harassing phone calls. He had come back to Canada under another name. The official was delighted to have tracked

Jonas down and he started deportation proceedings. He was sure Jonas would be deported on the spot for coming back into Canada under an assumed name. Shortly afterwards, this official was replaced and it seems that nothing has happened since.

The three of us, Yvette, Isabel and I, have been sending letters to the Minister of Immigration and our members of parliament. Jonas has already gone through six appeals and has one more chance, and then, if all goes well, I will feel safe.

Isabel took Jonas to court for the money he owed her. For his revenge, Jonas sent pornographic pictures and a video of himself and Isabel to her boss and wrote that she was an informant and couldn't be trusted. This was a big mistake. Isabel's reputation is impeccable and she had the support of her superiors. Isabel's boss immediately resealed the envelope of pictures and hired a lawyer on Isabel's behalf to help her get rid of Jonas. Jonas doesn't harass her anymore because he knows she can win.

One day, Isabel and I went out and I drove her home. Jonas was there and he came over to the car and spoke to me, "Why did you leave me?" I didn't want to infuriate him so I told him I had to run and get the babysitter and I'd call him and make plans so he could visit Danny. I got Danny and went to Interval House immediately. I had the shakes. I was so nervous that he would force Isabel to tell him where I was. He thought she had no use for me, and when he found out that we had been in contact, he was very, very angry. He really blasted her but he didn't hit her. And she didn't tell him where I lived.

I stayed at Interval House for two more weeks.

Through my lawyer's work, we've learned that Jonas has at least six children by five women. He told a woman in his church that God put him on earth to procreate—that it was his duty to procreate. Just like Moses who had many wives, it was his duty to continue his line. He used the Bible to show that in marriage women have to stay faithful to the man but the man doesn't have to be faithful to the woman. He tried to get a deaf girl pregnant and had it planned that, when the baby was born, he would have her pronounced incompetent, declare his fatherhood, and then take the baby to his current wife and have her raise the child. He's a sick man.

He told a psychiatrist that a woman in his country squealed on him and that was why he was put in prison. He blames all women for that. He can never forgive women, which is how he explains his violence.

Jonas knows how to charm older women. He'll offer his help, drive them home and then seduce them. He married a woman who had cancer of the uterus. That wasn't for procreation. That was for money.

He worked as a male prostitute for elderly women. He mentioned it to me one day—said he needed money and didn't care to keep up his business. Told me he charged $60 a night. Those nights he would go away with a change of clothing and come back in the morning. I don't know if he did it, maybe it was just a con for me. I had no right to ask him about that. I was pregnant at the time. I cried all the time. I cried every day I was with him. I kept everything to myself.

I figured out how much money I've lost because of Jonas. I took loans out for him, plus all my pay cheques and then there's the money I lost because I had to quit my job and go into hiding. It comes to about $25,000. My lawyer found out that Jonas had a life insurance policy on me as well.

I've gotten to know some of the other women in Jonas' life and, surprisingly, am very close to two of them. We are all very successful women who have money or who can get credit. One owns her own business, another is a manager in the communications field, another, like me, had a high position in government. He's a very, very charming man.

Of all the women, I was the only one who became submissive. The others fought back, argued back and consequently got beaten a lot more.

In his country, the morals are not the same. Men are allowed to beat their wives and the police would never interfere. Jonas thought it was perfectly normal for him to beat me. But in some places in his country, when a man beats a woman, the woman goes to a group of women and they together go after the man and beat him up. The police don't interfere then, either.

Jonas' father is the same as Jonas. He was married with a full family and then he fooled around with a woman and got her pregnant with Jonas. He went to England and there he married another woman. Jonas has many half-brothers and -sisters.

My life is very good right now since I've moved back to Ottawa, but it's very different because I have a child. I have to consider him in every decision I make. Danny is in subsidized day care and he's a wonderful child.

When I went to Interval House, I told them I want to become me again. That was my goal. I'm not me yet, and it's been two years. I'm still dependent on welfare and this job that I've just started is too new for me to feel comfortable about my future. And Jonas is still in the country.

I like my job. I don't have the house I want yet, but that will come in a year. I'll be able to rent a place then that I'll be proud to show.

I got my pension from my other job and was able to clear off some debts and buy a car.

What about friends?

I don't have many friends yet except for Yvette, Emma and Isabel. I took Isabel to one of the support group meetings at Interval House and others were shocked that we were friends. But we've come to respect one another. We were both abused by the same man at the same time. By speaking with Jonas' former wives and girlfriends, I affirmed what happened to me. The sharing I had with the other women in the group was good, but it was never as good as the sharing I have with those three women. Because together we're strong, apart we're all scared. Only one is standing back, but she's with us, she supports us. She lives in the same little village that Jonas comes from. He's checking up on her all the time. She won't allow her three-year-old daughter (his child) outside alone. She's afraid he'll pick her up, and he would. It's a terrible life.

Emma's son was five years old when she was living with Jonas and she only lived with him for six months. Jonas mentally abused this child. I don't know if there was any sexual abuse; the boy hasn't said. The boy is nine years old now and he has a fit if Jonas' name is mentioned. He's been undergoing psychiatric help at the Royal Ottawa for the past four years.

I've been gone too long from my old friends. It's been four years since I've been able to see them. I'm still in hiding from Jonas. I'd like to get back to my old friendships and talk about something other than Jonas. I'd like to have normal conversations again.

I don't feel comfortable with my family anymore. My mother died before I met Jonas and I think I'm still grieving. I miss her a lot. Her cancer was diagnosed two months before she died. My father remarried when I was living at my brother's. His wife is a wonderful woman, but it's not the same. We call each other, but we don't visit. I've hurt my father so much. Twice my dad visited me when I was living with Jonas and he cried both times—in front of Jonas. I think he saw through him, what I didn't see.

I have two brothers close by and that's a little bit easier, but I haven't invited them over. That would be quite an accomplishment for me. I feel I owe them a lot and I can't repay. Maybe it's because I'm still on welfare and I don't want them to see how empty my fridge is. They like to drink beer and I can't afford beer. Actually, they invited themselves over. They called and said, "We'll be over on Sunday to see you." They don't act as if I owe them, but I guess I have a lot of pride.

When Jonas is deported, I will go back to his church. I like the feeling there because you can talk about the Bible. You can argue it, and you can discuss it. And there's no such thing in the Catholic religion. They don't even give you a Bible to read.

But there's another reason. I'm a white person. Danny will be going to a mostly white school. I've got to give him some black influence and I think that church is the best place. He'll always be looked upon as black and I don't want to ignore that.

It took some time to locate Jackie for the update as she had moved to Sudbury. Fortunately, she was visiting friends in Ottawa when she learned that I needed to see her. She phoned and I was delighted to hear her lovely voice again. We met at a Tim Horton's restaurant and, over double chocolate doughnuts, I asked her what had been happening in her life over the past six years.

Nothing much has happened except my trying to find work. It's been very hard. I was never able to get back into the position I had. When I left Interval House, I found work right away and then I got laid off. I took a six-month computer course, found work again and then was laid off after ten months. Contracts don't last very long.

Now I'm in a different field. I worked with the Canadian Hearing Society for over one year. It's work I always wanted to do because my brother is deaf. I took an English sign-language course (ASL). What I really wanted was French sign language (LSQ). The only place in Canada to obtain a diploma in LSQ is in Sudbury so we moved. It's a three-year program. I will graduate in '96. I'm enjoying the course, but school is very hard, you know. The other students are in their early twenties and I'm forty.

If I can find a job, I'll be fine—regain my pride, job security and all that. A lot of deaf women are abused by their husbands and families. I think my experience will be helpful.

I asked her about her son.

He's very beautiful. He's eight now. He looks very much like his dad, but he's even-tempered, like me—not at all aggressive. Danny is having trouble in school. He just failed grade two. His self-confidence is low. He's the only black student in his school, but he's treated fairly by the other children.

I've always told Danny about his father—warned him—don't go near to any black man. But he's attracted to black men nevertheless. When we lived in Ottawa, I never let Danny go outside alone. In Sudbury, I do not have to worry because Jonas would never find us there.

I do want to move back to Ottawa. It's full of culture. There are very few black children in the north.

What about Jonas?

He married a French woman from Quebec on January 1, 1988, while I was still in Interval House. You see, when I went there, I cancelled all my credit cards and stopped the payments on the mortgage. So then he had no money. He had to find someone to pick up the mortgage. She had a good job.

But Jonas, being Jonas, was beating her also. I called her daughter once and told her that her mother could call me if she wanted to talk. The woman phoned and we talked all night. She seemed very strong, able to stand on her own two feet. She was going to press charges for his latest assault on her. The next day, she changed her story and no charges were laid so Jonas was free again.

Shortly thereafter, she quit her job and went with him, back to the Caribbean. The records do not show he was deported. He left before Immigration forced him to leave the country.

The last I heard, he is still there. I think she's not with him anymore. In October of '93, he sent a fax to Isabel for me saying how much he loved me, he wanted us to have a new life, that I should move down there.

We talked a little about the Bernardo trial, but another current trial had made more of an impact on Jackie. The O.J. Simpson case hits me very close. He is black and she was white. I thought he was guilty from the beginning.

What about friends?

I don't have too many friends, I'm too busy. My friends are still the same—Isabel, Yvette. We talk a lot about it still.

Advice?

Never go back. If he did it once, he'll do it twice—a hundred times. The choice you make by leaving is your decision for a better life for you and your family. I never went back and I've never regretted it.

IS THERE ANY HOPE?

Abuse is ugly and the many stories coming to light can make you feel overwhelmed, depressed and concerned for the future. But there is hope.

It is important to remember that it was just over twenty years ago when the first women's shelter opened in Canada. Twenty years ago, women were expected to do as their husbands dictated. If they were abused or even murdered they were routinely blamed for the act. "She provoked him," was the common justification.

That is no longer true. There has been change.

Due to the existence of many women's shelters and the resulting increased awareness, public attitude has changed. Now, when I talk to women's groups about abuse, seldom does anyone suggest that it is the abused woman's fault. And if that suggestion is made, others in the group are quick to respond, often giving personal examples of the difficulties of living with an abuser.

It goes deeper. The massacre of fourteen women at the Ecole Polytechnique in Montreal on December 6, 1989, by a man who blamed feminists for his anger, awakened our country to the rage of some men and the vulnerability of all women. That terrible act legitimized the issue of abuse and raised its status on the public agenda.

Change is taking place partly because women are taking their place in all areas of society. Their need and demands for safe learning and working environments have made an impact. For example: nurses are making public the abuse they have endured from male patients and doctors; young women in high schools, colleges and universities are becoming vocal about sexual harassment by male students and staff; women in the trades are exposing the often daily harassment by their co-workers. Church women, women in business, women in the arts, women in the legal system and women raising children are working for change and making their voices heard.

Another signal of change is that all of this has become news. The influence of the women's movement and the presence of women in the fifth estate are changing the definition of what is important and therefore newsworthy. The abuse of women and children has been given a higher profile within the media so that now, on a daily basis, we learn about situations that weren't reported in the past.

But there is a backlash. I can see it in the eyes of some young men who resent being told that male violence is a problem in our society. They don't see themselves as abusive and they don't want to be lumped in with the rest of the guys. They are particularly angry when they perceive that there are preferential hiring practices for women and minorities. They see women's increased power as a direct blow to their own power.

There have been major efforts in many areas of society to stop the abuse of women; however a barrier to this progress comes from the judicial system itself. At times, it appears that this monolith is based on abuse. It is an adversarial, confrontational system. The truth seems to get lost in the game of winning and losing, with defence lawyers badgering witnesses in order to 'break them down' and make them seem less credible.

If the abuser is found guilty, sometimes the judge's decision places the woman in even greater danger. Rarely is a sentence given that reflects the seriousness of the crime, the need for a real change in the abuser's behaviour, or the need to provide true safety for the victim. Instead, the most common sentence requires the abuser to sign a Peace Bond, whereby he promises to stay away from his partner for a year. But this piece of paper has little effect on the violent man who believes that his wife or girlfriend is his property and that she is to blame for all his woes.

On the positive side, the police are beginning to take an active role in laying charges against abusers. No longer are women expected to charge their partners, but they are still required to testify if the case goes to court. Even the strongest individual finds it a test to endure the length of time between when the charges are laid and when the case is actually heard. Defence lawyers know that if they can remand (postpone) the case for several months, the woman may give up and give in to whatever deal is presented, just to get it over with.

The justice system has yet to find an appropriate way to deal with the children of abusive fathers. Too often, abusive men are given access, including unsupervised access, to their children. Incredibly, some abusers even win custody of their children. There seems to be a belief within the legal system that children need the influence of a father regardless of how harmful that influence may be. Sitting with a woman who is waiting for her abusive partner to return the children after a Sunday visit gives one understanding of the true meaning of stress.

Our justice system often doesn't work, especially for abused women. Most want nothing to do with it. Only approximately five per cent of women who come to our shelter have involved the police and the courts.

But here, too, one can look forward to change. There are many demands from both inside and outside the halls of justice for a more prompt, fair and respectful judicial system.

The revolution continues.

In spite of all the difficult challenges that lie ahead, it is exciting to be part of the movement that is helping women to take their place in society. Not only to take their place, but to use their influence to change the structure of our society so that it meets the needs of both genders and all peoples.

The evolution will be complete when women are treated with respect in their own homes by their partners. When that day comes, it will be a very different world.

SEVEN TYPES OF ABUSE

This list of abuses is based on one made by men who described how they controlled or harmed their wives or girlfriends. A single act may not be abusive. What is important is the intention behind that act. Most abusers use many different tactics to manipulate their partners' behaviour and repeat those techniques over a long period.

*Indicates acts that are clearly criminal or may be criminal, depending on the circumstances.

Please feel free to photocopy this list.

Emotional/Verbal/Psychological Abuse

- making her do illegal things*
- making false accusations
- name calling, finding fault
- verbally threatening her
- overpowering her emotions
- yelling at her
- intimidating her
- making her think she's crazy, stupid
- ridiculing her taste in food, books, etc.
- disbelieving
- bringing up old issues
- displaying inappropriate jealousy
- degrading her
- turning a situation against her
- brainwashing
- laughing in her face
- using silence to punish or degrade her
- refusing to do things with her or for her
- always getting his own way
- having a double standard for her
- saying one thing, meaning another
- denying or taking away her responsibilities
- insisting on accompanying her into the doctor's office
- deliberately making a mess for her to clean
- preventing her from taking a job
- not keeping commitments
- threatening to report her to authorities
- making her drop charges
- telling woman-hating jokes
- refusing to deal with issues
- minimizing her work or contribution

- pressuring her to stay around during drug or alcohol abuse
- not coming home
- coming home drunk or stoned
- displaying woman-hating or violent pictures, videos, games
- egging her on, challenging her to physical violence
- being friends with men who are abusive
- demanding an account of her time/routine
- putting her on a pedestal
- never really forgiving, holding grudges
- lying
- treating her as a child
- starting arguments
- pressuring her
- neglecting her
- expecting her to conform to a role
- comparing her to others
- real or suggested involvement with other women
- making her feel guilty
- certain mannerisms, eg. snapping fingers, pointing
- threatening to get drunk or stoned unless . . .
- not passing on messages
- manipulating her
- withholding affection
- threatening her with loss of immigration status

DURING PREGNANCY AND CHILDBIRTH

- forcing her to have an abortion*
- insulting her body
- refusing sex on the grounds that her pregnant body is ugly
- denying that the child is his
- refusing to support her during the pregnancy
- refusing to support her during the birth (not being there, showing up at the birth drunk, sleeping around while she is in the hospital)
- not showing up to bring her home from the hospital
- not supporting her or helping out after she comes home with the baby
- demanding sex after childbirth
- blaming her because the infant is the "wrong" sex
- refusing to allow her to breastfeed
- pouting, sulking or making her feel bad for time spent with the baby

Environmental Abuse

IN THE HOME

- breaking things, smashing the walls*
- harming pets*
- ripping her clothing*
- locking her in or out*

223

- throwing out or destroying her possessions*
- mowing over her flower garden
- slamming doors
- throwing objects, food
- taking the phones or denying her use of the phones

IN THE VEHICLE

- driving too fast (while she is in the car)*
- driving recklessly*
- driving while intoxicated*
- forcing her into the vehicle (when he's angry)*
- pushing her out of the vehicle when it's in motion*
- threatening to kill her by driving off a bridge, into an oncoming car*
- chasing her or hitting her with a vehicle*
- prohibiting her from using the vehicle by tampering with the engine, chaining the steering wheel, taking the keys

Social Abuse

- controlling what she does, who she sees, who she talks to, what she reads, where she goes
- put-downs or ignoring her in public
- not allowing her access to family or friends
- interfering with her family or friends
- changing his personality when others are present
- being rude to her family or friends
- embarrassing her in front of her children
- dictating her mode of dress
- dictating her behaviour
- habitually choosing friends, activities or work rather than being with her
- making a scene in public
- making her account for herself
- phoning to make sure she is at home, at work
- censoring her mail
- treating her like a servant

USING CHILDREN

- forcing her to stay home with the children
- teaching children to abuse mother through name calling, hitting, etc.
- insulting or assaulting her in front of the children
- not sharing responsibility for the children
- threatening to abduct children or telling her she'll never get custody
- putting down her parenting ability

USING CHILDREN DURING SEPARATION OR DIVORCE

- buying off kids with expensive gifts, promises
- not showing up on time to pick up kids, not having them back on time
- pumping kids for information about Mom,
- telling kids that Mom is responsible for breaking up the family
- using kids to transport messages
- denying her access to the children

USING RELIGION

- justifying abuse or dominance because of religion
- using church position to pressure for sex or favours
- using her, then demanding forgiveness
- excessive spending for religion
- interpreting religion his way
- forcing her to or preventing her from attending church
- requiring sex acts or drug use as religious acts
- mocking her beliefs

Financial Abuse

- taking her money*
- withholding money
- spending money foolishly or beyond means

- pressuring her to take full responsibility for finances
- not paying fair share of bills
- not spending money on special occasions, ie. birthdays etc.
- spending on addictions, gambling, sexual services
- pressuring or controlling her working conditions
- keeping the family finances a secret

Physical Abuse

- any unwanted physical contact*
- kicking, punching or pinching her*
- pulling or pushing her*
- slapping, hitting or shaking her*
- cutting or burning her*
- pulling her hair*
- squeezing her hand, twisting her arm*
- choking or smothering her*
- forcing her to eat*
- spitting on her*
- throwing her*
- throwing things at her*
- hitting her with objects*
- restraining her in any way*
- tying her up*
- urinating on her*
- breaking her bones*
- knifing or shooting her*
- murdering her*
- threatening to kill or injure her*
- pushing her down stairs*

- ignoring her illness or injury
- denying or restricting food or drink
- pressuring her or tricking her into alcohol or drug use
- standing too close/intimidation
- hiding or withholding her necessary medication

Sexual Abuse

- any unwanted sexual contact*
- forcing her to have sex*
- forcing her to have sex with others*
- forcing her to have sex with animals*
- forcing her to shave her pubic hair*
- uttering threats to obtain sex*
- pinching, slapping, grabbing, poking her breasts or genitals*
- forcing sex when she's sick, after childbirth, an operation etc.*
- badgering or hounding her for sex *
- sleeping around
- knowingly transmitting a sexual disease
- treating her as a sex object
- being rough
- pressuring or forcing her to pose for pornographic photos, videos
- displaying pornography that makes her feel uncomfortable
- using sex as a basis for argument

- using sex as a solution to an argument
- criticizing her sexual ability
- unwanted fondling in public
- purposely not washing and expecting sex
- name calling (whore, slut, frigid, bitch)
- accusing her of having affairs
- degrading her body parts
- telling sexual jokes which make her feel uncomfortable
- making sexual comments in public
- demanding sex for drugs or alcohol
- demanding sex for payment or trade
- using drugs or alcohol for sexual advantage
- insisting on checking her body for sexual contact

Ritual Abuse

- mutilating her or others*
- mutilating animals*
- forcing her to participate in cannibalism*
- sacrificing humans*
- forcing her to participate in rituals*
- forcing her to witness a ritual*
- suggesting or promoting suicide

SUGGESTED READING

I have limited this list to a selection of Canadian resources and listed them in order of their first publication. The information in many of the early books is still relevant today. It is interesting to note when the various issues were acknowledged by Canadian writers.

1972   *The Battered Child in Canada*
         Mary Van Stolk
         McClelland and Stewart

1977   *Rape: The Price of Coercive Sexuality*
         Lorenne Clark
         The Women's Press

1978   *The Secret Oppression: Sexual Harassment of Working Women*
         Constance Backhouse, Leah Cohen
         Macmillan

1980   *Wife Battering in Canada*
         Linda McLeod
         Canadian Advisory Council on the Status of Women

1982   *Women and Children First*
         Michele Landsberg
         Penguin

1987   *Battered but not Beaten*
         Linda McLeod
         Canadian Advisory Council on the Status of Women

1987   *My Father's House— A Memoir of Incest and Healing*
         Sylvia Fraser
         Tricknor & Field

1988   *Don't: A Women's Word*
         Elly Danica
         gynergy books

1988   *Ritual Abuse*
         Kevin Marron
         McClelland & Stewart

1989   *Pornography and the Sex Crisis*
         Susan Cole
         Amanita Publication

1991   *The Montreal Massacre*
          Louise Malette, Marie Chalouh
          gynergy books

1993   *Life With Billy*
          Brian Vallee
          Seal Books

1994   *Confronting Sexual Assault: A Decade of Legal & Social Change*
          Julia Roberts, Renate Mohr
          University of Toronto Press

1995   *Ending the Cycle of Violence:Community Response to Children of
          Battered Women*
          Einat Peled, Peter Jaffe, Jeffrey Edleson
          Sage

Our Canadian government has sponsored many studies
and, as a result, has excellent reports including:

1991   *Sexual Offences Against Children*
          Robin Badgley

1991   *The War Against Women*
          The Standing Committee on Health & Welfare, Social Affairs,
          Seniors and the Status of Women

1993   *Changing the Landscape: Ending Violence, Achieving Equality*
          The Canadian Panel on Violence Against Women

The National Film Board of Canada has many
excellent productions including:

1980	*Loved, Honoured and Bruised*	Gail Singer
1981	*Not A Love Story*	Bonnie Sherr Klein
1987	*To a Safer Place*	Beverly Shaffer
1988	*The Crown Prince*	Aaron Kim Johnson
1990	*Sandra's Garden*	Bonnie Dickie
1990	*After the Montreal Massacre*	Gerry Rogers
1993	*Without Fear*	Aerlyn Weissman
1994	*When Women Kill*	Barbara Doran

I recommend the National Clearinghouse on Family Violence for their
excellent resources. Call 1-800-267-1291, toll-free.

WOMEN'S SHELTERS IN CANADA

From *Transition Houses and Shelters for Battered Women in Canada*, Health Canada, 1995. Reproduced with permission of the Minister of Supply and Services Canada, 1995.

Newfoundland/Terre-Neuve

Corner Brook Committee on Violence
Corner Brook, Nfld
(709) 634-8815

Cara House
Gander, Nfld
(709) 256-7707

Libra House
Happy Valley, Nfld
(709) 896-8251

Labrador West Family Crisis Shelter
Labrador City, Nfld
(709) 944-3600

Iris Kirby House
St. John's, Nfld
(709) 753-1492

Naomi Centre for Women
St. John's, Nfld
(709) 579-8432

Prince Edward Island/ Ile-du-Prince-Édouard

Anderson House
Charlottetown, PEI
(902) 894-3354

Nova Scotia/Nouvelle-Écosse

Cumberland Transition House
Amherst, NS
(902) 667-1200

Harbour House
Bridgewater, NS
(902) 543-3999

Bryony House
Halifax, NS
(902) 422-7650

Tearmann House for Battered Women
New Glasgow, NS
(902) 752-0132

Leeside Society
Port Hawkesbury, NS
(902) 625-1990

Family Treatment Program
Shubenacadie, NS
(902) 758-3553

Cape Breton Transition House
Sydney, NS
(902) 562-4666

Third Place Transition House
Truro, NS
(902) 893-3232

Juniper House
Yarmouth, NS
(902) 742-4473

New Brunswick/
Nouveau-Brunswick

Passage House
Bathurst, NB
(506) 546-9540

La Maison Notre Dame
Campbellton, NB
(506) 753-4703

L'Escale Madavic
Edmundston, NB
(506) 739-6265

Fredericton Transition House
Fredericton, NB
(506) 459-2300

Crossroads for Women
Moncton, NB
(506) 853-0811

Miramichi Emergency Centre for
Women
Newcastle, NB
(506) 622-8865

Hestia House Inc.
Saint John, NB
(506) 634-7571

Fundy House
St. Stephen, NB
(506) 466-4485

Sussex Vale Transition House
Sussex, NB
(506) 432-6999

Woodstock Sanctuary House
Woodstock, NB
(506) 325-9452

Quebec/Quebec

La Passerelle d'Alma
Alma, QC
(418) 668-7917

La Maison Mikina
Amos, QC
(819) 732-9161

Maison d'hébergement d'Anjou
Anjou, QC
(514) 353-5908

L'Autre Chez Soi
Aylmer, QC
(819) 685-0006

Maison des Femmes de Baie-Comeau
Baie-Comeau, QC
(418) 296-4733

Maison Clair de l'Une
Buckingham, QC
(819) 986-8286

Collective d'action contre la violence
faite aux femmes
Carleton, QC
(418) 364-7782

La Ré-source de Châteauguay
Châteauguay, QC
(514) 699-0908

Auberge Camiclau de Chambly
Chambly, QC
(514) 658-9780

Maison d'hébergement l'Aquarelle
Chibougamau, QC
(418) 748-7654

Horizon Pour Elle
Cowansville, QC
(514) 263-5046

Maison Halte-Secours
Dolbeau, QC
(418) 276-3965

La Rose des Vents de Drummond
Drummondville, QC
(819) 472-5444

La Maison d'hébergement et de
transition l'Accalmie
Etang du Nord, QC
(418) 986-5044

Maison l'amie d'Elle
Forestville, QC
(418) 587-2533

L'Entourelle
Fort Coulonge, QC
(819) 683-3000

Aid'Elle
Gaspé, QC
(418) 368-6883

La Maison Unies-Vers-Femmes
Gatineau, QC
(819) 568-4710

Le Centre Mechtilde
Hull, QC
(819) 777-2952

Maison d'acceuil La Traverse
Joliette, QC
(514) 759-5882

Maison d'accueil et d'hébergement La
Chambrée
Jonquière, QC
(418) 547-7283

Association des Femmes Arnautiit
Kuujjuaq, QC
(819) 964-2080

La Jonction pour Elle
Lévis, QC
(418) 833-8002

Le Havre des Femmes
L'Islet-sur-mer, QC
(418) 247-7622

Le Toît de l'Amitié
La Tuque, QC
(819) 523-7829

La Bouée régionale du Lac-Mégantic
Lac Mégantic, QC
(819) 583-1233

Le Parados
Lachine, QC
(514) 637-3529

La Citad'Elle de Lachute
Lachute, QC
(514) 562-7797

Maison Vallée-de-la-Gatineau
La Peche, QC
(819) 827-4044

Maison Le Prélude
Laval, QC
(514) 682-3050

Carrefour pour Elle
Longueuil, QC
(514) 651-5800

Waseya House
Maniwaki, QC
(819) 449-7425

Passe-R-Elle des Hautes Laurentides
Mont-Laurier, QC
(819) 623-1523

Assistance aux Femmes de Montréal
Montréal, QC
(514) 270-8291

Auberge Shalom pour Femmes
Montréal, QC
(514) 733-7589

Auberge Transition
Montréal, QC
(514) 481-0496

Inter-Val 1175 Inc.
Montréal, QC
(514) 933-8488

La Dauphinelle
Montréal, QC
(514) 598-7779

Maison Dalauze
Montréal, QC
(514) 640-4210

Maison Flora Tristan
Montréal, QC
(514) 939-3463

Maison Marguerite
Montréal, QC
(514) 932-2250

Multi-Femmes
Montréal, QC
(514) 523-1095

Maison Secours aux Femmes de
Montréal
Montréal, QC
(514) 593-6353

Transit 24
Montréal, QC
(514) 383-4994

La Maison d'hébergement de Pabos
Pabos, QC
(418) 689-6288

Refuge pour les Femmes de l'île de
l'ouest
Pierrefonds, QC
(514) 620-4845

La Maison la Montée
Pointe au Pic, QC
(418) 665-4694

Maison Kinsmen – Marie Rollet
Québec, QC
(418) 688-9024

Maison de Lauberivière
Québec, QC
(418) 694-9316

Maison des Femmes de Québec
Québec, QC
(418) 522-0042

Regard en'Elle
Repentigny, QC
(514) 582-6000

L'Auberge de l'Amitié Roberval
Roberval, QC
(418) 275-4574

La Maison le Coin des Femmes
Sept-Iles, QC
(418) 968-6446

L'Escale de l'Estrie
Sherbrooke, QC
(819) 569-3611

Maison La Source
Sorel, QC
(514) 743-2821

Pavillon Marguerite de Champlain
St. Hubert, QC
(514) 656-1946

Maison Havre l'Éclaircie
St-Georges Ouest, QC
(418) 227-1025

La Clé sur la Porte
St-Hyacinthe, QC
(514) 774-1843

Le Coup d'Elle
St-Jean-sur-Richelieu, QC
(514) 346-1645

Mirepi Maison d'hébergement
St-Raymond, QC
(418) 337-4809

Le Centre Louise-Amélie
Ste-Anne-des-Monts, QC
(418) 763-7641

Maison d'hébergment pour Femmes
Immigrantes de Québec
Ste-Foy, QC
(418) 652-9761

Maison Hélène Lacroix
Ste-Foy, QC
(418) 527-4682

Maison d'Accueil le Mitan
Ste-Thérèse, QC
(514) 435-3651

La Gitée Inc.
Thetford Mines, QC
(418) 335-5551

Maison de Connivence
Trois-Rivières, QC
(819) 379-1011

Résidence de l'Avenue "A"
Trois-Rivières, QC
(819) 376-8311

Maison d'hébergement le Nid
Val d'Or, QC
(819) 825-3865

Centre d'hébergement l'Entre-Temps
Victoriaville, QC
(819) 758-6066

Centre Amical de La Baie
Ville-de-La-Baie, QC
(418) 544-7490

Centre des Femmes
Ville-Marie, QC
(819) 622-0111

La Méridienne
Weedon, QC
(819) 877-3050

Ontario

La Montée d'Elle
Alexandria, Ont
1-800-461-1842

My Sister's Place
Alliston, Ont
(705) 435-9400

Atikokan Crisis House
Atikokan, Ont
1-800-465-3348

Women and Children Crisis Centre
Barrie, Ont
1-800-461-1716

Mississauga Family Resource Centre
Blind River, Ont
1-800-461-2232

Muskoka Interval House
Bracebridge, Ont
1-800-461-1740

Family Life Resource Centre
Brampton, Ont
(905) 451-6108

Nova Vita Women's Shelter
Brantford, Ont
1-800-265-0764

Leeds – Grenville Interval House
Brockville, Ont
1-800-267-4409

Family Crisis Shelter
Cambridge, Ont
(519) 653-2422

Lanark County Interval House
Carleton Place, Ont
1-800-267-7946

Chatham Kent Women's Centre Inc.
Chatham, Ont
(519) 354-6360

Women in Crisis
Cobourg, Ont
1-800-263-3757

My Friend's House
Collingwood, Ont
1-800-265-2511

Maison Baldwin House
Cornwall, Ont
1-800-267-1744

North York Women's Shelter
Downsview, Ont
(416) 635-9427

Hoshizaki House Non-Profit Housing
Dryden, Ont
1-800-465-7221

Avoca Foundation
Eganville, Ont
1-800-267-8827

Women's Crisis Centre
Elliot Lake, Ont
1-800-461-4623

Women's Habitat of Etobicoke
Etobicoke, Ont
(416) 252-1785

Three Oaks Foundation
Foxboro, Ont
(613) 966-3074

Kenora Family Resource Centre
Kenora, Ont
1-800-465-1117

Survival Through Friendship House
Goderich, Ont
1-800-264-5506

Women's House of Bruce County
Kincardine, Ont
1-800-265-3026

Marianne's Place
Guelph, Ont
(519) 836-1110

Kingston Interval House
Kingston, Ont
(613) 546-1777

Pavilion Family Resource Centre
Haileybury, Ont
(705) 672-2128

Anselma House
Kitchener, Ont
(519) 741-9184

Hope Haven Homes
Hamilton, Ont
(905) 547-1815

Victoria's
Lindsay, Ont
1-800-565-5350

Inasmuch House
Hamilton, Ont
(905) 529-8149

Women's Community House
London, Ont
(519) 642-3003

Interval House of Hamilton– Wentworth
Hamilton, Ont
(905) 547-8484

Marjorie House
Marathon, Ont
(807) 229-2222

Maison Interlude House
Hawkesbury, Ont
1-800-267-4101

C.M.H.A. Family Resource Centre
Matheson, Ont
(705) 273-2339

Women's Shelter of Georgina Inc.
Jackson's Point, Ont
1-800-661-8294

Mattawa Family Resource Centre
Mattawa, Ont
(705) 744-5567

Habitat Interlude
Kapuskasing, Ont
1-800-461-8044

Huronia Transition Homes
Midland, Ont
(705) 526-4211

Halton Women's Place
Milton, Ont
(905) 878-8555

Manitoulin Haven House
Mindemoya, Ont
(705) 377-5160

Omushkegiskwew House
Moosonee, Ont
(705) 336-2993

Lennox & Addington Interval House
Napanee, Ont
(613) 354-0808

Nelson House
Nepean, Ont
(613) 225-0533

Nova House
Niagara Falls, Ont
(905) 356-5800

Nipissing Transition House
North Bay, Ont
(705) 476-2429

Ojibway Family Resource Centre
North Bay, Ont
(705) 472-7828

Women's Outreach
North Bay, Ont
(705) 494-9589

Neighbourhood Housing
Orangeville, Ont
1-800-265-9178

Green Haven Shelter for Women
Orillia, Ont
(705) 327-7319

The Denise House
Oshawa, Ont
(416) 728-7311

Interval House of Ottawa–Carleton
Ottawa, Ont
(613) 234-8511

La Présence
Ottawa, Ont
(613) 241-8297

Maison d'Amitié/Amity House
Ottawa, Ont
(613) 747-0020

Womens' Centre (Grey & Bruce)
Owen Sound, Ont
(519) 371-1600

Esprit Place
Parry Sound, Ont
(705) 746-4800

Bernadette McCann House for Women
Pembroke, Ont
(613) 732-7776

Crossroads I and II
Peterborough, Ont
(705) 743-3526

New Starts for Women
Red Lake, Ont
(807) 727-3303

Ernestine's Women's Shelter
Rexdale, Ont
(416) 746-3701

Women's Interval House of
Sarnia–Lambton Inc.
Sarnia, Ont
(519) 336-5200

Women in Crisis (Algoma) Inc.
Sault Ste. Marie, Ont
(705) 759-1230

Faye Peterson House
Thunder Bay, Ont
(807) 623-6600

Emily Stowe Shelter for Women
Scarborough, Ont
(416) 264-4357

Anduhyaun Inc.
Toronto, Ont
(416) 920-1492

Homeward Family Shelter
Scarborough, Ont
(416) 724-1316

Interval House
Toronto, Ont
(416) 924-1491

Haldimand – Norfolk Women's Shelter
Simcoe, Ont
(519) 426-8048

Women In Transition
Toronto, Ont
(416) 533-1175

Women in Crisis Sioux/Hudson/North
Sioux Lookout, Ont
(807) 737-1438

Woodgreen Red Door Family Shelter
Toronto, Ont
(416) 469-4123

Women's Place Inc.
St. Catharines, Ont
(416) 684-8331

YWCA Women's Shelter
Toronto, Ont
(416) 693-7342

YWCA Women's Place
St. Thomas, Ont
(519) 633-0155

Chadwic Home
Wawa, Ont
(705) 856-2848

Optimism Place
Stratford, Ont
(519) 271-5550

Women's Place
Welland, Ont
(905) 788-0113

Women's Crisis Shelter
Strathroy, Ont
(519) 246-1526

Naomi's Family Resource Centre
Winchester, Ont
(613) 774-2838

Sturgeon Falls Family Resource Centre
Sturgeon Falls, Ont
(705) 753-1154

Hiatus House
Windsor, Ont
(519) 252-7781

Geneva House/YWCA Sudbury
Sudbury, Ont
(705) 674-2210

Woodstock Women's Emergency Centre
Woodstock, Ont
(519) 539-4811

Manitoba

Parklands Crisis Centre and Women's
Shelter
Dauphin, Man
(204) 638-8777

First Nation Healing Centre
Koostatak, Man
(204) 645-2750

Nova House
Selkirk, Man
(204) 482-1200

Snow Lake Centre on Family Violence
Snow Lake, Man
(204) 358-7141

Eastman Crisis Centre Inc.
Steinbach, Man
(204) 326-6062

The Pas Committee For Women In
Crisis Inc.
The Pas, Man
(204) 623-7427

Thompson Crisis Centre
Thompson, Man
(204) 677-9668

South Central Committee on Family
Violence
Winkler, Man
(204) 325-9956

Ikwe-Widdjiitiwin Inc.
Winnipeg, Man
(204) 772-0303

Native Women's Transition Centres
Winnipeg, Man
(204) 989-8240

YM-YWCA Osborne House
Winnipeg, Man
(204) 942-3052

Saskatchewan

Qu'Appelle Haven Safe Shelter
Fort Qu'Appelle, Sask
(306) 332-6881

La Ronge Family Service Centre
La Ronge, Sask
(306) 425-3900

Moose Jaw Transition House
Moose Jaw, Sask
(306) 693-6511

Battleford Interval House
North Battleford, Sask
(306) 445-2742

STIWC Regina Safe Shelter
Regina, Sask
(306) 543-0493

Isabel Johnson Shelter YWCA
Regina, Sask
(306) 525-2141

Regina Transition House
Regina, Sask
(306) 757-2096

Saskatoon Interval House
Saskatoon, Sask
(306) 244-0185

Southwest Crisis Services Inc.
Swift Current, Sask
(306) 778-3692

Southwest Safe Shelter
Swift Current, Sask
(306) 778-3684

Shelwin House
Yorkton, Sask
(306) 783-7233

Alberta

Calgary Women's Emergency Shelter
Calgary, Alta
(403) 232-8723

Sheriff King Home (YWCA)
Calgary, Alta
(403) 283-5994

Camrose Women's Shelter
Camrose, Alta
(403) 672-1035

Edmonton Women's Shelter Ltd.
Edmonton, Alta
(403) 479-0058

Sucker Creek Women's Emergency
Shelter
Enilda, Alta
(403) 523-2929

Crossroads Research Centre Shelter
Fairview, Alta
(403) 835-2120

Unity House
Fort McMurray, Alta
(403) 743-4691

Grande Cache Transition House
Grande Cache, Alta
(403) 827-5055

Dr. Margaret Savage Crisis Centre
Grande Centre, Alta
(403) 594-5095

Odyssey House
Grande Prairie, Alta
(403) 532-2672

Hope Haven Society
Lac La Biche, Alta
(403) 623-3100

Harbour House (YWCA)
Lethbridge, Alta
(403) 320-1881

Lloydminster Interval Home Society
Lloydminster, Alta
(403) 875-0966

Eagle's Nest Stoney Shelter
Morley, Alta
(403) 881-2000

Peace River Regional Women's Shelter
Peace River, Alta
(403) 624-3466

Strathcona Shelter Society Ltd.
Sherwood Park, Alta
(403) 464-7233

Columbus House of Hope
St. Paul, Alta
(403) 645-5195

Wellspring Family Resource and Crisis
Centre
Whitecourt, Alta
(403) 778-6209

British Columbia/ Colombie-Britannique

Libra Transition House
Aldergrove, BC
(604) 532-0090

Maguerite Dixon House
Burnaby, BC
(604) 299-2488

Lakes District Transition House
Burns Lake, BC
(604) 692-7220

Ann Elmore House
Campbell River, BC
(604) 286-3666

Herstory House
Chetwynd, BC
(604) 788-3646

Ann Davis Transition House
Chilliwack, BC
(604) 792-3116

Comox Valley Transition House
Courtenay, BC
(604) 338-1227

Mizpah Transition House
Dawson Creek, BC
(604) 782-9176

Somenos Transition House
Duncan, BC
(604) 748-8544

Hope Haven Transition House
Fort Nelson, BC
(604) 774-3068

Meaope Transition House
Fort St. John, BC
(604) 785-5208

Boundary Women's Coalition
Grand Forks, BC
(604) 442-3131

Hope Transition House
Hope, BC
(604) 869-5191

Ishtar Transition Housing Society
Langley, BC
(604) 530-9442

Hans Kna Kst Tsitxw Transition House
Lytton, BC
(604) 455-2284

Cythera Transition House
Maple Ridge, BC
(604) 467-9966

S-Yem / Yi'M Transition House
Merritt, BC
(604) 378-0881

Abbotsford/Mastsqui Transition House
Mission, BC
(604) 852-6008

Mission Transition House Society
Mission, BC
(604) 826-7800

Haven House
Nanaimo, BC
(604) 756-0616

South Okanagan Women in Need Society
Penticton, BC
(604) 493-7233

Port Alberni Transition House
Port Alberni, BC
(604) 424-7111

Coquitlam Transition House
Port Coquitlam, BC
(604) 464-2020

Grace House
Powell River, BC
(604) 485-4554

Prince George & District Elizabeth Fry
Society
Prince George, BC
(604) 563-1113

Phoenix Transition House
Prince George, BC
(604) 563-7305

Prince Rupert Transition House
Prince Rupert, BC
(604) 627-8588

Amata Transition House
Quesnel, BC
(604) 992-3385

Revelstoke Women's Shelter Society
Revelstoke, BC
(604) 837-4362

Nova Transition House
Richmond, BC
(604) 270-4911

Xohlemet Society
Sardis, BC
(604) 858-0468

Sunshine Coast Transition House
Sechelt, BC
(604) 885-2944

Passage House
Smithers, BC
(604) 847-9000

Evergreen Transition House
Surrey, BC
(604) 584-3301

Liberty House
Surrey, BC
(604) 951-9925

Virginia Sam Transition House
Surrey, BC
(604) 572-5116

Three Sisters Haven Society
Telegraph Creek, BC
(604) 235-3113

Ksan House Society
Terrace, BC
(604) 635-6447

Terrace Transition House
Terrace, BC
(604) 635-2373

WINS Transition House
Trail, BC
(604) 364-2326

West Coast Transition House
Ucluelet, BC
(604) 726-2020

Emily Murphy Transition House
North Vancouver, BC
(604) 987-3374

Helping Spirit Lodge
Vancouver, BC
(604) 872-6649

Kate Booth House
Vancouver, BC
(604) 872-7774

Powell Place
Vancouver, BC
(604) 683-4933

Vancouver Rape Relief
Vancouver, BC
(604) 872-8212

Vernon Women's Transition House
Vernon, BC
(604) 542-1122

Victoria Women's Transition House
Victoria, BC
(604) 385-6611

Atira Transition House Society
White Rock, BC
(604) 531-4430

Chiwid Transition House
Williams Lake, BC
(604) 398-5658

Yukon

Dawson Shelter Society
Dawson City, YK
(403) 993-5086

Help & Hope for Families
Watson Lake, YK
(403) 536-2221

Kaushee's Place
Whitehorse, YK
(403) 668-2106

Northwest Territories/Territoires du Nord-Ouest

Katimavik Crisis Centre
Cambridge Bay, NWT
(403) 983-2129

Inuvik Transition House
Inuvik, NWT
(403) 979-3877

Qimavvik
Iqaluit, NWT
(819) 979-4566

Photo by Linda Martin

Fern Martin was one of the founders of an eastern Ontario shelter for abused women, Lanark County Interval House. During the past 17 years, she has worked as a member of the board, crisis counsellor and public educator.

Fern lives on a farm near the village of Pakenham with her husband, Peter. She has three grown children, Linda, Selina and Rusty, and a granddaughter, Holly.

For more copies of

THE NARROW DOORWAY

Women's Stories of Escape From Abuse

send $18.95 plus $4.50 to cover GST,
shipping and handling to:

GENERAL STORE PUBLISHING HOUSE
1 Main Street, Burnstown, Ontario
K0J 1G0

Telephone: 1-800-465-6072
Fax: 613-432-7184